Martin Breheny
Colm Keys

The
Chosen
Ones

Celebrating 1000 GAA All Stars

BLACKWATER PRESS

Editor
Frieda Donohue

Design & Layout
Paula Byrne

Cover Design
Melanie Gradtke

ISBN
1-84131-672-5

© 2004 Martin Breheny & Colm Keys

Produced in Ireland by
Blackwater Press, c/o Folens Publishers,
Hibernian Industrial Estate, Tallaght, Dublin 24

The authors and Publisher would like to thank the following for permission to reproduce photographic material: David and Jacqueline Kilcoyne, Brian Murphy and Sportsfile.

Acknowledgements

The first glimmer of the idea for this book flickered in that well-known citadel of GAA activity, Caesar's Palace, Las Vegas, during the Vodafone All Star American tour in January 2004.

A discussion on various All Star teams was as animated as usual and intensified when the question was raised as to who was likely to become the 1000th award winner. With 33 hurling and football All Star teams chosen since the launch of the scheme in 1971, the right half-forward on the 2004 All Star football team would become the 1000th recipient.

One thousand All Stars! Surely such a significant landmark had to be recognised in some way? Las Vegas wasn't quite the place to decide on the format, but shortly afterwards the concept for this project began to take shape.

Question was – how best to structure a book dealing with so many players? It clearly wasn't possible to interview every All Star, so it was decided to concentrate on a representative 20. But which 20?

We teased it out for hours, days and even weeks before settling on the final choices. We have tried to be as representative as possible. We interviewed hurlers, footballers, multiple and single All Star winners, while Cork's Brian Murphy represents dual players. It was vital to include Damien Martin (Offaly), who was goalkeeper on the 1971 All Star hurling team. Since the hurling team was announced a few weeks ahead of the footballers, Damien holds the distinction of being the very first All Star.

By their nature, the majority of All Star awards tend to go to the stronger power bases, but we took a deliberate decision to also include players from the so-called 'weaker' counties. To that end, we interviewed Kevin O'Brien (Wicklow) and David Kilcoyne (Westmeath), who were their respective counties' first All Star recipients.

Brian McEniff and Joe Kernan are featured as men who won All Star awards and later managed teams to All-Ireland success, while

Dermot Earley Senior and Junior represent an élite group of fathers and sons who won awards. We sincerely thank the 20 All Stars who agreed to be interviewed. All were hugely co-operative and very enthusiastic and we hope we have done them justice.

We felt that the book would be incomplete if it failed to honour Cormac McAnallen, who died so suddenly last March. Cormac was full back on last year's All Star football team and seemed certain to win several more awards, until his life was cut tragically short. We are deeply indebted to his family, who agreed to be interviewed for the tribute chapter.

It was vital to include detailed statistics of the All Stars, which involved a lot of painstaking research. We are very grateful for the help we received in this regard from Donal Keenan and Killian Keys. Donal was also a helpful presence in other key areas of the production.

The enthusiasm for the project shown by the Vodafone Ireland Team was typical of the energy and style they bring to the All Star scheme, while publishers, Blackwater Press, under the captaincy of Managing Director John O'Connor, were fit and ready for every challenge. Editor Frieda Donohue put in a performance of All Star proportions, while Margaret Burns, Paula Byrne and Melanie Gradtke played prominent roles too.

Thanks also to Seán Kelly, Paddy Downey, Seán Moran, Vincent Hogan, the staff at Sportsfile and Shane O'Brien from Simonstown Gaels, all of whom helped in various ways.

Not for the first time in a hectic year, our families have had to wait until last! Spare time was a luxury we simply didn't have this year, which impacted greatly on Rosemary, Alan and Linda (Breheny) and on Frances, Danielle and Lauren (Keys), but they bore it a lot more cheerfully than either of us would have done. Without their total support we could never have completed the project, or retained our sanity, in weeks when seven days weren't quite enough to get through various workloads. Thanks to all – this is as much your book as ours. A special word of appreciation too to Mary Keys.

Finally, we hope that readers enjoy this celebration of a truly great Irish sporting institution.

Martin Breheny & Colm Keys
November 2004

Contents

Message From Seán Kelly, GAA President

Whoever came up with the idea of the All Stars and, in particular, the title 'All Star' was a genius, or at the very least an All Star! It has become an instantly recognisable title, a much sought-after accolade and a distinguished brand name. It has penetrated the psyche to such a degree that a former player is often referred to in terms of the number of All Star awards that he won.

The reverence in which the All Stars are held was brought home to me last summer, when I attended an underage match in my native Kingdom. Pointing to a young kid, a trainer advised me to watch him closely, predicting 'He's an All Star in the making.'

Normally, prodigies of that kind would be singled out in such terms as 'He'll wear the county jersey,' or 'He'll play for Kerry.' Now there is an even more special élite – the All Stars. That's not surprising since, in an organisation of around 200,000 players, only 30 can get All Star awards in any season.

The All Star concept has grown dramatically over the years. It generates debate after debate and a few rows – rows of All Star proportions.

An All-Ireland medal and an All Star award are the two most prestigious honours in the game. Such status deserves special treatment. Thankfully the sponsors over the years – Carrolls, Bank of Ireland, Powerscreen, Eircell and Vodafone in particular – have added enormously to the prestige and value of the scheme since they came on board. Thus, such faraway places as Dubai, Argentina, San Diego, Phoenix and Las Vegas have been given the All Star treatment, while it will be Hong Kong's turn in January 2005.

It's great for the players and they truly deserve it. And, like true GAA sportsmen, they really appreciate it. Rewards are reaped in other ways too. Gaelic Games had all but died in San Diego prior to the visit of the All Stars in 2003. As if touched by the magic and aura of our greatest players, a revival followed and now they have highly successful ladies' and men's teams, many of the players being American-born. Watch out then for Hong Kong entering the Leinster championships in 2020!

People are so conscious of the importance of the great All Star accolade that it has now become a matter of continuous assessment, rather than an end-of-year examination. This year, we had newspaper columnists choosing teams in mid-season under the heading: 'If the All Stars were selected now.'

And the selectors! Oh, isn't it great when comment turns on the commentators? Yes, the selectors are indeed the finest selection of correspondents covering Gaelic Games. As Uachtarán, it is my pleasure to act as non-voting chairman at their deliberations. You thought these guys were cold and detached and unemotional. Far from it! Heated debates take place, as one journalist argues the merits of a player (not from his own county), another selector is arguing the superior merits of *his* preference (not from his county either).

I predict that this burden of selectorial objectivity will lead to a great falling-out some day. And rightly so! For everything to do with the All Stars has to be on a grand scale. An All Star selectors' row is not for the fainted-hearted. It should be verbal, intense and hopefully sponsored!

But, by and large, the selectors do a great job and few can quibble with the sincerity, integrity and profundity of the entire system.

It is fitting therefore, and further testimony to the importance of the All Star scheme that this book has been produced. It gives me great pleasure to congratulate the authors, the renowned, respected and knowledgeable correspondents Martin Breheny and Colm Keys, who have widespread experience of all aspects relating to the All Stars: the games themselves, the banquets, the trips abroad and the selection meetings. They are thus most qualified to produce this book.

As my friend from Kerry might say, 'Watch out for these men, for they are All Stars in the making.' Or have they arrived already? This book could mark their arrival as true All Stars *í lár na páirce*.

Míle buíochas agus dea mhéin.

Seán Kelly
Uachtarán CLG

From Little Acorn to Strapping Oak
GAA All Stars: 1971–2004

'The All Star scheme has stood the test of time and indeed every other test it encountered. Naturally, it has generated some controversy along the way, but the concept is so fundamentally strong that it will always have a place in the GAA.' Paddy Downey

When, on a wet Saturday afternoon in the spring of 1971, four GAA correspondents approached a caravan which was parked on the grounds of University College Dublin, they could never have envisaged that they were about to erect the first floor of a sports awards' skyscraper that has grown to dominate the presentation skyline.

The foundation for the GAA All Stars had been laid in the 1960s when the now-defunct *Gaelic Weekly* magazine ran its own awards scheme, honouring the best hurlers and Gaelic footballers in each position. It started in 1963 and ran until 1967, but when it ceased the following year, a large void was created which simply demanded to be filled.

And so, when GAA correspondents Paddy Downey *(The Irish Times)*, the late John D. Hickey *(Irish Independent)*, Pádraig Puirséal *(Irish Press)* and Mick Dunne (RTÉ) entered the caravan on the UCD campus in 1971, they had a plan in mind. The caravan was the administrative headquarters for the All-Ireland 7-a-side championships, which were organised by the UCD GAA club. Eugene McGee, the UCD secretary, had invited the four correspondents along to select the winners of various categories, such as best player, best-turned-out team and so on.

The championships were sponsored by the P.J. Carroll and Co. cigarette company, whose public relations manager was Pat Heneghan. The GAA took a rather jaundiced view of sponsorship at the time, but since the 7-a-side championships weren't regarded as an official part of the competition structure, backing by a commercial concern was allowed.

The four GAA journalists felt that Carroll's might just be ready to extend their sponsorship on a grander scale so, during a break in the action on that Saturday afternoon, they put their All Star idea to Heneghan, who immediately showed a keen interest and promised to discuss it with his company. A week later, Carroll's confirmed their interest, subject to the approval of the GAA.

'We feared that the GAA might not support the idea, especially since it was a cigarette company that was being proposed as sponsor, but we contacted Seán Ó Síocháin [the then General-Secretary of the GAA], who showed great interest, but he told us that he would have to talk to other senior GAA officials including Pat Fanning, who was President at the time. Anyway, we were pleasantly surprised when, in a relatively short space of time, word came back that the All Stars scheme, sponsored by Carroll's, would have the full backing of the GAA,' recalls Downey.

The journalists were delighted with the news as it brought to fruition an idea that had been floated almost a decade earlier. In the early 1960s, the Association of Gaelic Sports Journalists was formed and, some time later, with Gael Linn as sponsors, they launched an awards scheme to honour the best hurler and footballer of the year.

However, it quickly became apparent that it lacked the stature of the Caltex Award (the present day Texaco award), the high-profile scheme that covered all the main sports. The journalists decided they needed a new focus for their awards.

'Mick Dunne, who was GAA correspondent of the *Irish Press* at the time, was very interested in American sports and came up with the All Stars concept. We held a meeting of the Association of Gaelic Sports Journalists upstairs in a pub in Moore Street [Dublin] and, after a lively debate, the motion to press ahead with the All Stars idea was passed by a majority. However, the late Val Dorgan of the *Cork Examiner* was chairman and, for some reason, he decided that it needed a two-thirds majority. A fairly heated argument ensued and no final decision was reached that night. However, shortly afterwards, *Gaelic Weekly* announced that they were planning to run their own All Stars scheme. We were a bit miffed that our idea appeared to have been lifted, but most journalists still agreed to become involved in the selection process because we felt it was a good concept and would benefit the players. *Gaelic Weekly* ran it for five years but it didn't get much publicity in the national newspapers,' recalls Downey.

It ended in 1967 and, over the next few years, the GAA correspondents talked regularly of attempting to revive it.

'By now, Mick Dunne had moved from the *Irish Press* to RTÉ and Pádraig Puirséal was back as GAA correspondent of the *Irish Press* and, together with John D. [Hickey], we often discussed how we might resurrect the All Star concept. It finally came together in 1971 and has remained a hugely important part of GAA life ever since,' said Downey.

The first All Star hurling team was named in October 1971, followed a few weeks later by the football team.

The first presentation banquet was held on 15 December 1971, a glittering affair which set the template for future presentations.

The selection committee for the first All Star teams was as follows: John D. Hickey *(Irish Independent)*, Donal Carroll *(Evening Herald)*, John Comyn *(Sunday Independent)*, Pádraig Puirséal *(Irish Press)*, Seán Óg Ó Ceallacháin *(Evening Press & RTÉ)*, Eugene McGee *(Sunday Press)*, Jim O'Sullivan *(Cork Examiner)*, Mick Dunne (RTÉ), Micheál Ó Hehir (RTÉ) and Eoin McQuillan *(Belfast Newsletter)*.

GAA President Pat Fanning and General-Secretary Seán Ó Síocháin also sat in on the meeting, which was chaired by Pat Heneghan, representing P.J. Carroll and Co.

A steering committee, charged with drawing up and implementing the rules and procedures of the All Star scheme, was also put in place. It was comprised of Dunne, Downey, Hickey, Puirséal and O'Sullivan.

However popular the All Star scheme was among the players and public, it was inevitable that the selections would generate controversy. The tone was set after the first announcement, when various critics, including some of the selectors' journalistic colleagues, raised serious questions about the teams. Among the most strident was Mitchel Cogley, who castigated the selectors for their football selection in the *Irish Independent*.

He wrote: 'Since the announcement of the football 15, I have heard all sorts of cribs and, with due deference to those of my colleagues who made the final judgement, I heartily agree with what the "knockers" have to say. The selectors dropped a heavy clanger in the omission of Kerry's Mick O'Connell. He should, in my view, have been an automatic choice at midfield. I would have passed over Willie Bryan and would have gone for Jimmy Duggan of Galway in preference to his countyman, Liam Sammon. Much as I admired the excellent play of Galway left corner-forward, Seamus Leydon, I just cannot understand the omission of Kerry's Mick O'Dwyer. Of all the boobs pulled, however, surely the choice of Cork's Ray Cummins at centre half-forward takes the biscuit. Has he ever played the position at top level?'

Cummins had also been chosen on the inaugural hurling All Star team but his selection at centre forward on the football team surprised more than Cogley. Downey recalls that Seán O'Neill (Down) was the No.1 choice at full forward on the football team, but the selectors felt that Cummins, who was also a high-quality No.14, should be included on the team and, since he had switched out to centre forward on a few occasions, he deserved to be selected.

The issue of sportsmanship generated even greater controversies. It was decided that only players who were exemplary sportsmen were eligible for an All Star award, so anybody who served a term of suspension for any offence, however trivial, was barred from selection. This restriction lasted for many years and proved extremely divisive, as many GAA people thought it was excessively harsh. It even led to resignations from the selection panel in the mid-1980s.

While the principle behind the sportsmanship rule may have been valid, the lack of discretion allowed to the selectors meant that a player who had been sent off for a relatively minor incident in an obscure club game lost his chance of winning an All Star award in that season. In effect, it depicted the player in a negative light and punished him twice for the same offence, first through suspension and later through his ineligibility for the All Stars.

Those who opposed the non-negotiable nature of the rule argued that a degree of discretion should be allowed to the selectors, while still retaining an emphasis on sportsmanship. It was eventually decided to lift the automatic restriction on choosing players who had served a term of suspension, although good sportsmanship is still considered an important element when selecting All Stars.

Inevitably, the 'sportsmanship rule' led to some embarrassing incidents which arose when a player who had been selected as an All Star was sent off before the presentation banquet. He became, in effect, a non-person and wasn't allowed to attend the function. It happened to Kilkenny's Mick Brennan in the late 1970s and to Offaly's Pat Fleury in 1982. Brennan was under suspension at the time of the presentation banquet but Fleury's ban, imposed after being sent off for a relatively minor offence in an Oireachtas semi-final against Clare, had ended almost two weeks before the All Star presentation function.

It led to a huge controversy. The sheer injustice of preventing a player from receiving his award at the official presentation function, although he was no longer under suspension, enraged a large cross-section of the GAA community.

However, the All Star steering committee insisted that, under the rules of the scheme, Fleury could not be invited to the presentation. So, while 14 other top hurlers enjoyed the glittering banquet, Fleury attended a routine meeting of his club, Drumcullen.

In a hard-hitting column, criticising the manner in which Fleury had been treated, Eugene McGee wrote in the *Irish Press*: 'It is difficult to write about an episode like that without a feeling of total disgust that any group of people should publicly humiliate a great GAA person like Pat Fleury just by quoting the word "precedent". One is left to wonder if the key word in the whole affair should be PRECEDENT. How about another word instead, HYPOCRISY?'

When the rule was changed to allow players who had served a term of suspension to remain eligible for All Star selection, it removed one of the major points of controversy, although not all. Inevitably, disputes arose over team selections and, while they generally came down to a matter of opinion, the announcement of the 1994 hurling team caused huge embarrassment.

Offaly right half-back, Brian Whelahan was, by general agreement, the best hurler in the country that season, having played a hugely significant role in his side's successful march to All-Ireland glory. He would have been an automatic selection on virtually everybody's All Star team but, through a quirk in the selection process, he was omitted.

Instead, the right half-back position went to David Clarke (Limerick) while Whelahan's Offaly colleagues, Hubert Rigney and Kevin Martin were slotted into the No.6 and No.7 positions respectively. All three were outstanding hurlers but none had quite reached Whelahan's heights in 1994.

So why was Whelahan omitted? It appears he was the victim of a glitch in the selection procedure, caused by the fact that the team was chosen by secret ballot.

With Whelahan virtually an automatic choice in most selectors' thinking, the battle for the second wing-back spot was between Clarke and Martin. However, since it was a secret ballot, selectors didn't know how others were voting. It appears that those who thought Clarke and Whelahan should be the two wing backs, voted the Limerick man at No.5 and Whelahan at No.7. Those who supported Whelahan and Martin voted Whelahan at No.5 and Martin at No.7. Amazingly, Whelahan got squeezed between the two positions and ended up with fewer votes than either Clarke or Martin.

It was one of the most embarrassing omissions in the history of the All Star scheme as Whelahan had earlier been chosen as the 'Players' Player of the Year' and would later win the Texaco 'Hurler of the Year' award.

For the next two years, the All Star teams were chosen by votes from players, but reverted to the journalists again in 1997 and have remained in their control ever since.

Apart from the honour of being recognised as the best player in a particular position in any given year, the All Star scheme introduced another hugely important dimension in the form of tours to America. Right from the launch of the scheme in 1971, the GAA and the sponsors were keen that the All Stars and the All-Ireland champions in both hurling and football should be awarded with a trip to the US, where they would play each other in exhibition games.

The first trip, which lasted ten days, took place in late March/early April 1972 when the All Stars and the All-Ireland football and hurling champions (Offaly and Tipperary) travelled to San Francisco. Since the champions had several players on the All Star team it was necessary to bring others to deputise in various positions. This added another layer to the All Star scheme, since several players who lost out on the original selection would be rewarded with a trip as replacements for those who were required to line out with the All-Ireland champions.

The first tour to San Francisco featured two games in both hurling and football, with Offaly footballers winning on aggregate by 1-26 to 1-23, while the All Star hurlers beat Tipperary over two legs on an aggregate score of 11-24 to 8-26. In the early years of the All Star tours, the players stayed as guests in the houses of GAA enthusiasts in a particular city. However, that was later changed and the players stayed in hotels, which was good for team spirit and togetherness. The tours took in several American cities over a long period, but were eventually abandoned in the 1990s.

However, they were resurrected in 2001. The All Star football teams of 1999 and 2000 travelled to Dubai, where they played each other in an exhibition game and, a year later, the All Star hurlers of 2000 and 2001 undertook a similar tour to Buenos Aires. Since then, the footballers have played in San Diego (2002); the hurlers visited Phoenix, Arizona in 2004; while Hong Kong is the footballers' destination in 2005.

Now in its 34th year, the All Star scheme has had five different sponsors. P.J. Carroll & Co., who played such an important part in the launch of the scheme in 1971, remained as sponsors until 1978. They were replaced by Bank of Ireland, who sponsored the scheme for 16 seasons (1979–94). Powerscreen had two years as sponsors (1995–96) and were replaced by Eircell in 1997. Eircell were subsequently taken over by Vodafone, who have continued as enthusiastic and innovative sponsors of the scheme.

The All Star scheme has grown in stature over the years and its importance in the life of the GAA community is reflected in the amount of debate and analysis, plus the inevitable criticism, which accompanies the announcement of the team every year.

'The All Star scheme has stood the test of time and indeed every other test. Naturally, it has generated some controversy along the way, but the concept is so fundamentally strong that it will always have a place in the GAA,' said Paddy Downey who, together with his visionary journalistic colleagues, played such an important part in its launch 33 years ago.

When Character Comes First

Pat Hartigan (Limerick)

ALL STAR WINNER: **1971, 1972, 1973, 1974, 1975**

'I read it as I saw it and waited for the ball to drop into my hand, but it fell short by about ten yards. At that moment I knew I wouldn't make it. The game was up. It was all over.'

From the instant numbness in his left eye, Pat Hartigan knew he was in trouble. A routine clash of ash, as he was blocked while attempting to protect his lines during a Limerick training session, triggered such a vicious spin on the sliotar that the ridge caught the middle of his eye before he had time to react.

There was no pain, but the numbing sensation worried him deeply. He tried to open the eye with his hands but there was no vision. It was the longest day of the year, 21 June 1979 and Hartigan, still only 28 years old, had been looking forward to a Munster final with Cork and a chance to end the 39-year hoodoo the Rebels had held over Limerick in provincial hurling deciders.

As the evening wore on and the symptoms remained, Hartigan's fears for his sight increased. There was no improvement and not even the slightest sign that normal service would be resumed. For a week he lay in Limerick General Hospital, before the bleeding could be controlled and an exact diagnosis reached.

By then, Pat Hartigan, one of the greatest hurlers of his or any generation, didn't need to hear the voice of the surgeon Mr Shorten to confirm what he already knew. The same instinct that made him such an indomitable full back during 11 years of service to Limerick senior hurling and football teams was now telling him to prepare for one of the great traumas of his life. The sight was gone in one eye.

The warrior spirit in him wanted to go on, however. Out of hospital, and adapting to his new circumstances, Pat still felt he had something to offer. Ten days before the Cork game, he headed to the Gaelic Grounds with the then Limerick manager, the late Noel Drumgoole, to test out his new lines of vision. He stood in around the square and Noel pucked balls in his direction, checking his capacity to read and react swiftly.

'I was still adamant that I was going to play,' Hartigan recalled. 'Sure I was nervous. Noel was about 50 yards away, striking the ball and I had no problem catching it. But on one occasion, he didn't make proper contact. I read it as I saw it and waited for the ball to drop into my hand, but it fell short by about ten yards. At that moment I knew I wouldn't make it. The game was up. It was all over.'

For all the trauma and discomfort it would cause in his life, the greatest loss Pat felt was in those years just after that long June night in 1979. Would Limerick have beaten Cork in that Munster final if he had been commanding the square? Would they have succumbed to Galway a year later in the All-Ireland final, or in the 1981 semi-final? Would Limerick still be chasing their first All-Ireland title since 1973 if that ball had not shot up so suddenly and caught him in the only spot where it could inflict maximum damage?

'There was damage to the back of the retina and if the impact had been 1mm to the left or right it would have left me with sufficient vision to carry on playing.'

To this day, the vision he has in his left eye amounts to no more than dark shadows. A few years ago, his great friend from childhood, renowned businessman J.P. McManus, together with Dermot Desmond, arranged to make contact with a clinic in Russia on his behalf to see if successful repair work could be carried out. But, after analysis of scans and photos of the eye, it was determined that nothing could be done because of the damage to the optic nerve.

Such a debilitating injury could have left him bitter, but it didn't. Adjustments were made for driving and other aspects of his life. A career on the national and international shot-putting circuit, where he had displayed so much promise as a talented youth, was nurtured and pursued to fill the void left by hurling.

'I wasn't bitter. I accepted that I was in hard luck but that was it. But I had the athletics and I was still able to pull on a pair of togs and compete. If I didn't have that, then bitterness might have crept in.'

Such was the status he enjoyed in Limerick hurling that for the following two seasons he remained attached to the squad, as they hunted that elusive All-Ireland crown. But it never felt right.

'I would have to say that 1980 and 1981 were difficult for me because I always believed I should have been there. We beat Cork in a Munster final in 1980 and, while that was great, I missed out on it as a player and it hurt. We lost the All-Ireland final to Galway, who hadn't won one for 57 years and, a year later, we lost to them again in most unlucky circumstances in the semi-final, but they lost to Offaly in the final. To think that two years running,

Galway and Offaly won the All-Ireland and we ended up with nothing really drove it home.

'If I'd been there I would have been full back; it would have released Leonard Enright further up the field and there is no doubt the team would have been strengthened. Joe McKenna, Eamon Cregan, Liam O'Donoghue, Paudie Fitzmaurice and Seán Foley were all still playing, so there was no reason why Limerick should not have won one of those two All-Irelands.'

So where does Pat Hartigan stand in the pantheon of great full backs? He was overlooked for both the GAA's 'Team of the Century' and its 'Team of the Millennium', but his status in the game is still enshrined. When observers seek to judge modern-day giants of the No.3 shirt, such as Brian Lohan, Pat Hartigan becomes the automatic barometer.

Five successive All Star awards from the scheme's inception in 1971, one an automatic choice in 1973, stand testament to his great ability. He had immense natural power, but he had touch too, and the awareness to understand that a full back need not exclusively be a gatekeeper, an enforcer who offers protection to his goalkeeper and little else.

In essence, he was the first modern No.3, a player who changed full back play so much that he was considered one of the inspirations for the decision to delete the third-man tackle from the playing rules.

'When I started hurling for Limerick, the third-man tackle was in vogue, the goalkeeper was a target and your priority as a full back was to protect him. But, even though I was big enough and strong enough to offer that protection, I used to prioritise hurling the ball. I'd meet the ball anywhere up to 40 m out from our own goalmouth, so full forwards no longer stayed around the square because they were sent out after me.

'I didn't have to concentrate on the physical aspect of the game so much. I probably hurled more ball than any full back prior to that. It has been written in the past that my style revolutionised the position. Not long afterwards, the third-man tackle was dispensed with and, in my opinion, my style of play was instrumental in that.'

It's a source of immense pride to him that he was never sent off in a career that had its roots in the fields and roads around the parish of Donaghmore. Drombanna was home to the Hartigans. South Liberties was the local club, but it was in Sexton Street that his immense talent was carefully nurtured.

'It was only when I went to the CBS that I started hurling competitively. Up to the age of 13, I had never put on a team jersey of any description because there was no side in the local primary school. I hurled day and night on the road and down in the local fields with the lads, but never competitively.'

Reputations were built in Sexton Street. By the age of 15, he had White Cup (under 15 and a half) and Dean Ryan Cup (Munster junior colleges) medals in his pocket and had broken onto the Harty Cup team.

They won a third successive Harty Cup and All-Ireland colleges' title, beating St Mary's of Galway in the 1966 final and, a year later, when a fourth 'Harty' was claimed, a number of them took the decision to repeat and go for the elusive fifth in 1968.

No other college up to then had won five-in-a-row. St Flannan's and North Mon had both reached four, but five was the Holy Grail. It became an obsession for Hartigan and his young colleagues.

'We had a crack team. There was Seán Foley, Seán Burke, Christy Campbell and a number of lads on the periphery of subsequent Limerick teams. Pat McCarthy was going for a fourth successive Harty Cup medal, I was going for a third and there was an enormous effort put in.'

It ended in failure, however, when a Coláiste Chríost Rí team, the backbone of which included Martin O'Doherty, Brendan Cummins, Séamus Looney, Brian Murphy and other members of the Cork team that would go on to dominate hurling in the mid to late 1970s, denied them in the final. Even now, Hartigan can vividly recall the heartbreak of history passing his school and the team by.

'It was certainly one of the saddest days. To be hit with that at 17 years of age, it was like our whole world had collapsed. We had gone back to school to win it and the feeling was so strong that some of us contemplated repeating again. We weren't going to recover the sequence but we wanted to leave the school on a winning note.'

If that 1968 Harty Cup defeat was the year's trough, there were plenty of peaks to overshadow it. It was a breakthrough year for Pat, who played on eight different Limerick teams in six months. In a quite amazing season, he represented Limerick hurling and football teams at minor, U-21, senior and intermediate (hurling) and junior (football) levels. In all, he reckons that between club, county and college he represented 15 different teams that year. Once established on the senior hurling and football teams, he never lost his place, until that fateful night in 1979 ended his career.

In tandem with his meteoric rise in Gaelic Games, was a burgeoning shot-put career, hewn from the raw natural strength he possessed. Pat knew little of coaching or technique in a field discipline that had little following in this country. He lifted weights in a garage gym owned by his brother, Bernie, on nights that he wasn't involved with hurling or football and allowed his shot-put career to flourish in the slipstream of Limerick's famed green shirt.

'Track and field athletics were big in Limerick city. I suppose I took my influence for the sport from Bernie, who was involved in the discus and threw at the World Student Games in 1962. I was young and strong but had no specialised training or coaching. It was just raw natural ability. Limerick AC won national track and field league titles in 1979, 1983 and 1985. I didn't take part in 1979 because of my injury, but I captained the team in 1983. We went on to represent Ireland in the European club championships in each of the following years,' he recalled.

'Open sports were very much the thing in the Munster and western areas back then and we enjoyed the challenge of going along. But if it clashed with hurling, then there was no competition. Shot-put is a sport very much geared to the competitors, not to the spectators. I never gave it the time it deserved.'

Still the honours poured in. There were All-Ireland intermediate shot and discus colleges titles won in 1966, senior shot and discus titles won two years later, and he followed Bernie to the World Student Games in Portugal. Inevitably, the invitation to take a scholarship in America (Boston) followed. Phil Conway, an Irish champion at the time, was already in Boston and the offer was tempting. But it was 1968 and Pat's sporting career was already headed in a very definite direction.

'Around the same time as the scholarship offer, the trial for the Limerick hurling team came up. I did well and stuck with it. I was a home bird really. Moving away never appealed to me. I was helping out on the farm at home during the summer holidays. I enjoyed the summers, piking hay and milking cows, attending and playing matches on a Sunday and going to dances in local halls that night. The scholarship would have been a great opportunity if the hurling had not gripped me so much. I felt I could always throw in to the national championships and other events, once we were knocked out of the championship.'

It didn't take long for Pat to establish himself as a true Limerick great. He spent six years with the Limerick U-21s and, by the age of 21, he had a League medal and a first All Star on the inaugural team in 1971. There was massive interest in the composition of the team and he had an inkling that he would be selected when a photographer called a week before the team was due to be announced.

'The idea of the All Stars had captured the public imagination but, at the age of 21, I could never visualise myself being placed in the same category as someone like Jimmy Doyle. But then I got a call from a photographer who came out to Drombanna to take my picture. I tried to quiz him about who else's picture he was taking but he wouldn't say, and I was reluctant to ask any of the other Limerick players if he had called to them. I was very curious at the time, I have to admit.'

He heard nothing else until the team was released in the papers. One paper he glanced at carried his photograph in the full back position with Ray Cummins's name beneath it!

'My name was at full forward with Ray's picture. It took me a few moments to establish it was a misprint because I was so keyed up. I would have to say it was the greatest thrill of my sporting life. The scheme came too late for Jimmy Doyle, Ollie Walsh, Christy Ring and so many other great players. Here I was, in one of my early years, and I was on the first ever All Star team. No matter what else is said, that can never be taken away from me.'

Hartigan always felt the award carried a certain responsibility which he had to honour.

'I took it on board that, if I was selected, I had something to stand for. There was a level of sportsmanship attached to it. As it transpired, I was never sent off, had my name taken only once and never tried to play the game other than how it should be played. I am glad to look back on my own career and say I never engaged in foul play. That is as important to me today as any other part of my game. No one could ever say I was a dirty player.'

The early 1970s were arguably the busiest ever for Limerick hurling. They contested five League finals between 1970 and 1974, winning only one. They were also in five Munster finals in 1971 and in 1973–6, winning two. Then, there was the ultimate decoration of an All-Ireland medal in 1973.

Hartigan sensed that a solid team was evolving in the county in the late 1960s. Limerick's National League final success over Tipperary in 1971 was reversed by the same county in the Munster final a couple of months later. The following year, a disappointing loss to Clare led to a change of management. Mickey Cregan, brother of Eamon, was installed as trainer with Jackie Power, father of Kerry footballer Ger, as manager.

'There was a lot of unease around at the time and it caused a big disruption at the start of the 1973 League campaign. But once it ironed itself out, everyone got behind the new management. We eventually saw the light, understood that the Board were calling the shots and reached another League final, which we lost to Wexford.'

The signs were encouraging, however, and the 1971 Munster final defeat by Tipperary was avenged two years later, when the first provincial crown for 18 years was claimed. With London as their opponents in an All-Ireland semi-final, Limerick could begin preparing for an All-Ireland final and their cause was helped by the absence, through injury, of Eddie Keher, Jim Treacy and Kieran Purcell from the Kilkenny team. To this day, Kilkenny claim that Limerick owed their success to the absence of this influential trio, but Hartigan doesn't concur.

'We were very fired up for it. We had beaten that Kilkenny team in League and Oireachtas matches before. We won the All-Ireland final comfortably, 1-21 to 1-14, and, Kilkenny injuries or not, I believe we would have beaten them anyway. History says that we did, which is all that matters.'

One of the outstanding memories Pat has of that day in Croke Park was the first face he saw in the Limerick dressing-room afterwards, a person that in latter years has become as familiar on the business and sporting pages as it has in the parade rings of these islands.

J.P. McManus grew up in the same parish as Pat and their families enjoyed a close bond which has endured to this day.

'Somehow J.P. got into the dressing-room, as only he could, and he was the first face I saw and a welcome one at that. He's a great Limerick man from the Ballysheedy side of our parish and his love of Limerick GAA knows no bounds.'

McManus and Hartigan had the shared interest of the South Liberties club, with whom he won three Limerick senior hurling championship titles in 1972, 1976 and 1978 and he recalls how his friend, at the age of 21, was as progressive a chairman as any club could ever have wished for.

'Even then he was ahead of his time. If the club wanted something, even a new set of jerseys, J.P. knew how to go about it. He presented the club with a set himself at a very young age, when most clubs just had the one set between all adult teams. He was a bit ahead of all of us. We weren't able to move fast enough with him.'

Hartigan insists McManus has never forgotten his roots and even the naming of some of his horses after South Liberties' stars like Hartigan himself, Joe McKenna and Eamon Grimes is testament to that.

'It's a great sense of pride to us all what J.P. has gone on and done for himself. As a club, we're blessed to have him and I'm sure there are many envious of South Liberties in that regard,' says Hartigan of the man who gifted Limerick County Board €5 million for the redevelopment of the Gaelic Grounds in July 2004.

If 1973 was the high point of Hartigan's career, he was never to scale those peaks again. A year later, Limerick beat Clare in the Munster final to retain their title, with Pat having what he feels himself was his best ever performance against Gus Lohan, father of current Clare stars, Brian and Frank. However, with Keher and Purcell restored to the full forward line, Kilkenny gained revenge in the All-Ireland final, winning by 3-19 to 1-13. With the great Cork team of the 1970s also emerging, Limerick's powers began to fade.

'I was still only 25 and I had picked up a fifth consecutive All Star but, by that stage, we were on the way down.'

He never made it back to a Munster final again as a player and, in the aftermath of that terrible training ground accident, he began to focus more on shot-putting.

'I started into it in a more serious way around 1980 and, in the years that followed, I represented Ireland in Europa Cup meetings, captaining the team in the 1981 semi-final in Warsaw, and won national titles and over 40 indoor championship titles.'

He also went to the Cooley Mountains for the annual Poc Fada, winning the title in 1981 and 1983 and finishing runner-up in 1982 and 1984. His management stints have been restricted to club underage teams at South Liberties and, while it has been mooted, he has never linked up with a Limerick senior hurling management team.

His passion for the game in the county remains the same, however, and he was as hurt as anyone in 1994 and 1996 when All-Ireland titles 'were lost by Limerick'.

'Those defeats were hard to take. Traditionally I would have expected Limerick to beat Offaly and Wexford. If someone had told me that Wexford would score 1-13 in an All-Ireland final, I would have said that Limerick would win comfortably. But it was a very inept performance that day and I'm afraid Croke Park has been a very unhappy hunting-ground for us since 1973.'

His respect for the man who was the architect of the 1994 defeat, the then Offaly manager Eamon Cregan, is unwavering however, especially as a player.

'I didn't have the pleasure of seeing Mick Mackey, but if there was a better hurler than Cregan in Limerick in my lifetime, I would say show him to me. Cregan was a great forward and an equally good defender. He thought out the game very well and he was a tough competitor. He reverted to centre-back in 1973, having scored 2-2 in the Munster final. In the All-Ireland final I played behind him and there was never a gap between us. He could always get himself between the ball and the goalposts.'

In time, Hartigan feels Limerick can be a force in hurling again. But they may never have another Pat Hartigan.

---

*Pat Hartigan is National Sales Manager with Grasslands Irl. Ltd. He and his wife, Kate, live in Corbally, Limerick. They have two grown-up daughters, Faye and Sally Anne.

The Science of Subtlety

Mike Sheehy (Kerry)

ALL STAR WINNER: 1976, 1978, 1979, 1981, 1982, 1984, 1986

'It was absolutely crazy that so many sensible people started believing the nonsense that it was the northern way or no way. It irritated me because it made no sense whatsoever.'

Mike Sheehy couldn't believe what he was hearing. On the streets of his native Tralee, in the broader Kerry hinterland, and all across the media, an insidious heresy was being peddled. Kerry had lost the 2003 All-Ireland semi-final to Tyrone and were feeling emotionally raw. It was the second successive year that their All-Ireland dream had been shattered by an Ulster team, a double setback that inevitably led to a period of piercing self-analysis.

Sheehy considered it entirely appropriate that Kerry should conduct a detailed stocktake of their systems, values and priorities, but he was bewildered by the direction in which it had headed. A rather bizarre theory had taken root and, nourished by the sense of disappointment the previous few seasons had generated, was growing far too strong for Sheehy's liking.

The message was stark and simple. Kerry's style had become obsolete, a sporting dinosaur that had roared in other days but which was to be silenced forever by Ulster's power play. Clips showing a phalanx of Tyrone players surrounding bewildered Kerrymen, driving them sideways and backwards before eventually winning possession, were repeatedly shown on TV.

This was Gaelic football but not as Sheehy knew it, nor as he ever wants to recognise it. And yes, it was effective. Tyrone beat Kerry, just as Armagh had done in the 2002 All-Ireland final. Were it not for the fact that Kerry had been among the victims on successive years, Sheehy would have been pleased for Armagh and Tyrone. He had even tipped Tyrone to beat Kerry in his column in *The Kerryman* newspaper.

He knew how much Joe Kernan, Peter Canavan and everybody else in Armagh and Tyrone had endured over the years and understood the true worth of what the All-Ireland breakthrough would mean to both counties. However, he could never accept that the style of play being employed by Armagh and Tyrone was either attractive or good for Gaelic football. Nor could he countenance a situation where it would become the norm.

Yet even in Kerry, people were beginning to question themselves and it alarmed Sheehy.

'People were saying that the Kerry way was old-fashioned. Tyrone's swarmed defence and Armagh's power play were being hailed as the only way forward. It seemed to be a matter of all aboard the new bandwagon, without asking where it was going. Even here in Kerry, it was being suggested that we needed to radically alter our style. I couldn't believe it. We had won 32 All-Ireland senior titles, yet we still doubted ourselves. We seemed totally convinced by systems used by Armagh and Tyrone, who had won a single All-Ireland each.

'Good luck to Armagh and Tyrone, they deserved their titles but it was absolutely crazy that so many sensible people started believing the nonsense that it was the northern way or no way. It irritated me because it made no sense whatsoever.'

Sheehy makes no secret of the fact that he dislikes the Armagh and, to a greater extent, the Tyrone style. He believes that it's far too negative and, in Tyrone's case, is preventing them from reaching the peaks their vast array of talents are challenging them to visit.

'When Tyrone go out and play expansive, attacking football, they are the best around. They have more naturally gifted footballers than any other county, so why they want to stifle that talent is beyond me. Tyrone's defensive approach very nearly cost them the 2003 All-Ireland final. They were a better team than Armagh, yet they dug in for a tight, defensive game. If they had set their stall out and allowed their creative instincts to dominate, they would have won more easily.

'I recall watching that game with a sinking feeling for Gaelic football. It was an absolutely perfect day for a game yet, instead of sitting back to enjoy a great encounter, we were treated to a negative, defensive battle. It was awful to watch. This Tyrone panel is good enough to come back and win more All-Ireland titles, but only if they abandon the negativity and play to their creative strengths.'

Sheehy is a great admirer of Joe Kernan as a player and manager, but feels that Armagh also used negative tactics to optimum effect, not least in the 2002 All-Ireland final against Kerry.

'Let's take one very important example: Armagh's goal came from a one-two between Oisín McConville and Paul McGrane. McConville ran forward, knocked the ball on to McGrane, while continuing his run. McGrane flicked it back to McConville who finished to the net. Dara Ó Sé could easily have checked

McConville's run by barging into him. At worst, he would have given away a free, although that's by no means certain, but he would definitely have prevented the goal. Had it been at the other end, Armagh would have checked the runner. It's not allowed but they seemed to get away with it quite a lot of the time. The one-two is a great art in most field sports, but if the runner is checked without the ball, it's a victory for negativity. I can't understand why referees aren't harder on that.'

Sheehy is so concerned about the erosion of fielding skills that he believes it's time to introduce a 'mark' system, whereby a high catch is rewarded by allowing the fielder to play the ball away. It's quite common to see a spectacular catch, followed by unseemly congestion when the fielder returns to earth, where he is greeted by a tackling party. Often, he can't play the ball away and is punished for over-carrying. Sheehy regards that as a total insult to skill and imagination, yet nothing is being done to protect the high fielders.

It's all very different to his playing days when high catching was one of the great arts of the game. But then much has changed since the Sheehy era, which lasted from 1974 to 1987, a period in which Kerry's dominance was the most pronounced in the history of Gaelic football. Eight All-Ireland titles, 11 Munster crowns and four National Leagues mark the historical beacons in their remarkable reign as the supreme force over which Mick O'Dwyer presided so regally.

If it was an accident of birth that so many amazing playing talents arrived for Kerry duty at the same time, it was no coincidence that they gelled together so effectively under the Waterville wizard, whom Sheehy regards as untouchable in any poll to select the best ever Gaelic football manager.

'O'Dwyer was ahead of his time, but the amazing thing was that he always kept ahead and is still doing it to this day. His enthusiasm is unbelievable. I can never see a day when that man won't be in charge of a team. Some people will say that O'Dwyer was lucky with Kerry in that he had a very good squad to work with, but nobody can ever underestimate his contribution to making the whole thing work.

'There were times when lads might feel a bit flat, but O'Dwyer never did. He always had huge energy and enthusiasm, which kept the scene very positive.'

If O'Dwyer was the central force around which the Kerry squad orbited, there were so many component parts to the great adventure that it's unlikely to be replicated. Critics claim that Kerry were in a privileged position because Cork were their only serious rivals in Munster, which enabled them to time their campaign to perfection. Effectively, Kerry could win the All-Ireland title with three meaningful contests, although such was their dominance that they turned some Munster finals, All-Ireland semi-finals and finals into lopsided mismatches. With teams getting a second chance nowadays, it would be more difficult for Kerry to reign supreme for so long, especially since every county is preparing much better. Still, Sheehy would love to be playing under the new system.

'Players are getting more games nowadays. We seemed to be spending half our life training for very few games, even if most of them were big occasions. There's no doubt it would be much harder to win so many All-Irelands under the current system, but it would be more rewarding, from a playing viewpoint, because of the busier schedule. Also, all counties are putting in more effort now. In our time, there may have been seven or eight counties working as hard as Kerry, but they are all at it now.'

There was very little difference in how Sheehy dealt with weak or strong defences in a career that spanned 49 championship matches, during which he won every honour in the game including eight All-Ireland senior medals, seven All Star awards, plus the 'Footballer of the Year' honour in 1979.

It's unlikely that his scoring exploits will ever be repeated, as he supplemented his instinctive predatory skills from play with consistent accuracy from frees.

His famous goal, scored against Dublin in the 1978 All-Ireland final, when he chipped a free into the net over Paddy Cullen's head, remains very high on the hit parade of famous sporting moments.

It was the ultimate in cheeky improvisation, as Sheehy calmly put the ball down and lobbed it gently over Cullen as he galloped back towards an unprotected goal. It had a seriously demoralising impact on Dublin, who fell apart in the second half, eventually losing by 17 points. Sheehy still shivers when he thinks of what might have happened if he had missed the target.

'It was just one of those moments when the gap appeared and I took a chance. Thankfully, it went in because if it hadn't, I would have been eaten alive at half-time. As it was, O'Dwyer just kept looking at me and saying nothing, but I knew what he was thinking. If I'd missed, I dread to think what might have happened. Let's put it this way – O'Dwyer wouldn't have been best pleased and would have let me know about it.'

The 1978 success launched Kerry on a glory trail that lasted until All-Ireland final day in 1982, when they were pursuing a place in history by becoming the first county to win the five-in-a-row. Kerry supporters saw it as a formality and got into celebration mode well ahead of the big clash with Offaly. Five-in-a-row songs were penned and sung, and souvenirs began to appear in shops all over a county where defeat was not considered an option. And all the time, Eugene McGee and Offaly were plotting.

'The whole thing got to us. O'Dwyer did his best to limit the hype but it was impossible. I thought he would explode on the Thursday night before the final, when we came away from training to find five-in-a-row t-shirts being sold outside the gate. The whole scene had gone crazy. And it got worse. I remember getting off the train in Heuston station on the Saturday to be greeted by a man from Sneem [home club of team captain, John Egan], who said he expected to see us all in the town with the cup on Monday night. I remember thinking, *This isn't right, there's still a game to be played*.'

And what a game. Séamus Darby's late goal snatched victory for Offaly in a final that Sheehy remembers with no affection. He didn't reach anything like his usual high standard and, to crown his discomfort, he missed a penalty in the second half, at a time when Kerry were a point ahead. A goal would almost certainly have clinched the title but Offaly goalkeeper Martin Furlong made a fantastic save.

'My legs were like rubber all through the game. I felt stiff and couldn't get any real movement going. Maybe it was the occasion but, whatever the reason, I didn't get into the game and the penalty kick reflected the way I was playing. I have always held that penalties should be kicked by a player who is on his game. If your confidence is high, you're more likely to get the penalties right. I wasn't going well that day and it showed in the way I took the penalty, although I don't want to play down Martin Furlong's save in any way.'

While that defeat prevented Kerry from breaking through a new frontier, Sheehy is convinced that, had they won in 1982, they wouldn't have captured another three-in-a-row in 1984–86. But, having lost to Cork in the 1983 Munster final, they regrouped for a second coming and restored dominance for the following three years.

Sheehy considered retiring after the 1986 final in which Kerry made a dramatic comeback to beat Tyrone because, by then, a series of injuries had left him with problems in both legs. One moment at the end of that final hinted to him that the end of the road was beckoning.

His father, Jim, who died in early 2004, was a quiet man, not given to great shows of emotion but, a few minutes after the 1986 final, he walked up to his son on the Croke Park pitch.

'He had a serious heart operation earlier in the year so I don't know how he got onto the pitch, but suddenly he was there. He said nothing but gave me a quick hug and was gone. I have often thought since that maybe he knew the good days were coming to an end.'

Sheehy would probably have quit only for Austin Stacks' victory in the Kerry county championship, which meant that it was his turn to captain the team in 1987. O'Dwyer heard that he was thinking of retiring and quickly got to work on changing his mind. O'Dwyer's pressure, plus the thought of being captain, persuaded Sheehy to stay on for 1987, but the magic had gone. He scored a trademark goal to help Kerry snatch a draw in the Munster final in Páirc Uí Chaoímh, but had an absolute nightmare in the replay in Killarney. It was to be his last championship game, one that fills him with dread every time he thinks about it.

'I ripped one of my boots during the drawn game and brought it to a *gréasaí* here in Tralee the following week, but he couldn't repair it. I was still trying to make up my mind which of my other boots I'd wear when I spotted a spare pair Ger Lynch had brought to training on the Saturday morning. I tried them out and decided they were perfect. Later on, I fitted new studs and went back down to the field that evening to practise some free kicks, which all sailed over the bar.

'What I didn't realise was that the grass would be cut shorter in Fitzgerald Stadium for the following day's game, but I spotted the mistake I'd made with the studs the second I led the team onto the pitch. I couldn't go back in and change because I was captain and had various things to do. And anyway, the lads would think my head was gone completely if I dashed back into the dressing-room to switch boots.

'The first free arrived and I lined it up as usual. Disaster. I barely raised the ball. It was an awful feeling and it got worse. I missed a few other frees too because I simply couldn't get my toe under the ball. At half-time, O'Dwyer demanded to know what the hell was going wrong. I couldn't tell him the truth. I told him I wasn't feeling right and would be happy to go off but he wouldn't hear tell of it. However, he decided that "Bomber" Liston, who fancied himself as a place kicker, would take the frees in the second half and, sure enough, his chance arrived very soon. It was a straightforward free but he didn't even get a good wide! The ball trickled harmlessly over the endline and suddenly O'Dwyer is running along the sideline roaring at me, "What the hell are you doing? Why didn't you kick that free?" It was that sort of day for me. We were well beaten in the end. The great era was over.'

If Sheehy had any illusions about returning for a final fling in 1988, they were shattered by another knee injury. It was the latest in a long series of ankle, knee and Achilles' tendon injuries that plagued him during his glittering career. On several occasions he needed pain-killing injections to enable him to play and, while they gave him short-term relief, the problems continued to mount up. He still suffers from severe pain in his knee on long car journeys or on certain days, but accepts it as an unfortunate legacy which couldn't be avoided. The Kerry squad received the best medical attention of that era but it was still a long way short of what's available in these sophisticated days for sports medicine.

Sheehy has continued his lifelong involvement with Gaelic football, having served as a minor and U-21 selector with Kerry and still looks back with the warmest of memories on a marvellous playing career. He believes that it's most unlikely that any team will emulate that remarkable Kerry squad, not just because of increased competition, but also because of the demands and stresses of modern life.

'Football always came first with us, but there wasn't as much stress in young people's lives back then. Nowadays, they're under a whole lot more pressure in their careers so it's very hard for players to keep going as long as we did. We were lucky that such a talented group of players came together under such a great manager and the more we won, the more we wanted to win.'

His own contribution to that glorious run was quite exceptional, although he modestly plays it down. Instead, he dwells on the excellence of his teammates, singling out midfielder, Jack O'Shea for the ultimate accolade.

'Undoubtedly, he was the best footballer I played with or against. An unbelievable talent in every way.'

It's also a description that wraps itself very neatly around Sheehy's glittering career, in which his achievement in winning seven All Star awards puts him in second place on the overall football honours list, two behind Kerry colleague, Pat Spillane.

Kerry's remarkable run between 1975 and 1986 ensured that they dominated the All Star lists virtually every year. They won 65 awards during that special period in the county's history. Kerry have won three All-Ireland titles since then, with the 2004 success being especially sweet after the misery of the previous three seasons. For Sheehy, the reassertion of Kerry values was most welcome.

'It showed that Kerry football isn't old-fashioned or in need of a serious overhaul. But then that was never the case, despite what some peole seemed to think in 2003.'

Mike Sheehy runs his own Financial Consultancy in Tralee. He and his wife, Gráinne, have two sons: Mike (22) and David (19).

You're Never a Stranger
When You've Hurled

Damien Martin (Offaly)

ALL STAR WINNER: 1971

'Up to that, we didn't think of beating Kilkenny and Wexford. We played as individuals trying our level best to compete, but the prospect of winning anything didn't come into it.'

A raw, winter morning welcomed Damien Martin into Shannon Airport on his way back from America in late 1971. He had been in New York playing with the Offaly club and, as usual, had enjoyed the experience immensely.

Still, it was nice to be back, but as he walked through the arrivals lounge he had no idea that his return was about to be marked by one of the greatest thrills of his hurling career.

'I bought the *Irish Press*, turned to the back page and couldn't believe what I saw.'

His picture, accompanied by some of the biggest names in hurling, beamed out at him. He checked it twice to make sure it really was there. He had been selected as goalkeeper on the very first All Star hurling team. The footballers were high fashion in Offaly at the time, having won the All-Ireland senior title for the first time three months earlier. The hurling team, though, had continued its constant battle for third place in Leinster, behind Kilkenny and Wexford.

Offaly's new-found football status ensured a strong representation at the inaugural All Stars. Indeed, given the scale of their achievement, they might well have dominated the team, but they had to make do with four: Eugene Mulligan, Nicholas Clavin, Willie Bryan and Tony McTague.

None of those selections came as any surprise, but even Martin was amazed to find himself named as the hurling goalkeeper. It wasn't that he lacked confidence in his own ability, but he felt that goalkeepers from the more successful counties had higher profiles, which would stand to them in the selection process.

'I simply couldn't believe it. I had been going fairly well but to get in ahead of the likes of the great Ollie Walsh was something else. I often wondered afterwards how I managed it. I think it might have had a fair bit to do with my performance in the Leinster semi-final where we lost to Wexford. Still, it came as a huge surprise to actually get on the team although strangely enough I should have guessed something was going on from a few weeks earlier. Obviously the team was picked well in advance of the announcement back then because I remember being told before a League clash against Dublin in Croke Park some weeks earlier to make sure I behaved myself during the game. I thought it a bit odd, but it all made sense later as I wouldn't have got the All Star award had I been sent off. Something else happened which should have made me suspicious. The Offaly team stopped off at Barry's Hotel in Dublin where a photographer came in and asked to take a picture of me. I thought nothing of it, but it was the one that later appeared with the announcement of the All

Stars. There would have been hundreds of pictures of Mick Roche, Frank Cummins, Babs Keating, Eddie Keher and all the other top names on file but D. Martin from Offaly wouldn't have figured very much. If you look back at the All Stars poster for that year, I'm the only player pictured in a shirt – the rest were all in their county jerseys.'

Ironically, that was to be his only All Star award, which is quite amazing given the input and influence he had on Offaly's dramatic metamorphosis from enthusiastic hopefuls to confident deliverers. But then, the 1970s continued to be as barren for Offaly hurling as the 1960s, which had ended on an encouragingly high note when Offaly beat Wexford to reach the 1969 Leinster final, where they lost by two points to Kilkenny.

Martin, who had made his Offaly senior debut in a League game against Wicklow at the age of 17 in 1964, had developed into a goalkeeper of considerable stature after taking over from Andy Gallagher, who had been an excellent No.1 for many years.

There were lots of other fine players around in the 1960s but, for whatever reason, Offaly couldn't make the breakthrough. Martin attributes that, in part at least, to the ferocity of the club rivalry, which left the county scene lacking the sense of unity and purpose that other counties enjoyed. However, things gradually began to take a new direction.

'Brother Denis took over around 1967 and he changed the scene for the better. I would also say that the arrival of my own club, St Rynagh's, as a major force, was hugely important. We won our first title in 1965 and suddenly the traditional clubs had this shower of brats in their midst. Then along came Kinnitty, who were also a fine team.

'Brother Denis was the ideal man for the time. He ran excellent training sessions and always insisted we had tea and sandwiches afterwards. Gradually, we began to get to know each other as Offaly colleagues rather than rivals from different clubs, who belted lumps off each other. He managed to get everybody hurling for Offaly rather than for themselves. Up to that, we didn't think of beating Kilkenny and Wexford. We played as individuals trying our level best to compete, but the prospect of winning anything didn't come into it. Brother Denis changed all that and I have no doubt that if he had got that group of players some years earlier, Offaly would not have had to wait so long for the breakthrough. As it happened, some of them were past their best when he came along.'

What followed was a decade of disappointment through most of the 1970s. Several teams took turns at beating Offaly but, as time went on, there was a gradual improvement, culminating in what Martin regards as one of their unluckiest ever defeats, when they lost to Wexford by a point in the 1979 Leinster semi-final in Athy.

It was fiercely frustrating and Martin, among others, felt it was time for a different approach.

'I proposed at a club meeting that we should get a coach from outside the county. I had nobody in mind, but I felt that we were on a pendulum and, while I didn't know what would swing it our way, I liked the idea of an outside voice. We had nothing to lose. We hadn't won an All-Ireland in almost 100 years of doing it our own way so why not try an outside coach? I was asked to propose the motion at a County Board meeting where a lot of hurling clubs were opposed to it. Thankfully, the football clubs were supportive and it was accepted. The rest is history. Dermot Healy was brought in from Kilkenny and he transformed everything. I knew absolutely nothing about him prior to that, but found him a delight to work with. Tony Reddin [a former Tipperary star goalkeeper] used to train St Rynagh's and there wasn't a whole lot of difference between himself and Healy in terms of how the game should be played. Both put a huge emphasis on getting the first touch right at top speed. It might sound simple enough but we hadn't been doing that.

'However, I'd say Healy's biggest contribution to Offaly hurling lay in his ability to change mindsets. He talked us into winning matches we had no right to win. He repeatedly made the point that if, as had happened so often in the past, Offaly teams could match Kilkenny for 50 minutes, why not for the full game? He convinced us that we were as good as Kilkenny, but that we would have to work that bit harder to beat them. If we were prepared to do that and managed to keep calm when the big teams came at us, we could achieve anything.

'Healy wouldn't take the paint off the dressing-room walls in his team talks. There was no screaming or cursing or show-boating. He would outline in detail what he wanted from us but he always got his point across very forcibly.'

If Offaly were convinced that they had the right man, they were doubly reassured at half-time in the 1980 Leinster final against Kilkenny. They had targeted that game for the big breakthrough and, while Kilkenny still looked to be playing comfortably in the first half, they were now facing an Offaly team that knew how the black-and-amber mindset worked.

More than that, Offaly knew what adjustments Kilkenny would make.

'Dermot had predicted exactly what they would do, who they would change and when. He told us how they would react to certain situations and outlined how we could counteract them. Kilkenny probably thought that we wouldn't have the conviction to stick with it in the closing ten minutes, but we were ready for them this time. They threw everything at us, but we held on to win by a point.'

Less than 10,000 spectators turned out for the 1980 Leinster final, since Kilkenny supporters assumed that victory was a formality, while only a small number of their Offaly counterparts had genuine faith in their side.

A month later, Offaly lost the All-Ireland semi-final to Galway and, 13 months on, found themselves facing a second defeat by their near neighbours in the All-Ireland final, only this time the lessons learned in 1980 were put to good use.

Martin was – and indeed remains – a big fan of Galway hurling and was pleased to see them end 57 years without an All-Ireland title in 1980. Twelve months on, Galway had a double success on their agenda, but Offaly were driven by demons that weren't going to be denied, not even when facing a seven-point deficit early in the second half.

'I know people may find this hard to believe, but I was still convinced we could win. We had nearly beaten them with a ten-minute burst a year earlier and I felt that, sooner or later, we would get a run on them. When we did, we made it count, even if Johnny Flaherty left it late to get the winning goal!'

Martin had made some crucial saves which were probably just as important as Flaherty's goal, even if they don't figure as high on the folklore charts. For instance, a second-half block from Noel Lane was quite remarkable and possibly decided the outcome of the game.

While it was a great day for Martin and Offaly, it was a sad occasion for John Connolly, one of Galway's greatest-ever hurlers. It turned out to be a last championship game for a man whom Martin still regards as one of the true giants of the game.

'People may have forgotten what John Connolly did for Galway in their bleaker years. I remember watching in absolute awe at his performance against Tipperary in the 1971 All-Ireland semi-final at Birr. It was as good as I have ever seen. The man was a genius.'

Just as Connolly won his All-Ireland medal at a time when his career was nearing an end, Martin admits that his own standards began to dip a little in the 1980s. Galway supporters, in particular, might disagree with him, but with work pressures increasing all the time, he decided to retire after the 1980 All-Ireland semi-final defeat.

However, he was coaxed back after the narrow 1981 Leinster semi-final win over Laois and went on to contribute enormously to a special season for Offaly hurling. A year later, they had a third Leinster and second All-Ireland title in their sights, when they came up against Kilkenny in the provincial final. It's a game that still evokes passions whenever it's discussed. Offaly were protecting a three-point lead with six minutes to go, when Martin attempted to nurse a speculative Kilkenny shot out over the end line.

However, Liam Fennelly chased the 'lost' cause and flicked the ball across to Matt Ruth, who slammed it into the Offaly net. Two Kilkenny points followed and Offaly's reign was over, leaving their bewildered goalkeeper to declare that he would have plenty of time to keep the crows away from the barley that summer.

Arguments rage to this day as to whether the ball had crossed the line before Fennelly whipped it across to the goal. Martin has no doubts that it had gone wide.

'No question – it was comfortably a few inches over the line. I got criticised for not playing it but I knew exactly what I was doing. Unfortunately for us, a wide wasn't given and Kilkenny exploited it.'

Martin got one more chance to win a second All-Ireland medal as a player but, after reaching the Centenary final in Thurles in 1984, Offaly left their form at home and were easily beaten by Cork. Rather bizarrely, the team assembled in the Anner Hotel, Thurles, a few hours before the game to be greeted by Offaly supporters and assorted others, whose minds were very much on All-Ireland-day fun, not the serious business of playing. It was such a carnival atmosphere that even when the squad went for a puckaround in a field near the hotel, they were accompanied by supporters, many of whom dispensed briefly with their pints to accompany their heroes and remind them of how good they were.

Whether it had any impact on the All-Ireland final performance is a matter of conjecture, but Cork were far too polished for Offaly, winning easily by 3-16 to 1-12.

It was to be Martin's last All-Ireland final as a front-line player, although he would win his second All-Ireland medal as a sub to Jim Troy in 1985. Martin worked extremely hard with Troy that year, especially on the squash court, where they spent hours locked in combat. It was to prove hugely beneficial. Troy had an outstanding year as Offaly powered their way to All-Ireland glory, beating Kilkenny and Laois in Leinster, Antrim in the All-Ireland semi-final and Galway in the final. Martin is still convinced that the failure to select Troy on the All Star team that year was a dreadful injustice. The award went to Cork's Ger Cunningham, a goalkeeper for whom Martin has the utmost regard, but he insists that Troy was very definitely No.1 in 1985.

Martin himself had one more big day out in the 1986 Leinster final, when he deputised for Troy, who had broken his thumb. Kilkenny won by 4-10 to 1-11 in a game that marked the end of an inter-county career that had begun almost 22 years earlier in a National League game against Wicklow at Ashford. Westmeath had beaten Offaly by six points in the 1964 Leinster championship, so morale wasn't especially high in the green, white and gold camp heading into the new League season. With Andy Gallagher unavailable, Martin got his chance to achieve a long-cherished dream of playing for Offaly when he came on as a sub in a game that Wicklow won.

'Naturally, since it was my first game I remember it well, even the embarrassment of being asked for my autograph on the way into the ground. I hadn't even made my debut, but obviously the kid who wanted me to sign his autograph book didn't know that. I played fairly well when I came on but we still lost so I'm sure he wasn't very impressed. Neither were Offaly people.

'But then, it wasn't the only time that Wicklow caused us problems. We beat them in a League game in Aughrim by two points in the late 1970s, which might sound like an exciting game until you look at the score line: Offaly 0-3 Wicklow 0-1. And Pádraig Horan got two of our points from centre-back!'

Martin has mixed memories of the days when forwards were allowed to 'challenge' the goalkeeper which, in many cases, was an excuse to virtually assault the unfortunate No.1s. It led to some thundering battles between brawny full backs, whose brief was to protect the goalkeeper from determined full forwards intent on getting at him.

'I had good men minding me, but I still ended up with loads of stitches. Even if the full backs held their men out, the forwards would pull one-handed over them and very often make contact with the unfortunate goalkeeper. It was even worse when the rule was changed. The backs had to be more careful in case they gave away a free by stopping the forwards coming in on the goalkeeper, but forwards didn't give a damn. They knew that a free out was the heaviest price they had to pay, so for about a year after the rule was changed, it was pure bedlam.

'Still, I liked the old system because it made you feel really involved but, having said that, there were lads playing in full back and forward lines back then who wouldn't get on junior teams now. Plenty of them are walking around with All-Ireland medals too, while some very good hurlers, who would thrive nowadays, got nowhere then because they were thought to be a bit windy.

'The truth is that some outstanding stickmen were half-killed. The abuse the likes of Jimmy Doyle and Eddie Keher took was unreal, but they survived it. I wonder how some of the star names of the modern game would have coped in that era? I was in dressing-rooms where I heard fellas being told to take certain opposition players out of it. I remember being so pumped up going home from training on a Wednesday night that you'd eat thorny wire there and then, never mind on the following Sunday.'

Different times, different attitudes. It amuses Martin when he hears some modern-day players complaining when, in fact, they are living in a privileged world that didn't exist for the previous generation.

'Don't get me wrong. I'm all for looking after players well, but it has to apply right across the board. It seems to me that the players who complain loudest are those whose careers have benefited most from hurling and football. Good luck to them, but the games are there for all the players not just a high-profile minority. When you think of the many fine players from weaker counties, players who put in so much without ever getting a chance to sample the big time, it puts things in perspective. I'm thinking, for instance, of players like Pat Dunny and Tommy Carew [Kildare], Paddy Quirke [Laois], Johnny Carroll [Laois], Declan Lovett [Kerry], Pat Jackson [Westmeath], plus, of course, lads like Paddy Spellman, Barney Moylan, Paddy Molloy and Tommy Errity from Offaly. Great players all.'

Current players can have no appreciation of how times have changed, but Martin paints a vivid picture of life in the real GAA in the late 1960s.

'I was working in Clifden in the summer of 1969 and I used to drive up to Birr on Wednesday and Friday nights for training. It was quite a run in my old Anglia car, especially as the roads weren't very good at the time. We reached the Leinster final that year and I remember driving to Birr for training on the Friday evening before the game and back to Clifden that night to work a half-day on Saturday. Can you imagine that happening now? The mileage rate, in Offaly at least, was 3p [4 cent] so you wouldn't exactly make a fortune, especially when you consider the wear and tear on an old car. Anyway, I got a cheque for £103 [€130] travelling expenses coming up to Christmas that year and it was as if I'd won the Lotto. I'd have to say that the late John Dowling was very good to us. John always held that no player should be out of pocket and made sure it didn't happen.'

Hurlers enjoy a much better lifestyle nowadays, but the trappings of a more sophisticated age should not be mistaken for a belief that the game is more solidly based. On the contrary, Martin believes that the game is in trouble and needs urgent attention.

'It's only getting lip service at present. The standard of club hurling in many counties has gone way down. There are too many senior clubs in some counties, several of which would have been of intermediate standard 20 years ago.

'For all that, hurling will survive in the strongholds, but the nearer you get to the towns and cities, the less hurling you see. The only way to promote and develop hurling is to invest in clubs and coaching. That will take big money, so why don't we use Croke Park to generate it? You'll hear lads talking about keeping foreign games out of Croke Park, but if they spent as much time worrying about hurling, the game would be much stronger. I can't see any reason why Croke Park couldn't be rented to other sports, with the money earned by the GAA going to develop hurling.

'While I'm on the subject of Croke Park, I made a suggestion to a very senior GAA official some years ago that a section of the new stadium should be set aside for former players, who would be allowed to buy tickets for big games. It would be a nice gesture of recognition for their contribution over the years and would also give ex-players a chance to meet each other. It wouldn't be that difficult to administer. Anyway, I put my thoughts in writing and sent them off to a top official, who was in a position to at least have the idea considered, but I never even got a reply, which was bad form.'

Martin's concern for hurling is born of a deep devotion to the game, which continues to fascinate him as much now as when he was a kid. The highpoint was, of course, the 1981 All-Ireland final triumph, but he always viewed hurling life in a far broader context than success or defeat.

'I remember going down the streets of Tullamore on an open-top bus the night after we won the 1981 final. The place was thronged, with thousands of faces beaming broadly up at us. Pádraig Horan turned to me and said: "Lord, Damien, isn't it all worth it now?"

'I replied: "It would be worth it anyway Pádraig, whether we won or lost." That's the way I felt about hurling. It was fantastic to win All-Ireland medals but, for me, there was more to it than that. It was about enjoyment, competition, making friends, seeing places, being part of a team. You see, wherever you go, you're never a stranger when you've hurled.'

---

*Damien Martin is a businessman. He and his wife, Josephine, have a grown-up family: Aimee, Eunan and Michael.

Another Day, Another Challenge

Brian McEniff (Donegal)

ALL STAR WINNER: 1972

'What we needed was to lose the fear of winning, not the fear of losing. That was an inherent problem for Donegal teams. We were afraid of winning. We needed to be mentally tougher.'

I f you want anything done in life, ask a busy person. That old adage is wholly appropriate for any account of Brian McEniff's life as a player, inter-county, provincial and international manager, GAA administrator, husband, father of ten children, Chief Executive of a hotel group and director of a number of semi-state bodies.

The more stress and pressure McEniff experiences, the more he appears to thrive. He admits he is hard on himself. The daily grind of running an inter-county football team, combined with the responsibilities of keeping a watchful eye over the 12 hotels in the chain he operates with older brother Seán, who acts as chairman, and the interaction with such a large family leave him with very few spare hours in the day. But from an early age, McEniff has never known it any other way.

His success in football gives him far more pleasure than his rise in the business world. He was his county's first All Star in 1972 and the manager for each of Donegal's five Ulster senior championship triumphs in a 21-season period.

The crowning glory for McEniff will always be the 1992 All-Ireland title success, but the sum of the various parts of his life adds up to much more than one glorious September day.

To acquire a taste of McEniff's love of responsibility, it's best to go back to late 1971 when one Sunday newspaper ranked Donegal at No.31 in their football order of merit. Only Kilkenny wallowed below them. Donegal had come off the back of a terrible pre-Christmas League run, culminating in an embarrassing 2-14 to 1-4 defeat by Leitrim.

In McEniff's words, they had 'hit the wall'. They were managerless off the field, leaderless on it and in dire need of direction.

Only two years earlier, they had reached a National League semi-final against Offaly, which they lost badly and the slide that followed was alarming.

McEniff was only 28 years old at the time, but he was one of the county's most prominent players – he had been part of an unofficial All Star team which travelled to San Francisco the previous year – and his hotel business in Bundoran was beginning to thrive.

The local St Joseph's team were the first winners of an unofficial All-Ireland club title in 1968 and, with a willingness to take the burden on his shoulders, McEniff was appointed Donegal player–manager.

'When I was young I was always putting teams together in my head, combining great players from Donegal with those from around the country. I liked the responsibility of putting structures together. I suppose at the time I took over Donegal I was playing good football. St Joseph's were successful, I was a regular on the Ulster team and business was good. I took over the running of the family hotel, The Holyrood, when my father took ill and had bought The Hamilton Hotel beside it as part of an expansion. I had learned to accept responsibility and how to deal with issues and people and felt like having a crack at the Donegal job.'

He set about putting a management team together and came up with some interesting names. Mick Higgins had initially been approached to manage, but opted instead to advise. Jim 'The Natch' Gallagher, Connie Maguire, Gerry McCafferty and Columba McDyer, the Glenties man who won an All-Ireland medal with Cavan in the famous 1947 Polo Grounds final, all came on board as selectors. The rest is history.

Within eight months of McEniff's appointment, Donegal were crowned Ulster champions for the first time. To him, it remains a more emotional day than 20 years later when the Sam Maguire Cup headed for the Hills.

'Tears flowed in Clones that day. After where we had been in the League it was a remarkable achievement by everyone. It was the first time that real self-belief had been shown by a Donegal team. It was a great challenge, although difficult at the start because of the club factions in the county. I had to learn more about the politics of Donegal football than about management itself.

'I had been to boarding-school in St McCartan's in Monaghan, then hotel school in Dublin, before I went to Canada in the early 1960s, so I hadn't grown up understanding the politics of Donegal football. There was a lot of bitterness there which I wasn't totally aware of, but I worked my way around it. It's what would have earned me respect in Donegal. It wasn't so much the success, but the even-handedness with which I managed the county team's affairs. People knew I would pick the best players without any parochial influence.'

His role off the field in 1972 was surpassed by his contribution on it. In the Ulster final, Donegal found themselves five points down to Tyrone at half-time on a wet, miserable day. He kicked an early point and, when Seamus Bonnar's speculative delivery found its way to the net through the Tyrone goalkeeper's hands to level the match midway through the half, it was McEniff who claimed the kick-out and drove over the lead score. They won by five points, lost an All-Ireland semi-final against Offaly to a controversial goal and, later that year, the player–manager was honoured with the right half-back position on the second All Star team. At 29, he was already a legend among his own people.

Bundoran has always been home to McEniff, a name that is almost the signature to one of Ireland's most popular holiday resorts. His father, John, originally from Newbliss in Co. Monaghan, was on his way to America when he decided to go to Bundoran to say goodbye to his sister Katie, who was married and living there.

During the brief visit, he met a Carrickmore woman, Elizabeth Begley, who was working in a local pub and consequently his plans to go to St Paul in Minnesota were shelved. He later married Elizabeth and, at the age of 95, she is still living in Bundoran.

Brian was the youngest of five children in the McEniff household and acquired a great love of sport from his father.

'He was born in Scotland, but returned home to Monaghan at just three months with his uncle Terry, after his own father had died. The Scottish roots never died. Through my father, I was well versed in Scottish soccer and that naturally spilled over into English soccer as well,' said Brian.

Another icon of McEniff's youth was the renowned Irish golfer Christy O'Connor, who played on the Ryder Cup team during his time as the professional at the local Bundoran course.

McEniff grew up on a diet of soccer as much as Gaelic football and had as many trips to see Sligo Rovers as the Donegal football team. He recalls long, hot summer evenings when the local boys would take on teams of Scots who were on vacation in the town.

Some formative years were spent on his grandparents' farm in Carrickmore, where his love and affinity for Tyrone developed.

He also learned to play the piano and organ, which remains one of his favourite pastimes to this day. How many inter-county managers have that in their repertoire?

'I took piano lessons for eight years. I'd have a big love of music. There was great contrast in our house when I was growing up. My father had a quiet, gentle type of Fine Gael background but my mother was a strong republican. She admired De Valera and, later, Neil Blaney and as the stronger personality in the house, we would have followed her in that thinking.'

For years, the young McEniff wrestled with his love for two counties but, on Ulster final day in 1956, he realised his devotion to Donegal was far greater.

'Tyrone won the Ulster senior title that day against a great Cavan team, but Donegal won the Ulster minor title for the first time. My father took me to Clones and I remember being far more excited about Donegal's win.'

He would later spend three years on the Donegal minor team that yielded little success, at a time when he was fulfilling his parents' wishes to attend hotel school in Dublin.

'I was the youngest and they were keen on someone coming into the business. They had made The Holyrood out of nothing and were very proud of themselves for that. My mother was a tremendous worker. To be honest, my preference would have been to do law at that time.'

In Dublin he played youth soccer for Bohemians and club football for Clan na Gael, although technically illegal. Still, he enjoyed himself alongside such great names as Mickey Whelan and Paddy Holden of Dublin, Kevin Coffey of Kerry and Paddy Reilly of Leitrim.

'I never bothered to transfer properly to Dublin. I just played away. You could do it back then. If you had a pair of boots, you played. There were no official checks. I played in a lot of different places, even with Trinity College. The great Mickey Whelan played with Clan na Gael, but he wouldn't have mixed freely with the young country boys. I get on great with him now, but I remember giving out to him about his attitude towards us when the matter came up in a New York taxi in about 1974!'

Back home in Donegal, McEniff made his debut for the senior county team in a 1961 Lagan Cup match against Armagh. For McEniff, the match was memorable, not just because it was his debut, but because it also marked the return to Armagh of well-known Celtic goalkeeper of the time, Eamonn McMahon.

McEniff's first stint with Donegal was short-lived, however, as he headed for Canada and a job in the landmark Royal York Hotel in Toronto.

With 1800 bedrooms and a staff of 2500, it was then the biggest hotel in the British Commonwealth and the fifth largest in the world.

'I could and should have worked in management but, for some reason I got it into my head that I wanted to work in the kitchens. For a qualified person, as I was, they couldn't understand it over there.'

McEniff immersed himself in hard work in Toronto and, even then, the business acumen in him surfaced quickly when he bought an apartment as an investment and filled it with tenants.

He also played for a local GAA club with whom he won three championship and three League medals. He made regular forays to New York where he played with the local Cavan team. He won an NFL medal with New York in 1964, but by 1965 he was yearning to return home.

'I went back that year and stayed long enough to win my first Donegal championship with St Joseph's [a Bundoran–Ballyshannon combination]. I knew then that my heart was in Bundoran.'

With his father taken ill, he made a permanent return to Donegal, took over the running of the hotel business and collected eight more county medals over a 15-year period, winning the last with Bundoran in 1979.

He continued to dabble in soccer and during the years of 'the Ban' he played soccer for Cork Hibernians under the assumed name of John Rooney, with whom he had shared accommodation in Toronto. Brian's wife, Catherine, hails from Ballinhassig (Cork) and on visits there McEniff would regularly take the field with Hibs.

'My mother-in-law used to laugh at it. I was known as John Rooney and it wasn't until Finn Harps joined the League that I phoned up the then Hibs secretary, the late John Crowley, and told them who I really was. I wanted them to stay in the hotel in Bundoran whenever they travelled up to play Harps.'

McEniff also retained contact with his friends in New York and, inadvertently, those links earned the first of his three sackings as Donegal manager in 1974.

On a visit to New York early that year, McEniff made a pact with John Kerry O'Donnell (Mr GAA in the Big Apple) that if Donegal won the Ulster title, the team would be brought over to the US. O'Donnell honoured that promise after Donegal won the replay against Down but, during the trip, the Kerry club, with whom McEniff had strong links, were fixed to play Donegal (New York) in the local final. McEniff played for Kerry, who won the game and when he returned home, he was unceremoniously sacked.

John Hannigan, who McEniff regards as one of Donegal's greatest ever players, took over but, within a year, he was back as player–manager for a second term. He was dispensed with again in 1977 and his playing days with Donegal were coming to an end as the burning pace for which he was renowned began to ebb.

With his hotel business thriving, McEniff cut his ties altogether, but returned for a third coming in 1981 and, within two years, Donegal were Ulster champions again. Two years later, Monaghan knocked them out of the Ulster championship and McEniff was made redundant for a third time. On this occasion, he had no argument.

'I was disappointed at the time but, on mature reflection, it was a correct decision. Tom Conaghan deserved his chance. He had won an All-Ireland U-21 title with a good group of lads in 1982 and was entitled to have a go.'

The Conaghan years didn't work out for Donegal and, by 1989, McEniff was back for his fourth and ultimately his most successful stint. With the basis of two All-Ireland U-21 winning teams (1982 and 1987) to work with, he believed he was on to something.

'I knew we were beginning to make real progress at that stage. A craftier Meath team beat us in the 1990 All-Ireland semi-final but we weren't far away. What we needed was to lose the fear of winning, not the fear of losing. That was an inherent problem for Donegal teams. We were afraid of winning. We needed to be mentally tougher.'

When they reached a fifth All-Ireland semi-final against Mayo in 1992, McEniff knew their time had come.

'Manus Boyle came on against Mayo and steadied the ship with some vital frees. He hadn't been selected for the Ulster final against Derry. Barry Cunningham also made an impact off the bench. Once we'd won the semi-final, I was confident we could beat Dublin. We had a good record against them in the League. We went out to play football and decided we weren't going to stand back from them.'

McEniff rates the influence of Martin McHugh as the central factor in the success.

'Anthony Molloy was the captain and leader but McHugh was the man that made it happen. I recall the great Seán O'Neill phoning me on the Sunday before the final. Seán doesn't talk to you, he talks at you and I remember him saying to me that if McHugh went down the barrel of the gun, we would win. I put that exact phrase to McHugh on the morning of the match. He didn't know where I got it from, but he did exactly what I asked. I think for all of us the joy on the faces of the Donegal people for weeks afterwards surpassed the football or the honour of winning itself.'

For the homecoming, McEniff walked the Sam Maguire across the bridge over the Bundrowes river that divides Donegal and Leitrim and into his home town of Bundoran though, ironically, his own chosen route would have been through the border village of Pettigo.

The scenes of revelry that followed were something that he, the most meticulous of planners, could not have legislated for.

'By the Thursday, I was laid up in bed and just about got to Martin "Rambo" Gavigan's wedding on the Saturday. I got away to Cork and then Majorca for a week but, when I returned, all hell had broken loose with the Sam Maguire Cup. It was going everywhere and anywhere and, as a result, we had to get the second cup out of Croke Park. But things got out of hand and that was quickly recalled. We probably didn't handle it all that well, but there was no holding back in the celebrations around Donegal in the following months.'

Donegal's good form continued during the League and they reached the final the following April, only to lose to a vengeful Dublin side after a replay. McEniff feels this may have cost them a second All-Ireland.

He insists he should not have continued in 1994 but, with trouble flaring in the background, he carried on and regretted it.

McEniff got out after the 1994 championship but continued to take charge of the Ulster team, a role he has retained since 1983, yielding 10 Railway Cup titles in all. Then, in 2000, he was appointed as International Rules manager for two years, which completed his remarkable managerial C.V. Ireland lost the home series but avenged those defeats spectacularly in Australia the following year.

By early 2003, with no replacement on the horizon for Mickey Moran, who had quit after the 2002 campaign, he was back for a remarkable fifth term as Donegal manager, a role he combined for a year with his duties as County chairman.

'I was already Central Council delegate, but became County chairman in 2003 to sort out difficulties the county were e riencing and I ended up being manager of the county team s well.'

The difference that 30 years makes struck home in one of his first meetings with the players.

'They were looking at me and saying to themselves, "What is this old fogey at?" And I was saying in my own mind back at them, "What am I at here?" We were poles apart, but gradually we hit common ground except for the odd disruption like we had after this year's [2004] Ulster final.'

Reaching an All-Ireland semi-final in 2003, which they lost to Armagh, and defeating Tyrone in the Ulster semi-final in 2004 have been the highlights so far of his fifth coming.

The McEniff business empire continues to grow. He owns six of the 12 hotels in the group and many of his 10 siblings are involved. He pools the hotels together with brother Seán, also owner of six across the country, for marketing and purchasing reasons.

'It's a successful group, but it's not something I ever set out to do,' he admits. As a director of Knock Airport, North West radio and Acorn Life, his workload is massive.

The pressure of business and football caught up with him briefly in January 2004, when he had stents inserted to correct a heart problem. It flattened him psychologically as much as physically because he thought his own body, which runs on four to five hours sleep a night, was 'indestructible'.

But he's had reassurance from someone close. 'My brother Liam is a doctor in Dublin and he told me I'm a better man now than I was before.'

He is also ready to write the next chapters of a remarkable and busy life.

---

*Brian McEniff is one of the country's most prominent hoteliers.
He is married to Catherine and they have a grown-up family of ten:
Mary, Catherine, Seánie, Fiona, Joanne, Brian Jnr, Tara, Barry,
Deirdre and Frances.

Dual in the Crown

Brian Murphy (Cork)

ALL STAR WINNER: 1973, 1976 (FOOTBALL); 1979, 1981 (HURLING)

'Players with the natural talent to excel in hurling and football are being forced to make a choice nowadays and I, for one, regret that. I believe it should be possible to accommodate them in both codes.'

It's one of the most elite clubs in Irish sport and Brian Murphy is justifiably proud of his membership. In fact, it's such an exclusive club that only three others have earned the right to enter the private lounge reserved for dual All Star winners.

Murphy's Cork colleagues, Jimmy Barry-Murphy and Ray Cummins, with whom he enjoyed so much success in the 1970s, and Liam Currams (Offaly), also hold the unusual distinction of having reached such levels of excellence in both hurling and football that they were selected as All Stars in both codes.

Winning an All Star award in one code is a lofty summit for any player to reach, but to be honoured in both sports is truly remarkable. To achieve it more than once really is something special. Attaining that level of excellence in two highly competitive field sports demands a massive amount of natural talent, combined with a physical and mental flexibility and limitless determination that relatively few possess.

Murphy, Barry-Murphy, Cummins and Currams had it all in glorious abundance in an era when the dual player slotted quite neatly into the fixtures' schedule. Cork was always the capital of dual player territory, being one of the very few counties with sufficient talent to have a realistic chance of winning an All-Ireland title in both codes on an ongoing basis. Of the 18 players who have won All-Ireland senior hurling and football medals since the foundation of the GAA in 1884, 11 were from Cork.

While Brian Murphy shares the dual All Star honour with three others, he stands alone in terms of All-Ireland success in both codes. He is the only player to have won All-Ireland medals in hurling and football at minor, senior and U-21 level, a truly amazing feat. Given the restricted opportunities for dual players in the modern game, it is most unlikely to be ever repeated. There's a whole lot more too. He won All-Ireland senior colleges' titles and Railway Cup medals in both grades and also enjoyed extensive football success with Nemo Rangers, including four All-Ireland titles. Quite simply, Murphy can present a very solid case to be considered the most successful dual player of all time.

His list of achievements is so long and varied that it's almost inconceivable that one individual could accumulate so many titles. Some players go through their entire careers without ever winning a major final but, astonishingly, Murphy won either a national or provincial title every year between 1968 and 1984. Quite often, he managed both. Long after his retirement, his greatness was further acknowledged when, in 1996, he was chosen at left full back on a team drawn from the previous 25 winners of the All-Ireland club football title.

Fate dealt him a lucky hand in that he was born into a club, county and college environment that not only encouraged and nurtured his wide range of skills, but also surrounded him with so many other exceptional talents that it was virtually certain he would amass a big title haul.

'I would be the first to admit that I was fortunate to have been living in an area where hurling and football were so strong and well organised in club and college. You often wonder how many other lads, who might have been just as talented, didn't get a chance to develop their skills because the proper structures weren't in place in their particular area,' said Brian.

For all that, his family and coaches could only do so much to provide a progressive sporting environment. The rest was down to him and, as his extraordinary list of achievements testifies, he used his talents to maximum effect across a wide variety of grades and competitions. His massive title haul, which excludes club successes within Cork, is as follows:

1968 – All-Ireland & Munster senior football colleges; Munster senior hurling colleges.

1969 – All-Ireland & Munster minor football.

1970 – All-Ireland & Munster minor hurling; All-Ireland & Munster senior football colleges.

1971 – All-Ireland & Munster U-21 football.

1972 – Munster senior hurling.

1973 – All-Ireland & Munster senior football; All-Ireland & Munster U-21 hurling; All-Ireland club football; All Star football award.

1974 – Munster senior football; National hurling League.

1975 – Munster senior hurling; Munster club football.

1976 – All-Ireland & Munster senior hurling; Railway Cup football; All Star football award.

1977 – All-Ireland & Munster senior hurling; Railway Cup football.

1978 – All-Ireland & Munster senior hurling; Railway Cup football.

1979 – Munster senior hurling; All-Ireland club football; All Star hurling award.

1980 – National hurling League.

1981 – National hurling League; Railway Cup hurling; All Star hurling award.

1982 – Munster senior hurling; All-Ireland club football.

1983 – Munster senior hurling.

1984 – All-Ireland club football.

A top-line senior dual player between 1972 and 1979, he concentrated on hurling for the remainder of his inter-county career, which ended in 1983. Like so many other Cork players in particular, he combined the dual role quite easily, something that is virtually impossible to do nowadays. Murphy regrets the loss of opportunities for dual players, believing that it is seriously detracting from the GAA menu.

'I had seven great years playing senior hurling and football for Cork. It was getting tougher to combine the two later on, which is why I gave up football, but I enjoyed both sports for as long as I could. I was lucky enough in that I didn't pick up many injuries, so I was able to have an extended run in both codes. Times have changed and the new structures for the hurling and football championships make it virtually impossible for players to combine the two nowadays. Present-day managers also take a different view. In my time, the dual player was regarded as a natural feature of GAA life and was accommodated as much as possible. Now, managers want players to concentrate on one sport only and while that's understandable up to a point, they are putting their own interests ahead of the player.

'There was a lot more give and take in my time, so I was able to balance the two sports. Cork were always good at making sure the dual players were accommodated and they gained as a result. Cork, and indeed the GAA in general, would have lost out heavily if players like Jimmy Barry-Murphy, Ray Cummins, Denis Coughlan, Dinny Allen, Teddy McCarthy and many others had to concentrate on one sport only.

'Players with the natural talent to excel in hurling and football are being forced to make a choice nowadays and I, for one, regret that. I believe it should be possible to accommodate them. Look at the situation which developed in Limerick this year. Some of their footballers were good enough to be on the hurling panel but, for whatever reason, it didn't happen. People in Limerick have to ask themselves the question – would the county have been better served if top-class dual players were encouraged and facilitated to play both sports?'

Murphy admits to having had a slight preference for hurling, yet it was football that provided him with one of the most special moments of his entire career. It arrived in his Leaving Cert year in 1970 when he was captain of the Coláiste Chríost Rí team that reached the All-Ireland colleges' final against St Malachy's, Belfast. It's a game that has gone down in history as one of the most dramatic in the long history of the famous Hogan Cup competition.

St Malachy's, inspired by Martin O'Neill, the former Northern Ireland soccer international and current Glasgow Celtic manager, led by 1-8 to 0-3 at half-time and, while Coláiste Chríost Rí launched a spirited revival in the second half, they were still two points behind in the final minute. However, in one last desperate fling, the Cork boys worked the ball downfield and Noel Miller kicked the goal that won the game by a single point, 4-5 to 1-13.

Murphy's love affair with Croke Park was underway and, over the next 14 years, he was a regular visitor, bringing his ultra-competent style to bear on the right and left corner of Cork's defensive operations. He was, it seems, destined to be part of the biggest Cork days, including the 1973 All-Ireland senior football final, when they won the title for the first time since 1945. Later, he would provide a crucial link in the chain that pulled Cork hurlers to the All-Ireland three-in-a-row in 1976–78.

While the hurlers delivered a big title haul, he feels that Cork should have got more out of their footballers in the post-1973 era.

'We won the Munster title again in 1974, but lost the All-Ireland semi-final to Dublin. We probably took them a bit for granted because they had come from nowhere, whereas we were All-Ireland champions and had beaten Kerry in successive years. Then, Kerry arrived on the scene and Cork didn't win another Munster final until 1983. We were very unlucky against Kerry in the 1976 final, which went to extra-time in the replay and, in many ways, that was a watershed for us. We had a very good team, but far too many changes were made for the following year and we lost momentum. That became the pattern for quite some time after that. Good players were let go purely on the basis that it was better to try out some new faces against Kerry when, very often, it would have been more advisable to get a bit of experience into the team. I have no doubt that if the current system were in operation back then, Cork would have done well in the qualifiers and been serious All-Ireland contenders most years. As it was, we just couldn't get past Kerry, which was very frustrating.'

Despite the subsequent disappointments with the football team, the memory of the 1973 All-Ireland success remains fresh in Murphy's mind. It had been all of 28 years since Cork had won the All-Ireland title, but they left nothing to chance in 1973. In fact, they out-scored all opponents so comprehensively that it seemed certain they would develop into double or possibly even triple champions. They beat Waterford by 2-14 to 0-3, Kerry by 5-12 to 1-15, Tyrone by 5-10 to 2-4 and Galway by 3-17 to 2-13 in the All-Ireland final.

'Some of those games weren't as easy as the scoreline suggests, but yes we played some wonderful football in 1973. We had some great goal-scoring forwards, who could pick their way through any defence. It really was a most enjoyable year, one that put Cork football back on the map. Unfortunately, we didn't build on it over the next few years, which was a great pity and a great loss to the county.'

Luckily for Murphy, Cork hurlers emerged as such a dominant force that they won three All-Ireland titles in a row in 1976–78 and five successive Munster titles in 1975–79. It was the third time that Cork had won the All-Ireland three-in-a-row and remains quite a landmark, even in a county where major success is a common currency.

'The three-in-a-row was very special. We had a great squad of players in that era and everything came together at just the right time. People say we should have completed the four-in-a-row but, on the other hand, we might have been caught on a few occasions in the 1976–78 period, so we were delighted with what we achieved rather than regretting that we didn't win more titles.'

They beat Wexford in both the 1976 and 1977 All-Ireland finals and edged out Kilkenny in 1978, a victory that was especially sweet for Murphy, who was based in Kilkenny as a Garda. Kilkenny has, in fact, become Murphy's home, as he still lives and works in the city and is heavily involved with the O'Loughlin Gaels club with whom his son, Brian, won a Leinster club medal in 2003.

'Living in Kilkenny always gave the rivalry with Cork an extra edge for me. I loved beating Kilkenny, but of course there were times too when I had to return to work after losing and you can imagine what that was like. The lads would be quite happy to let me know I was from Cork! That was definitely the case in 1972, when Kilkenny staged a fantastic comeback to beat us in the All-Ireland final. It was my first senior final and I certainly learned a few things that day against one of the great forwards lines of that era.'

Murphy often trained with Kilkenny clubs James Stephens, Dicksboro and O'Loughlin Gaels, but never considered leaving Nemo Rangers. The regular journeys back to Cork were tiring and time-consuming, but the draw to home and Nemo Rangers was so binding that the prospect of playing elsewhere simply didn't arise.

'We had a very tight bond in Nemo. We won the county title in 1972 and added the All-Ireland title a year later and, from there on, we were a very powerful unit. I won four All-Ireland club medals with Nemo and I really treasure every one of them. There's something special about winning an All-Ireland title with your club. It's the sense of achievement by a local community that makes it so unique. Whatever else the GAA does, it has to nurture the local scene because that's the bedrock of the entire Association.

'That's why I'm very concerned over the direction things are taking for club players nowadays. They are getting a bad deal in many counties because they have to fit their games around the county scene rather than the other way around. Hundreds of club players are left idle for long periods, simply to accommodate the inter-county programme. How can that be right? Why should the elite minority dictate to the majority? I see this as one of the biggest problems facing the GAA, one that has to be tackled and sorted because it's a threat to the future well-being of hurling and football.'

He also has concerns over the trend in hurling, fearing that a few leading counties such as Kilkenny, Cork and Tipperary will dominate to such a degree that the game will suffer nationally. New systems are being introduced, which will provide more championship games for all counties, but Murphy believes that the traditional superpowers will benefit most of all in the longer term.

'I'm not sure if we will ever have a situation where 10 or 12 counties have a genuine chance of winning an All-Ireland hurling title, but that has to be the aim. It's great for hurling in Kilkenny and Cork to contest so many All-Ireland finals, but the broader interests of the game would be helped by a much wider spread of titles. It's disappointing to see so many counties slipping further back down the rankings every year.'

As a keen student of trends and innovations, Murphy keeps a close watch on how both hurling and football are evolving. He has no doubt that football has undergone far more changes than hurling since his playing days, not all for the better either.

'We played a far more direct type of game. Nowadays, the priority is to retain possession, which has led to a big increase in hand-passing. There's also more "professional" fouling in modern-day football. Hurling hasn't changed that much other than in terms of speed. Players train longer and harder nowadays, so the game is played at a faster pace, which makes it very exciting. However, on the downside, I'm not sure if some of the skills are as refined as they used to be. For instance, it's rare to see a player execute an overhead pull anymore, which is a pity because it's a fantastic skill when done properly.'

Whatever the era or the style, Murphy would have slotted comfortably into any top side in either hurling or football. A quiet, methodical defender, he brought a great sense of order and discipline to his play, qualities that sustained him at the top of his trade for a very long time.

His devotion to Gaelic Games continues through his involvement with O'Loughlin Gaels, where he is a senior hurling selector. His son Brian has played at minor and U-21 level for Kilkenny, while his three other children are also heavily involved in hurling and camogie.

When it comes to looking for advice on the art of excellent defence, they need look no further than their father, a man who contributed so much to college, club, county and province in a truly remarkable career.

Brian Murphy is a Detective-Garda based in Kilkenny.
He and his wife, Ann, have a family of four: Brian (23),
Ciara (21), Orla (17) and Stephen (14).

Sharing a
Family Dream

Dermot Earley Senior (Roscommon)

ALL STAR WINNER: 1974, 1979

Dermot Earley Junior (Kildare)

ALL STAR WINNER: 1998

'He is more mobile. He has a much better engine, is a higher jumper and a more creative player than I was.' Dermot Earley Senior

'I have been on the Kildare team for a good few seasons now but I still pick up lots of constructive tips from him.' Dermot Earley Junior

Dermot Earley, Senior grew up with a dream. In it, Croke Park was ablaze with primrose and blue on All-Ireland football final day; he played at midfield and turned in a commanding performance as Roscommon ended a generation of disappointment by winning the All-Ireland title for the first time since 1944.

At the age of 32, fifteen years after making his senior debut, part of the dream was realised. Roscommon reached the All-Ireland final in 1980; Earley played at midfield, but they didn't win, becoming the latest team to be ensnared by the sheer efficiency of a great Kerry side. It was to be Earley's one and only senior All-Ireland chance.

Dermot Earley, Junior inherited much the same dream from his illustrious father. The only difference was that in his version he would be wearing the Lilywhite Kildare jersey when they finally ended a long wait for All-Ireland glory.

At the age of 20, in his first full season as a senior player, Earley found himself lining out in Croke Park on All-Ireland final day. Nineteen minutes into the game, he swept into the Galway square and flicked the ball into the net. Croke Park danced on a sea of white, as that goal looked as if it might be Kildare's launch pad to a whole new world. It wasn't. Galway rallied bravely and skilfully and eventually won by four points.

Dermot Jnr is still waiting for a second All-Ireland final chance but the ambition remains very much alive. Both father and son are convinced that, however long the wait, All-Ireland glory will be achieved.

Already, the Earleys have joined an exclusive club, occupied by fathers and sons who have won All Star awards. Dermot Snr was chosen at midfield in 1974 and 1979, while Dermot Jnr was the choice at left half-forward in 1998. The Earleys are also members of an even more exclusive All Star club involving a third family member, because Dermot Earley Snr's brother, Paul, won an award at full forward, after having an excellent season with Roscommon in 1985. However, unlike his brother or his nephew, Paul never got a chance to play in an All-Ireland final.

While there is a vast difference in terms of the stage of their careers in which All-Ireland opportunities presented themselves to father and son, there are so many other similarities between them that it's almost as if their paths were synchronised by outside influences.

Dermot Earley Snr played for Roscommon minors at the age of 15; Dermot Earley Jnr played for Kildare minors at the age of 16. Snr made his senior inter-county debut at 17; Jnr at 18. Snr became an Army Cadet after leaving secondary school; so did Jnr.

Of course, there are differences too, not least that they represent successive generations in a game that is constantly changing and evolving. It's quite common for players from former years to denigrate the modern approach, depicting it as a soulless, running game that lacks the touch and flair of previous times.

However, while Dermot Snr harbours reservations about certain aspects of the modern game, he has no doubt that, in general, it has altered for the better.

'The standard of fitness is so high; the game is much faster and it has never been more competitive. Contrary to what some people suggest, I believe that the execution of skill is much better too. I'd love to be able to play in the modern environment to see would my abilities come up to the mark. The attitude to the game is more obsessive now. We worked very hard in our day but it's even more intense now. I'd also say that modern-day players are better at handling pressure. They are part of a more confident, adventurous generation, which helps them to cope with challenges extremely well.'

While there is always a tendency to look back on previous generations of sportspeople with a misty-eyed view, Dermot Snr insists that, in terms of tactical planning, the past had its experts, too.

'I remember back in 1980 how Tom Heneghan [Roscommon coach] presented all the players with a white card, outlining a whole range of points that were relevant to your particular game. It was really detailed, stating what was expected when you had the ball, when the opponents had the ball, when you lost possession etc. It was simple, yet sophisticated; basic, yet smart.

Also, the entire squad took holidays at the same time coming up to the All-Ireland final. We trained morning and evening for seven days. I'm not even sure if it was allowed under GAA rules, but we did it anyway. It showed how driven we were, so it would be wrong to think that this is the first generation which has gone in for very careful planning.'

Dermot Jnr takes mixed signals from the past anytime he watches videos of his father's games.

'Sometimes, you look at a certain player and wonder how he ever got on a senior inter-county team, but then you see some spectacular catches or fantastic long kicks and you have to ask if they were better executed than nowadays. In some cases, the answer is yes. The big difference, I suppose, is in terms of preparation. Back then, teams trained maybe three or four times a week, whereas it can be anything up to six times a week nowadays. Also, there's an awful lot more scientific analysis going on. Computer software is now being used to provide an incredibly detailed level of information, which obviously would have been unheard of in the past.'

Dermot Snr is a big fan of in-depth analysis but fears that it's being used too negatively.

'The balance may be tipping in the wrong direction. As much emphasis is placed on what to do when the opposition has the ball, as to how to create when your own team is in possession. There's a place for that but it can be overdone. Take high fielding, for example. It has always been one of the great skills of Gaelic football but, nowadays, when a player makes a high catch, he is usually surrounded by a few markers when he arrives back down. Very often, he can't move. That encourages fielders to flick the ball to a colleague in a rehearsed move because it switches the point of play. It's a natural reaction to an evolving situation, but it has tended to rob the game of high fielding and that's everybody's loss.'

It's inevitable that comparisons are made between the Earleys, a battle that Dermot Jnr is always likely to lose on the basis that fathers are generally deemed to have been better than their sons. Every promising son has been told at some stage or another that he isn't 'a patch on' his father. Dermot Earley Jnr has heard it too, but no longer takes any notice. Besides, his father has a totally different view, contending that his son possesses quite a few attributes that he lacked.

'For a start, he is more mobile. He has a much better engine, is a higher jumper and is a more creative player than I was. That probably comes from his ability to get around the field so easily. However, there's one area where I would hold an advantage – I was better on my left side than he is.'

That came from the influence of his late father, Peadar Earley, who founded Michael Glavey's GAA club in Roscommon in 1955. Under constant pressure from his son to join him for a kickaround, he would promise to play once Dermot could kick the ball properly with his left foot, whereupon the eager youngster would practise intently before requesting another inspection. Dad would stand at the door and assess progress, but he didn't join in until his son was equally comfortable with left and right. It was a highly effective way of inculcating a precious skill.

Dermot Jnr accepts that his father had a better left-sided game and also believes that he was a superior passer and finisher. Still things to work on then for one of the most industrious players in the game. Dermot Snr remains so closely involved in the game that he can keep the advice tap open virtually on a day-to-day basis. He is chairman of the Sarsfields club in Newbridge, so Dermot Jnr is still likely to hear the occasional whisper during a game.

Having spent so much of his life as a Roscommon player and later as manager, prior to taking charge of Kildare for two seasons, it was inevitable that Dermot Snr would remain immersed in the game even if his sons Conor, David (who also played for Kildare) and Dermot had chosen other sporting pursuits.

Still, it was never likely that the Earley boys would ignore Gaelic football and, from the moment David and Dermot were called to U-14 trials with Kildare, white became the Earley household's theme colour. Dermot Snr will always have an abiding passion for his native Roscommon but for as long as his family's Kildare careers last, Lilywhite action will naturally take priority.

The line between constructive suggestions and excessive interference can be difficult for a parent to negotiate, but Dermot Jnr has always regarded his father's advice as a hugely positive influence.

'He has seen and done it all at every level, so there isn't anything he doesn't know about how the game should be played. I have been on the Kildare team for a good few seasons now, but I still pick up lots of constructive tips from him. If we're playing in Croke Park, I would spend the night before a game at home and we would talk things through. My mother would also have a word or two to say on the morning of a game and always something very relevant, too.'

Dermot Snr derives just as much pleasure from watching his son deliver at the lofty peaks of his potential, as he got from playing well himself. The 1998 All-Ireland semi-final against Kerry is a specific example. With Niall Buckley injured, Earley Jnr was told by Mick O'Dwyer, when the squad got to the Croke Park dressing-room, that he would be playing at midfield.

With quite a long time to go to the start of the game, he joined his father on the stand for a briefing session on how he should react to the new responsibility. Dermot Snr, a veteran of so many midfield tussles in big games, laid out a series of basic priorities and guidelines. A few hours later, Kildare had reached the All-Ireland final and Jnr was man-of-the-match. As Snr left Croke Park, he felt as happy as if he had actually been playing.

Memories of the 1998 final still weigh heavily on the whole of Kildare. Galway's second-half burst eroded Kildare's half-time lead and, while they finished strongly, a disastrous third-quarter left them with too much left to do. Scoring a goal was a personal highlight for Dermot Jnr but, in the end, it counted for nothing as Kildare's great adventure had ended in disappointment – even if the year would later be regarded as a major success since they had won the Leinster title for the first time in 42 years.

'In hindsight, it was almost as if Galway's name was on the title all along. We had some injury worries going into the game, which proved very disruptive. We did well enough up to half-time and were actually leading by three points at the interval, but when Galway hit their purple patch in the second half, they could do no wrong. They got one point that almost defied logic. Glenn [Ryan] was shepherding Ja Fallon further and further out towards the sideline. It was the perfect defence but, just when it looked as if Ja had nowhere to go, he turned on his left and fired over a point from under the Cusack Stand. Later on, I let fly with a shot that flew just over the bar, while Brian Murphy hit the post. It was that sort of day for us, certainly in the second half. We tried everything but just couldn't get it right, while Galway landed some unbelievable scores. Mind you, I'm not taking away from Galway in any way, they played some wonderful football in the second half,' said Dermot Jnr.

Dermot Snr has a slightly different view, believing that Kildare contributed to their own downfall.

'I had doubts from very early on when I saw the way Kildare responded to the changes that were necessary to counteract Galway's areas of dominance. Frankly, they didn't do a whole lot to address the problems that Galway were causing them. For example, Martin McNamara was allowed to repeatedly find midfielder Kevin Walsh with his kick-outs. He was able to bounce them in front of Walsh and it just seemed to go on and on, without any response from Kildare. It was one of the major factors in giving Galway the initiative, which they used extremely well.'

It wasn't the first time Galway had thwarted the Earley family, although Dermot Earley Snr did enjoy some good days against the maroon-and-white too. Not least the 1978 Connacht final in Pearse Stadium, which Roscommon won. It was a particularly happy time for Dermot Snr, as Dermot Jnr had been born a few days earlier.

'It was one of those days when we couldn't go wrong. We started very well and got in for two goals, so Galway changed their defence for the second half. They brought in Stephen Kinneavy, who was one of the longest dead-ball kickers in the game. I knew that because he was based as a Garda here in Newbridge and I had played with him. Anyway, he took a kick-out just after half-time and, as he did, I dropped back a few yards behind midfield. The ball sailed over the heads of the other lads and dropped into my hands. I couldn't believe I was unchallenged, but it was all down to the fact that I knew how far Stephen could drive the ball.'

That was, of course, a glory period for Roscommon football, during which they won four successive Connacht titles, culminating in an All-Ireland final clash with Kerry in 1980. It's a game that still evokes sadness among Roscommon supporters. Roscommon led by 1-2 to 0-0 after 12 minutes, but failed to exploit an excellent start. It turned into a sour war of attrition from there on, with Kerry eventually winning by three points. It was the end for that particular Roscommon team and, after losing a League final to Galway in 1981, the county went into a downward spiral and failed to win another Connacht title for ten years.

It was Roscommon's bad luck that they came up against a special Kerry team in 1980. In fact, it's generally felt that they would have won an All-Ireland title in any other era, a view with which Dermot Snr concurs.

'In hindsight, we should have done things differently against Kerry. We should have been more positive after we opened up an early lead, because we really had them going. Of course, that Kerry team was something special, which made our task all the more difficult. But we had our chance and didn't exploit it, which was very disappointing. We had a very strong team back then and certainly there have been All-Ireland championships since then when I reckon the Roscommon team of 1980 would have been good enough to win the final.'

While he was destined to end his days without an All-Ireland senior medal, he won virtually every other honour in the game, including two All Star awards, while he was also selected as a replacement on no fewer than seven occasions.

Ironically for a man who had a reputation as an exemplary sportsman (a key requirement for All Star selection), Dermot Snr ran into controversy after being sent off for the only time in his career, following a clash with Bobby Doyle in a League game against Dublin in early 1975.

He was suspended, rather harshly, for two months and suddenly the question of whether he should be permitted to travel with the All Stars arose. The GAA seemed uncertain on the issue but, before it was resolved, a telegram arrived. Addressed to *Dermot Earley, Croke Park, Dublin,* it read: 'Cordial invitation hereby extended to Dermot Earley to travel with All Stars. All expenses paid by me. Red-blooded men always welcome in Gaelic Park.'

The sender was 'Mr GAA' in New York, the late John Kerry O'Donnell. Earley travelled with the All Stars as assistant to team manager Seán Purcell, a decision he later regretted. He understood that while playing was not an option, he would be part of the official party. He had a shock in store for him. A welcoming committee greeted the team and each player was summoned forward and presented with details of the tour, plus an allowance. Earley was called forward but there was no envelope for him. It was deeply embarrassing and, to make matters worse, it happened on three other occasions during the trip.

It was a shabby way to treat one of the game's great ambassadors but it didn't change Earley's view that the All Star scheme has added greatly to the GAA scene. So too have the international links with Australia but, unlike his son, he never got a chance to play an International Rules game, something that he greatly regrets. He was especially disappointed in 1984 when, as player–manager with the Connacht football team, he missed out on an opportunity to play against Australia.

The Australians were scheduled to play a game in Galway but, instead of taking on a Connacht side, they had a practice game against an Irish selection. Earley was very annoyed with the Connacht Council for their failure to push for the provincial team to provide the opposition. He still regards it as a lost opportunity for a whole squad of Connacht players.

Dermot Jnr has been luckier, having actually played for Ireland against Australia, experiences he thoroughly enjoyed.

Nowadays, as he looks at the football scene from the height of his considerable powers, he can scarcely believe that it's almost 20 years since that emotional day in Dr Hyde Park when his father quit inter-county football after Roscommon lost the Connacht final to Mayo. Dermot Jnr had only just turned seven years of age at the time and, although living in Newbridge, he considered himself very much a son of Roscommon.

Together with his older brothers, David and Conor, he travelled to training sessions and games, both of them dressed in their Roscommon jerseys. They saw themselves as unofficial subs and could never have foreseen a day when Kildare would be their county.

Dermot Jnr recalls the 1985 Connacht semi-final against Galway in Tuam Stadium, when his father sustained a fractured jaw. He had just blocked down an atttempted point by Galway when he was caught in an accidental clash, which forced him to leave the action. The sight and sound of 12,000 spectators giving his father a standing ovation as he walked up in front of the stand, on his way to the dressing-room, is still fresh in the memory.

The following day, the *Irish Independent's* match report by Donal Keenan noted: 'Earley may not have the pace of old, but he is still a very important component in this machine. However, he suffered a depressed fracture of the jaw near the end, which will threaten his availability for the Connacht final against Mayo in two weeks' time.'

Predictably, it didn't keep Earley out and, while he kicked six points from frees in the final, Mayo still won by nine points. It was time to quit the inter-county scene at the age of 37.

Using that criterion, Dermot Jnr still has 11 years to go, although it's doubtful if anybody could survive that long in the modern game. Not that retirement lurks anywhere on his agenda, as he looks forward to continuing the battle to land the great prize of an All-Ireland title with Kildare.

Up until 2004, Croke Park hadn't been a happy hunting-ground for the Earley family on All-Ireland final day. Dermot Earley Snr and Jnr both lost All-Ireland senior football finals there, while Noelle was on the Kildare junior football team which was beaten by Donegal in the 2003 final. However, she made the big breakthrough in 2004, helping Kildare to win the All-Ireland Ladies' junior football title.

Emulating his sister by winning an All-Ireland title in Croke Park remains top of the priority list for Dermot Earley Jnr who, like his father, is convinced that it will be achieved by Kildare at some stage over the next few years.

If so, it will be difficult to figure out who is the more proud, father or son.

---

*Major General Dermot Earley is Deputy Chief of Staff of the Defence Forces. He and his wife, Mary, have a family of six: David, Conor, Dermot Jnr, Paula, Anne-Marie and Noelle.

---

*Dermot Earley Jnr is an Army Captain in the 5th Infantry Battalion.

Home Is Where the Hurley Is

Noel Skehan (Kilkenny)

ALL STAR WINNER: 1972, 1973, 1974, 1975, 1976, 1982, 1983

'There were times when we only had one sliotar, so if it got lost in the long grass or in a drain, we would become one big search party.'

If the forces of darkness were ever to extend their influence on the world into total control, Noel Skehan knows what form it would take.

They would move stealthily overnight, creeping quietly into houses, seizing every hurley and sliotar in the country, before transporting them to Croke Park, where they would be carefully stacked. A petrol hose would be turned on the massive ash pyramid, followed by a dramatic torching, sending colourful flames billowing into the sky.

Some hours later, when Croke Park had been razed to the ground, an announcement would follow that every other GAA ground in the country faced similar demolition, after which the Association would be closed down permanently.

An Ireland without the GAA, a desolate land, where its people could no longer dance to the thrilling rhythm of club v club, county v county, spirit v spirit, would, in Skehan's eyes, be as close as it comes to hell on earth.

Hurling is, of course, his special devotion, but he knows that, just as he adores the sound of ash on leather, there are others who have equal affection for the delights of Gaelic football. Either way, it's an obsession that underpins so much of the sporting life of this country that Skehan believes it's not fully appreciated.

'We all give out about aspects of GAA life from time to time and that's as it should be because it's such a big part of what so many of us are. It wouldn't be natural if we didn't argue about certain things among ourselves, but it should always be seen for what it is – good, healthy debate.

'Imagine a world without the GAA. God Almighty, half of us would go mad in a week. The GAA is not without its faults, but it's doing a whole lot more right than wrong and we should always remember that.'

There isn't a single day of the year when Skehan doesn't think about hurling. In or out of season, it's always there, either very much to the forefront of his consciousness, during the playing season or simmering away quietly in the background, during the winter months.

It has been that way for as long as he can remember. Now, at the age of 59, his devotion and passion for the game is as finely tuned as when he held his first hurley as a toddler in Bennettsbridge in the late 1940s. Between the covers of that book dwells a fascinating tale of a man who can answer proudly in any roll-call of hurling legends and who still holds the record for having won the most All-Ireland senior championship medals in either hurling or football.

The fact that he won three of his nine medals as sub to Ollie Walsh is sometimes used to demean his achievement, but that's of absolutely no concern to Skehan, who looks back in joy at the bountiful harvest hurling bestowed on him.

'I have nine All-Ireland senior medals, three of which I won as a sub in 1963, 1967 and 1969, and six that I won on the pitch in 1972, 1974, 1975, 1979, 1982 and 1983. I know the pleasure I got from every one of them and that's all that matters to me.'

They are only part of the success story for Skehan, who also won 11 Leinster senior titles, three National Leagues, four Oireachtas titles, one All-Ireland minor medal, six county championship titles, seven All Star awards, four 'Player of the Month' awards, and one Texaco award, plus four Railway Cup medals and several 'Sports Star of the Week' honours in the *Irish Independent*.

He would later busy himself as a Kilkenny minor and U-21 selector and an intermediate manager, prior to becoming a senior selector at the end of 2001.

It's a truly amazing contribution to hurling, but he still talks as if he is in heavy debt to the game, rather than the other way around. But then that's the way he was brought up. A young kid in Bennettsbridge felt privileged to have been born in such fertile hurling country, a place where there were no other distractions and where dreams always started with a hurl in your hand.

'It's so different now, not just in Bennettsbridge, but in most towns and villages all over the country. Back then, you hurled or you played football, depending on where you were brought up, but now there are soccer and rugby clubs in most areas, not to mention all the other attractions and, indeed, distractions that modern life throws up. We grew up on hurling and nothing else. It was our whole life. Still is in many cases, certainly mine anyway.'

Skehan's uncle, Dan Kennedy, captained Kilkenny to the 1947 All-Ireland title, so from the moment Noel took his first steps down to the local GAA field, it was inevitable that he would be consumed by the pride and passion of his area.

Nowadays, competition is structured from an early age, but back then it was far more spontaneous as groups of young men assembled on weekday evenings and Sunday mornings to hurl among themselves.

'I would wander down to the field to see the older lads playing and hoping to get the occasional game. They would start off playing backs and forwards, so they needed a few young fellas to keep the ball pucked into them. I'd get down early hoping to be asked. As the evening wore on and more players arrived, they would play a full game, so you might be asked to play in goal. That's how I ended up there.

'Modern-day players have no idea of what it was like back then. There were times when we only had one sliotar so if it got lost in the long grass or in a drain, we would become one big search party. We'd go back playing if we found the ball but, when we didn't, things ended for the evening. It was as simple as that.'

It's a world that the current generation could never envisage but, however rudimentary it may have been, it cultivated hundreds of magnificent players through all the hurling heartlands.

In normal circumstances, Skehan would have established himself as Kilkenny's first choice early in his career, but it was never going to be easy since the man holding that position at the time was the legendary Ollie Walsh. Skehan slipped in quietly as No.2 to Walsh in 1963, winning an All-Ireland medal in his very first senior season. A year earlier, he had won an All-Ireland minor medal.

With the exception of 1965–66, when he was out with a neck injury sustained in a bad car smash, it was a role he would fill up to the end of the 1971 season, which ended with Tipperary beating Kilkenny in the All-Ireland final.

A year later, Skehan would return to Kilkenny, clutching the Liam McCarthy Cup. Kilkenny's long-standing tradition of awarding the captaincy to a player from the county champions benefited Skehan, who received the honour in his first full season with Kilkenny.

The 1972 All-Ireland final developed into a truly remarkable game, where Cork looked as if they were certainties to gallop to the easiest of victories when they opened an eight-point lead with 13 minutes remaining.

It would have been far higher only for Skehan's excellence. Yet, as he watched the ball sail high over his crossbar for yet another Cork point, he was feeling thoroughly miserable.

'I can still see Con Roche winding himself up in front of the Cusack Stand and launching a mighty point from around 80 yards. I reckoned that was that. We were eight points behind, Cork were rampant and there really didn't seem any way back. I was fed up pucking the ball out, only to see it return almost as quickly, so I just belted it out again, expecting the pattern to continue. And then, all changed. I didn't touch the ball again for ages. By the time I did we nearly had the game won. Our forwards took off and landed some fantastic scores and, before we knew it, we were ahead. We won by seven points in the end, which was unbelievable.'

Amazingly, Kilkenny had out-scored Cork by 2-9 to 0-0 in the final 12 minutes. It was a remarkable season for Kilkenny and for Skehan, who was later chosen as 'Hurler of the Year', while also winning the first of five successive All Star awards, which he increased to seven in 1982–83.

An injury-ravaged Kilkenny side lost the 1973 All-Ireland final to Limerick, but Skehan would win five more medals before finally retiring in April 1985 at the age of 39. He was still playing well but he had lost the appetite for the game, following the death of his mother, May, who had passed away earlier in the year.

Anyway, he felt it was time to go. He had been around the scene a very long time and the last thing he wanted was to stay on too long, possibly lose his edge and be remembered for a bad season.

'You never know when things could start to go wrong. I had enjoyed a great career so there was no point pushing it. I had got a whole lot more out of it than I ever expected when I took over from Ollie in late 1971. That was one hell of a challenge in itself, as Ollie was one of the best goalkeepers the game had ever seen.

'One of the interesting things that happened during my career was the change of rule regarding goalkeepers. Prior to that, the goalie was fair game for forwards, who were allowed to charge in on top of him while the backs did their best to keep them out. It could get fairly hot around the square but, once the rule was changed, giving goalkeepers more protection, we all had to readjust.

'Goalkeepers had to learn to deal with additional space and to avoid letting play develop anywhere near the goal. We had to become more mobile and better prepared to come off our line. Modern-day goalkeepers have to be even more vigilant still, as many teams use two-man full forward lines, so there can be an awful lot of space to cover close to goal. You can't expect two defenders to deal with that, so the goalkeeper has to play his part, too.

'Giving the goalkeeper more protection improved the game but, in general, I think that GAA rules should be very rarely tampered with. With one or two exceptions, they're fine as they are. Sometimes, I think they're changed just for the sake of it.'

With the playing span of modern-day players growing increasingly shorter, the sheer longevity of Skehan's career offers a fascinating glimpse into the mood of the time and his own dedication to the game.

'People often ask me how I survived so long. There was no great secret to it. I trained harder and harder every year, not by slogging around fields but on squash courts, in handball alleys and anywhere else I thought would help keep me sharp. I played squash in the Premier Division in Leinster and I found it a great help with my hurling. In fact, I'd strongly recommend it for every hurler. I found it amusing that people thought I could live off experience alone. Experience is all very fine in its place but it's damn all use to you if you can't get to the ball. It might tell you why you let in a goal, but it won't show you how to keep it out.

'The older I got, the harder I worked to keep sharp every year. I would go into training a half-hour early just to get a bit of extra practice. I used to plague Joe Hennessy, Brian Cody and some other lads to come in early, too, just to belt balls at me. But it had to be done. You simply can't cut corners or you'll get caught out.'

Although he has served as a player and selector, Skehan finds it impossible to make comparisons between Kilkenny teams from different eras, for the simple reason that hurling has changed. It's a quicker, more intense game now, but he believes that has had a negative impact on skills such as overhead striking, which is all but a lost art in hurling.

The relentless march towards fitness means that players train harder too. With all counties embarking on heavy schedules, there is no way of stepping off the carousel. It's a non-stop circuit, one that Skehan suspects may be shortening players' careers.

'I never heard of a hamstring or a groin problem in my time, but now they're cropping up every week. It makes you wonder if all the training is contributing to the injuries. There's also a danger that players burn out sooner than they should because of the demands being placed on them.'

For all that, he believes that hurling is healthier than it has ever been, not just in Kilkenny, where the production lines virtually guarantee a seat at the top table, but also in several other counties.

'I have been involved in this game a very long time and I can never remember a time when there were so many contenders for the All-Ireland title. And just below the top band, you have some decent sides coming along too. Hurling has to be nurtured, but I'd be quite confident that it has a very bright future.'

It is 32 years since Skehan won the first of his seven All Star awards, achievements of which he is immensely proud. He believes that the introduction of the All Star scheme was a hugely important development for GAA players, as it was the closest they got to being selected on an international team. Significantly too, the scheme was launched at a time when the Railway Cup, a competition for which he has a great affection, was beginning to decline in terms of public interest.

'I couldn't believe the first time I was chosen as an All Star, especially when I heard that we were to travel to San Francisco. That might be no big deal to players nowadays but, back then, there were no team holidays after winning All-Ireland finals. The All Stars were the only route to these faraway places. That's not the case anymore, but the All Stars have retained their prestige and I can never see it dwindling. OK, so you will have rows and debates over team selection, but isn't that part of the fun? It doesn't matter what group of selectors you ask to choose a team, everybody won't agree with it. I believe the journalists generally do a good job and I'm absolutely certain the present-day players get as much of a thrill from being selected as we did in our day.'

While conditions for players have changed immeasurably over the past decade, Skehan remains passionately in favour of retaining the GAA as an amateur organisation. He believes that any move towards professionalism would be a step towards the ruination of the Association at all levels.

'By all means, look after the players well, but the day we go down a professional, or even semi-professional route, is the day we lose everything. The GAA is part of what we are. It's owned by all its members, it's buried deep in every parish and community, so we have to be very careful not to do anything that disrupts the balance. That doesn't mean that we can't keep our players happy, but we don't have to start paying them.'

While Skehan is very much a man of traditional values in most respects, he grows animated at the mention of his pet hate in hurling. It's something that has irritated him all his life, because he believes it's not only unfair, but also dangerous.

'I can't understand why the striker is allowed to run in several yards before taking a 21-yard free or a penalty. I know people will accuse me of complaining because I was a goalkeeper, but it's not just that. Surely a 21-yard free should be taken from the line, not from several yards closer to the goal. Yet, if a goalkeeper steps outside the small square when taking a puck-out, he is penalised. That's plain daft. It can be dangerous allowing a player to run in towards the 14-yard line before making his strike, but nothing is being done about it.

'A penalty or 21-yard free should be taken from the line and not from much closer in. I was always on to Eddie Keher about that during our playing days but naturally, as a free-taker, he didn't agree! I still haven't changed my mind though, and I never will.'

It's a small complaint amid a myriad of memories from a lifetime in hurling. And still the obsession lives on. Whether it's a club or county game, a training spin, a coaching session, or simply sitting at home watching videos of games, Skehan retains an emotional attachment to the sport he has served with such distinction.

'It has been everything to me. My life has been greatly enriched by hurling and not just through winning titles and awards. I have made wonderful friends all over the country and I've seen the world, from San Francisco to New York, to South Africa, to Australia, places I would never have got to in ordinary circumstances. I owe an awful lot to hurling.'

It owes him quite a lot too.

---

*Noel Skehan lives in Bennettsbridge and is a HR Manager. He and his wife, Mary, have two sons, Brian and Niall, and one daughter, Noelle.

Ranger Who Never Roamed

Joe Kernan (Armagh)

ALL STAR WINNER: 1977, 1982

*'I have never been afraid to ask for help and listen to ideas from others.
Show me the manager who knows everything. There isn't one.'*

For a split second, time stood still. The shrill blast of John Bannon's whistle was slow to resonate. It was one of those eerie moments when the sounds around him became increasingly distant and he was left alone with a flurry of thoughts buzzing in his head.

By the time he turned around, his backroom team, including Armagh secretary Paddy Óg Nugent, John McCloskey and Paul Grimley had descended upon him and the orange haze beneath the Hogan Stand was thickening fast. Then he remembered his captain, who had sunk to his knees at the joyous sound of that same whistle, raising his hands to the heavens in celebration of an All-Ireland final victory over Kerry.

Kernan thought of him and moved in his direction. Through the gathering crowds, they managed to converge and embrace. Joe Kernan, the manager, and Kieran McGeeney, his frontline commander, celebrated the liberation of Armagh football.

For Kernan, it is perhaps the most vivid memory of the afternoon of 22 September 2002, when Armagh became the eighteenth county to win an All-Ireland senior football title, a day when his status as a managerial legend was guaranteed. And it is perhaps the most appropriate place to begin the chronicle of a career in Gaelic football that has been built on so many ground-breaking achievements, both as a player and manager with club and county.

History will be kind to Joe Kernan the player. He won three Ulster championship medals (1977, 1980 and 1982), scored two goals in the 1977 All-Ireland final against Dublin, and won All Star awards at midfield in 1977 and at centre half-forward five years later. It was a period in which he was one of the more instantly recognisable faces in Armagh football.

History will be generous, too, to Kernan the manager, who has already landed three Ulster and All-Ireland club titles with Crossmaglen Rangers, plus one All-Ireland and two Ulster inter-county crowns with Armagh.

Sometimes 'Big Joe', as he is affectionately known across the length and breadth of the country, looks back on his career and expresses relief that circumstances didn't steer him off the path he has travelled so successfully for the past 30 years. At the age of 20 and looking for work around his beloved Crossmaglen, the temptation to emigrate to Australia, where two sisters, Olivia and Annette, and his brother Raymond (now deceased) had already gone, was almost overpowering. His father, Joe, had died when his second son was just 11 years old and his mother, Joan, had developed a routine of spending two to three months of the year in Australia with the rest of her family.

By his own admission, he wasn't an educational success and, with such a downbeat prognosis for the future of a troubled Northern Ireland, he thought long and hard about making the break. Like so many other young men before him, football was the magnet that kept him at home. A burgeoning career was preserved, much to the benefit of Crossmaglen and Armagh.

'I'm glad now that I didn't go to Australia. I felt at the time that if I went, I might like it so much that I wouldn't come back. I wanted to stay at home for the football. There were a lot of reasons why I should have gone. So much was falling apart around Northern Ireland, but the football kept us sane. When my mother went over there, I was the only one left behind. So football connections became family-like connections and I've always looked at football that way ever since.'

To this day, he considers the Armagh players as additional sons to the five he and his wife, Patricia, already have. More recently, he thinks how his management career could have been diverted off course if he had landed either the Cavan or Louth jobs which he sought. On the advice of his long-time friend, Ollie Brady, he applied for the vacancy in Cavan but Down's Liam Austin was preferred. He still doesn't know why Louth turned him down but appreciates that 'some things happen for a reason'.

And when, within a year of that rejection, he was asked to fill the vacancy in his native county, that reason became apparent. Fate had played its part. His popularity has soared to the point where he is now perceived as the ambassador for Armagh. When, a few months after Armagh's 2002 All-Ireland success, the Abbey CBS Newry Past Pupils' Society made him the focus of a 'This Is Your Life' special in the Carrickdale Hotel, some 780 guests, drawn from all areas of Irish sport, descended on the border venue to honour his contribution to Gaelic football.

It was a far cry from the days when he watched locals walk by the front door of his Crossmaglen public house, taking their custom to another premises up the street. Despite being the town's most recognised football figure, he couldn't take that custom for granted and his inn-keeping days ended in the early 1990s.

By that stage he had already served three years as assistant to the then County manager, Paddy Moriarty. 'Paddy Mo' had asked him in after Joe had quit playing in 1988 but, in each of the three subsequent years, Armagh were beaten by the eventual Ulster champions: Tyrone in 1989, Donegal in 1990 and Down in 1991. When 'Paddy Mo' quit, Joe opted out too, resisting the temptation to remain on as manager.

'After I quit playing for the club in 1988 – the year after I had finished with Armagh – Paddy asked me in as assistant and I jumped at the chance. It was a great learning curve. Maybe it was a mistake leaving after three years, but when Paddy said he was going I decided I wasn't going to remain on my own. I look back now and say maybe we should have stayed on.'

He had made his inter-county playing debut against Donegal in a McKenna Cup game at the Armagh Athletic Grounds in 1971 and ended it against Derry in the 1987 Ulster final, which they lost. It was the third provincial final defeat he had suffered in six attempts. Reaching the 1977 All-Ireland final against Dublin was the obvious highlight, but if Joe has a single biggest regret, it was losing to Roscommon by 2-20 to 3-11 in the 1980 All-Ireland semi-final.

'We lost that game by six points, having led by five points at one stage. If we were ever going to win an All-Ireland, it was that year, more so than in 1977 when we were just outclassed by Dublin.'

With a first taste of inter-county management behind him in 1991 and the hassles of running a pub in the past, the local club came calling for a manager and the invitation was swiftly accepted. Kernan had been one of Crossmaglen's most celebrated players, winning five Armagh titles between 1971 and 1988. He didn't make the team for the 1971 county championship but was introduced for the Ulster club championship and was an 18-year-old midfielder when they crashed out in the semi-final against Down champions, Bryansford.

When he took over management of the senior team, Crossmaglen, the most successful club in the county, were stuck in a barren spell and Kernan sensed the need to advance from their traditional catch-and-kick style. For three years, he laid the foundations for a more fluid type of game that was alien to what Crossmaglen people had become accustomed. It was a difficult transition.

On the night that the breakthrough finally came in 1996, when they claimed a first Armagh championship in 11 years, Kernan's eyes were opened in a way that would shape the dynamic of future dressing-rooms in which he was involved.

'Crossmaglen football was at an all-time low prior to that. Then, with eleven U-21s on the team, most of whom had won four successive U-21 county titles, we won a senior county championship, playing a particular brand of football. That night three of the parents, including two mothers, cornered me and said, "Joe, fair play to you, but we thought you were wrong." I was taken aback by this. What was I wrong about? They thought it was a mistake to try and change the style of play. It dawned on me then that players were going home from training and discussing the methods with their families. The point was that they didn't believe. Seeds of doubt were being sown at home. They were coming away from training and saying, "this is wrong". From then on, I preached to every team I sent out on a field that you have to believe and trust the system.'

'Believe' became the key word. When Crossmaglen went to Croke Park, Joe would urge them to look around for the Guinness advertising hoarding carrying that same message and draw inspiration from it.

Six months after Crossmaglen landed the 1996 Armagh championship, they won an unexpected All-Ireland title against Knockmore of Mayo. The momentum was now gathering for what would become the most successful chapter in the history of the All-Ireland club football series.

There were rare dips along the way. When Errigal Ciarán (Tyrone) dethroned Crossmaglen in November 1997, it provided the motivation for Kernan and his players to re-dedicate themselves to regaining the All-Ireland title.

'We thought we had a divine right to steamroll through Errigal because we were All-Ireland champions. We closed the dressing-room door that evening and there was a sense of devastation all around. Everyone shed tears. To me that was great. We were all hurting, which showed that nobody was satisfied with just one All-Ireland. I said to them to watch the All-Ireland final on St Patrick's Day and if you're still hurting then, you'll go on and win more.'

On St Patrick's Day, 1999, they claimed a second All-Ireland title, playing poorly against a profligate Ballina side. For Kernan, it was perhaps the most significant of the three Croke Park finals that Crossmaglen won.

'Armagh teams would have been renowned for playing well in big games and losing. But against Ballina, "Cross" were beaten off the field from start to finish, yet won the match. It was the best of the three title wins for the simple reason that an Armagh team had played badly and still won in Croke Park.'

The Ballina game was the inspiration for the third All-Ireland final win a year later. Crossmaglen were playing Na Fianna (Dublin) and Kernan urged them to win with a swagger, which they duly achieved. Crossmaglen lost Jim McConville early on and suffered other injuries to Donal Murtagh and Anthony Cunningham, but still won in splendid style.

'I'd say we produced the best football that any club team ever played in Croke Park. Na Fianna thought they had us that day when Jim went off, but we scored three points in five minutes in quick response. It was a great flourish. We had won a third All-Ireland in four years and, in that time, we made just three changes in personnel to the team.'

Crossmaglen continued winning county titles but, as the wear and tear of those years caught up and the focus of their better players shifted towards the county team, the scene changed. When Monaghan neighbours, Castleblayney, toppled them in the

Ulster championship in late 2000, Kernan stood down after eight seasons at the helm. He took a well-earned break, holidayed regularly at his Spanish home and dusted himself down for his next and greatest challenge.

He was the logical successor when Brian McAlinden and Brian Canavan vacated the managerial seats after Armagh lost to Galway in 2001, but Kernan himself had doubts because of the fractured nature of the relationship he had with elements in the County Board, arising from his days as Crossmaglen boss. He need not have worried. Within half an hour of meeting the executive, he was appointed. But, on taking over from the McAlinden–Canavan axis, Joe's greatest fear was that he would be 'trying to teach an old dog new tricks'.

There were plenty to warn him off the job, claiming that the squad had big mileage on the clock, had been to the well too often and had appeared to be on the descent when they lost to eventual All-Ireland champions Galway in a closely contested third-round qualifier clash in the summer of 2001. He listened, as he always does, but didn't heed the advice. From his initial soundings, he decided that the will to succeed was still very strong. One of his first trips was across to Mullaghbawn, where Benny Tierney had all but retired as the team's goalkeeper.

'Crossmaglen and Mullaghbawn would be bitter rivals but when I went to his house, asking him to stay on I got a warm welcome. I knew then that things could be made to happen.'

Another early trip he made was south to Dublin to seek assurances from Kieran McGeeney about his Armagh future and install him as captain. It was a profitable visit.

'I took soundings from some of the senior players – Kieran [McGeeney], Diarmuid [Marsden] and Paul [McGrane] and liked what I heard. I believed there was more in them, but I felt I had to work on the hurt they had suffered in the previous three years.'

He also played the Crossmaglen card cleverly. He didn't indulge the success or offer it up as the perfect and only template. He kept it at a safe distance and, in seeking Tierney for another year in preference to his own young club-mate Paul Hearty, he sent out a clear message – Armagh was far more than just Crossmaglen.

'There was no negativity with "Cross" and I felt that a positive attitude was the one thing I had to transfer to the Armagh dressing-room. I'd say to the lads, "Get us to Croke Park and we'll help you do the rest." It was all positive, positive, positive. I didn't want negative people around us.'

Having wound himself up for the challenge, Joe began to build his pyramid of helpers. A renowned coach in a variety of sports, John McCloskey was taken in as trainer, having worked with Joe at club level. And after two refusals by potential assistants from the desired mid/north Armagh area, Paul Grimley, brother of former Armagh players Mark and John, was recruited.

'Paul had worked with a lot of clubs in Armagh. I needed someone from that area because I didn't want the whole emphasis to be on the south of the county. Anywhere he went, he had commanded respect. I had been with John [McCloskey] before and his insight into training is really incredible. His contribution to Armagh's success can't be overstated. He is always up to date with everything. If Real Madrid or the English rugby team are employing the best and most modern methods, then so are we.'

Having put a selector and trainer in place, Kernan still wasn't finished. Eamonn Mackle, a Newry-based businessman and the man who had first approached Joe about taking over the Armagh team, has been his trusted sidekick, fulfilling a host of important duties. During championship time, Kernan and Mackle would meet every day and often devote up to eight hours to Armagh preparations. Statisticians, dieticians and 'performance developers' (as opposed to psychologists) were regularly employed. Even the smallest detail was afforded careful attention by Kernan, who operated on the principle of listening carefully and taking every idea on board. He has never been afraid to pick up the phone and ask for help.

In the build-up to Crossmaglen's first All-Ireland final, Colm O'Rourke was a regular visitor to the camp and his impassioned speech at the Grand Hotel in Malahide on the morning of the final is fondly remembered.

'He really struck a chord with the lads when he told them he would swap his two All-Ireland medals with Meath for one with his club, Skryne. His voice was breaking as he said that and we found it very moving. I have never been afraid to ask for help and listen to ideas from others. Show me the manager who knows everything. There isn't one.'

In time, Martin McHugh, Seán O'Neill and Seán Boylan would all respond to Joe's call and visit Crossmaglen. Even when he took over Armagh he was still amenable to outside influences.

For Kernan, life is a perpetual learning curve and, in seeking that outside help, he was doing something he had been prevented from trying as an Armagh player by a suspicious County Board.

'In 1982, we won an Ulster title for a third time in five years. I went to the Board, on behalf of the players, to ask about getting someone in to talk to us who had experience of winning. We felt it would have helped us to hear from the likes of Kevin Heffernan. The chairman at the time told me that they didn't want anyone stealing their thunder. I said, "What happens if there is no thunder?" We lost that year's All-Ireland semi-final to Kerry by ten points and the players felt very let down because when we asked for help we didn't get it.'

Things were different under Kernan's managership. Their landmark season in 2002 was peppered with different devices that helped the preparation and spirit of the squad. The trip to La Manga, prior to their championship opener against Tyrone, was a gamble that paid off spectacularly.

'None of us had one drop of drink for the entire week. I love a glass of wine myself but in La Manga I never touched it. We said to ourselves that if we have a drink, we won't beat Tyrone.'

They stuck by the self-imposed rules and ended up beating Tyrone after a replay, before adding a third Ulster title in four years later in the summer.

But they still had to negotiate Croke Park, where no Armagh team had won a senior championship game for 25 years.

A poor performance against Sligo in the All-Ireland quarter-final in Croke Park yielded a draw and a replay in Navan, which they duly won. By the time Armagh arrived back in Croke Park for the All-Ireland semi-final against Dublin, they were ready to break the hoodoo.

At half-time, Kernan pulled the first of two famous stunts designed to inspire his team. For 25 years, his 1977 Armagh shirt had been stashed away in his house. He now produced it and told the players this was his prize for reaching an All-Ireland final. Did they want an All-Ireland final jersey for themselves? Armagh went on to beat Dublin by a point.

Four weeks on and with Kerry leading by four points at half-time in the All-Ireland final, Kernan grabbed his runners-up plaque from 1977 and smashed it against the wall of the shower room. He then produced an All-Ireland medal that was almost 90 years old, which Mackle had managed to procure. The players stood, listened and learned. Within 40 minutes they were All-Ireland champions.

The celebrations and the sense of achievement were special, but the desire for a second All-Ireland title has remained strong in the two intervening years. In 2003, Armagh missed out on two-in-a-row, losing the final to Tyrone and in 2004, after producing a devastating Ulster final performance against Donegal, they were caught cold by Fermanagh in the All-Ireland quarter-final.

Still, 2002 has had an uplifting effect in a more peaceful Northern Ireland. Kernan notices it even at checkpoints on the roads around south Armagh.

'There was a time when it was "boot and bonnet" when you were stopped. Everybody knows about the British Army presence in Crossmaglen and how it almost broke the club. But the spirit survived and, with great people like Gene Larkin, Gene Duffy and the former GAA president Con Murphy working tirelessly to improve the situation, we came through it. Nowadays if you're stopped, you're asked how the Armagh team is going. We brought the Sam Maguire Cup to Stormont and, while some people didn't agree with that, we were made to feel very welcome. Derry or Down could not have done that eight or nine years earlier.'

Although he twice came close to managing other counties, he now feels he could never work against his beloved Armagh.

'I could never see myself sending someone out to mark Stevie McDonnell or one of the lads out of a game. I don't think I'd be able to plot Armagh's downfall after what we have achieved together over the past few years. But maybe things change, but you would need to have the appetite for it. I'll be 51 years old next year and I find it hard to believe that I would have the appetite to do it for someone else, other than Armagh. I think I would feel like a mercenary if I were to go somewhere else.'

Comforting words for a county he has served with such distinction as a player and manager.

---

* Joe Kernan is a self-employed estate agent and mortgage broker. He and his wife, Patricia, have five sons: Stephen (21), Aaron (20), Tony (18), Paul (17) and Ross (12).

Lake Star Trail Blazer

David Kilcoyne (Westmeath)

ALL STAR WINNER: 1986

'If everyone got up and left their roots to chase success,
there would be no GAA.'

Had he been born in Bennettsbridge, Johnstown or Tullaroan, David Kilcoyne would probably be spoken of in the same revered tones as the best Kilkenny hurlers of his generation.

Had he even been brought up on the other side of his own county, hard by a border with Offaly that stretches in excess of 30 miles, he could, in the unlikely event of the mood taking him, have slipped across at the appropriate time, joined a club and helped himself to an All-Ireland medal.

If the transfer market had ever existed in hurling, Kilcoyne's skill and dexterity would not have been allowed settle on Westmeath soil for too long. He could have named his own price and still attracted interest from the superpowers.

But Gaelic Games are essentially about place and identity. And few respect that more than this quiet, unassuming character from the northern part of a county that, for the most part, can only look in on hurling's fast lane.

Nonetheless, the 'what ifs' of his career don't add up to one single regret. David Kilcoyne has the distinction of being Westmeath's first All Star. For 15 years, he was their only winner, until footballer Rory O'Connell sprang from the pack to join him in the exclusive club.

Kilcoyne remains Westmeath's only hurling All Star, a distinction unlikely to be challenged in the foreseeable future. So how did a hurler from Kiltoom, near Castlepollard, end up sharing the most esteemed podium of individual excellence in his sport with such luminaries as Jimmy Barry-Murphy, Ger Cunningham, John Fenton, Pete Finnerty and Joe Cooney, the player he regarded as the best he had ever come across?

Of all the All Star awards handed out since the inception of the scheme in 1971, David Kilcoyne's achievement in 1986 must rank among the most unique: a celebration of a time when the Lake County, all too briefly, rubbed shoulders with the game's aristocrats. That included a National League quarter-final against Kilkenny and a subsequent season in the top flight. It was a time when they felt that, with a slight upward push and a few lucky breaks, they might have been kings.

He was undoubtedly one of the most consistent forwards of his generation, a supreme marksman who chalked up big scores as a matter of course, mostly in the game's backwaters, although he rose to the greater challenges too.

Even when Westmeath were exposed to the highest levels of League activity for that brief period during 1986 and 1987, Kilcoyne's talent held up comfortably under the most intense scrutiny.

When future hurling development committees seek to audit the game, they will hold the Kilcoyne account up as evidence of considerable profit in an area of recession. The necklace of villages and towns in the east and north-eastern part of Westmeath – Castlepollard, Raharney, Brownstown, Collinstown and Delvin – are rich in hurling tradition and interest. Having an All Star in their midst enhances their status as one of the most passionate pockets of the game. What makes Kilcoyne's story all the more remarkable is that he wasn't nurtured through any streamlined underage or college system.

He doesn't recall playing a club hurling championship game until he lined out with the Ringtown U-21 team as a 15-year-old in the mid-1970s. An U-14 tournament game offers a vague recollection of the only time he had ever pulled on a jersey for full underage combat up to then. His talent was natural, shaped by the love of the game that ran through his family, in the fields adjacent to their home. No one ever told him how or why. He was self-taught and self-tested.

'We survived on pucking balls in a local field. At the time there was little else for us to do. We didn't play against other teams, simply because there were no underage structures there, so we had no opportunity to measure ourselves against anyone.

'It gives substance to the argument that hurling is probably a natural gift to some. If a fella is generally awkward and behaves as if he has two left hands, you won't make a hurler out of him. I would always feel that hurlers are good at most sports. It's a natural coordination that can't be manufactured. When you look at a player like D.J. Carey, he is a class handballer, can play good golf and doesn't look out of place on a football field.'

The 2004 Féile na nGael was part hosted in Westmeath and David found himself drawn to many of the centres to watch the games. He was amazed to find dieticians and physical trainers in tow with some of the teams and it brought him back to his own journey, some 30 years earlier. It was all so different then.

The Kilcoyne family has made a big impact on Gaelic Games in their area. David's parents (the late Joe, who died in February 2004, and Ann) relocated from Louisburgh, Co. Mayo to north

Westmeath in the 1950s. There, they watched each of their five sons – Michael, Pádraig, James, David and Seán – represent the county hurling team for the best part of two decades.

The extended Kilcoyne family contributed seven members at one stage, including two cousins, to the Ringtown senior hurling team that would enjoy brief dominance in the county.

David's older brother, Michael, was a noted dual player in Westmeath for many years before joining Blackrock in Cork, where he won a county hurling championship in 1985, partnering Jim Cashman at midfield. Michael also won an All-Ireland club football title with Thomond College in 1978 on a star-studded team that included Mick and Pat Spillane (Kerry), Brian Talty (Galway), Jimmy Dunne (Offaly) and Eddie Mahon (Meath).

It was to Michael that David regularly looked for guidance and inspiration as he mapped out a career for himself.

'I suppose I took up hurling because Michael was playing it. I played more football than hurling in my teens. I played for Coole at the time and represented the Westmeath minors. Even then, you always felt football was being pushed that bit harder in the county. I would always feel it was given preferential treatment. Carmelite College in Moate was very successful around then, which was an influential factor.'

Football was, however, quickly put to one side as the hurling bug bit David that bit harder. An U-21 title with Ringtown in 1977 was followed by a senior title in 1980, plus promotion to the inter-county scene.

By 1984, Westmeath hurling was beginning to feel good about itself and an All-Ireland 'B' title was evidence of promising growth. It earned them an All-Ireland quarter-final clash with Galway and, although they lost by nine points, David Kilcoyne underlined his ability to prosper against top line defences by scoring 2-2.

Westmeath's momentum was growing and, when promotion to Division One of the NHL was secured in 1986, they felt they were on to something.

For a few celebrated months they enjoyed a couple of peaks that teasingly toyed with their ambitions. In the 1985–86 National League, they beat Kerry, Down, Roscommon, Meath and Antrim, but it was a victory over Tipperary that really caught the imagination. Kilcoyne scored 1-8 as Westmeath ran out seven-point winners (1-17 to 1-11) against a Tipperary team that included Ken Hogan, Nicky English, Pat Fox, Noel Sheehy and Bobby and Aidan Ryan.

It helped Westmeath to finish second behind Wexford on the Division Two table and earned them a quarter-final clash with Kilkenny, whom they ran to two points (3-8 to 0-15). It's a game they arguably should have won too, according to David, as Mick Cosgrove had a goal disallowed at a crucial stage in the second half.

'We genuinely felt that if we had beaten Kilkenny, we could have won the League. They went on to win the title some weeks later.'

David headed to America for the few weeks between the Kilkenny game and Westmeath's opening Leinster championship game with Laois.

'We had expectations of beating Laois, but they gave us a right hammering. It was a big setback. We felt we were gaining ground all the time but, of all the results, this one hurt hardest,' he recalled. 'Maybe we codded ourselves into thinking we were better than we were.'

They enjoyed another peak later that year, when they went to Loughrea and beat Galway in a League match, 2-12 to 1-12. But, even if they didn't sense it at the time, the decay was beginning to set in and the win over Galway was the summit of their achievements.

'We went back a lot in the following years with retirements and injuries. I struggled with injuries to the hip, back and groin. But I felt that one of the biggest factors was the loss of our trainer, Tom Donoghue, after the championship in 1986. We weren't given a reason why Tom was let go. It was a backward step. He had a great way with training, a great way with players and I don't think I have trained under anyone as good since then.'

Still, the achievements of securing promotion, running Kilkenny to two points in a League quarter-final and beating Galway were rewarded with All Star recognition for David.

His brother Michael, and Willie Lowry, had both been replacement All Stars previously, but expectations were high in Westmeath in the weeks before the announcement of the teams that David would gain full All Star recognition.

'There was a lot of talk about it. Westmeath was viewed as something of a success story that year and because I was running up some big scores I was being mentioned. It was the nearest we were going to come to getting some recognition for the efforts of the team. I regarded the All Star award as a reward for the team rather than for any individual excellence.'

Modest by nature, David never made any presumptions about himself. His main concern in the build-up to the presentation night was to get his important dental work completed, after suffering a facial blow in a League match against Cork!

The All Star gave him some status in the midlands.

'It didn't make me a rich man and it certainly didn't change me, as I think anybody who knows me would agree. It was nice to be known as an All Star, nice for the county, but I would feel it is probably forgotten about now.'

Naturally it attracted interest from elsewhere. He was 24 years old and at the top of his craft.

'A possible move was mentioned a few times but nothing concrete. Fellas would say it to you but it would be nothing direct. Contrary to speculation, I never heard anything from Offaly. Michael was hurling away in Cork at the time and it was mentioned that I might follow him down. But I was happy where I was. Maybe I was a lad in my own little world.

'I'd often be asked if I regretted not being born in Offaly or Tipperary or some other top hurling county and the answer has always been the same: no, I never regretted it. It was a big challenge playing for Westmeath and we probably got out of it all that we could at the time. If everyone got up and left their roots to chase success, there would be no GAA.'

Within a season of his All Star success, Westmeath were in decline, but David's prominence on the national stage continued with a Railway Cup medal with Leinster in 1988. A second All-Ireland 'B' title in 1991 hinted at another resurgence, but it never materialised.

He played his last game for Westmeath in 1995, when they suffered a humiliating defeat by Wexford in the championship and he came out of retirement in 1997 to help Ringtown regain their senior status. His return didn't last long, however, as the build-up of back, knee cartilage and groin injuries took their toll. In more recent years, he has turned successfully to management and had spells with the Brownstown and Turin sides.

But his most satisfying times on the sidelines were alongside Clonkill man Peter Curran, when they took charge of a Westmeath U-15 team. The squad developed into a really compact unit so that by the time they reached minor level, they were ready for big challenges. In fact, many of them were on the team that almost took down an impressive Kilkenny side, losing by just two points in 1999.

'We put in a lot of work with those young lads. We had contacts in Tipperary and organised regular challenge games. We kept them together and they performed really well at minor level. A few of them are doing well with the current Westmeath senior side.

'But ultimately a team like that is always going to struggle to survive against football. That same year [1999] Westmeath won an All-Ireland U-21 football title; a year later, they were Leinster minor football champions. And now, Westmeath are Leinster senior football champions. The young people have real heroes to look up to. And the natural draw is to football.

'That's the battle hurling in Westmeath will always face. Unless you win big, you'll quickly be forgotten about. I even see it in my own son Niall. For him, the likes of Finian Newman, captain of the 2004 U-21 team, is somebody he can identify with. Young lads need to have something to aim at and players they can look up to.

'But maybe sometimes we feel too sorry for ourselves in Westmeath hurling and spend too much time looking for help instead of helping ourselves. We should push the game in the county and do more for ourselves instead of making easy excuses.'

He enjoyed Westmeath's brief renaissance under Tom Ryan in 2004 but, as a keen student of local club games, he knew there was only so far Ryan could take them.

'Ultimately we're not good enough and there's not a lot coming through. I don't think the structures are there for us to prosper. Even at club level, I don't think the rivalry is anywhere nearly as intense as it used to be. When we were playing, we had a fierce rivalry with Castlepollard. Whether it was League or championship, it was serious business. But players don't seem to care as much now when they're beaten. If Castlepollard beat us now, it's a case of "well and good". I don't understand that.'

David's own legacy is altogether different: a class hurler who stuck by his roots when the temptation to chase gold would have lured others away from home. For Kilcoyne, the attraction of faraway green hills never could compare with the lakes of Westmeath.

---

*David Kilcoyne is a technician with Eircom. He and his wife, Jacqueline, have six children: Aimee (18), Niall (16), Darren (15), Ian (7), Laura (3) and Emma (1).

A Trick for All Seasons

'Nudie' Hughes (Monaghan)

ALL STAR WINNER: 1979, 1985, 1988

'They might go out to hurt you, but they would never go out to permanently damage you. A lot of it was intimidation.'

There are many by the name of Eugene Hughes in Monaghan, several even in Castleblayney. But there's only one 'Nudie'. The moniker, which has been with him since birth, acts almost as a brand for the man who is arguably the most gifted and most effective player Monaghan football has ever known. It also serves as a term of endearment for the standard bearer of a glorious, unforgettable decade.

Even in the drinks trade, where he has worked for almost 20 years, he answers to nothing else, as his business cards will testify. He thinks his mother is now the only person who still refers to him by his real Christian name.

'You would be wasting your time looking for me in this part of the country under Eugene Hughes,' he says with an impish smile.

A cocky sort on the field, a character off it, the nickname 'Nudie' aptly fits the lovable rogue who was at the epicentre of Monaghan's most successful days. A member of the exclusive set of players who have won All Star awards as defenders and forwards, Nudie was also the first in his province to win three awards, when he claimed his third in 1988. He was the antithesis of the straight-talking, authoritative figure of Seán McCague, the former GAA president and the man widely regarded as the person who united Monaghan football for its most successful spell between 1979 and 1988.

This determined pair were huge influences in putting Monaghan football on the map, making them a force to be feared during a glorious decade that yielded three Ulster titles and a first-ever National League success. Even on a team renowned for their hard physical edge, Nudie was one of their most polished acts, possessing a stocky frame that protected him from hard tackles and a confidence that was sometimes mistaken for arrogance by opposing teams.

The name 'Nudie' helped. It was almost as if it gave him the roguish confidence to get away with things others could never dream of – the 'Artful Dodger' of his day. By his own admission, he was a 'talker' on the field. If he could distract an opponent and break his concentration at any opportunity, he would. And often did!

'It was one of my best tricks,' he recalls. 'John Egan caught me with it when we played Kerry one year. He started to ask me about one of our players. I thought he was showing genuine interest but, before I had a chance to answer, he had slipped away from me and put the ball in our net.'

It was a harsh lesson for Nudie, but one he would use to his own advantage in the years that followed. He exploited it to particular effect *en route* to their last Ulster championship in 1988. Monaghan met a Cavan team managed by Eugene McGee, who had led Offaly to All-Ireland glory six years earlier. With more than 20,000 supporters packed into Clones for one of the sharpest football rivalries in the game, the atmosphere crackled with expectation.

'I'll never forget it. I was going well at the time and Damien O'Reilly, a fine young player, was marking me. The second half was a few minutes old when I turned around and said: "Damien, I'm playing football a long time but I've never, ever seen a crowd like it up on that yon' hill. How many would you say are up there?" As he looked up, I shot out to take a pass off Eamonn McEneaney and put the ball over the bar.

'The crowd went bananas because they knew I had been talking to Damien. Cavan took him off me and put Eugene Kiernan on me instead. I said to Eugene: "the best of luck". But he fixed me with a stare and told me fairly colourfully that there was no room for luck out there.'

The story reflects the essence of Nudie Hughes at his cheeky best. For all his tricks, McCague knew that no Monaghan team was complete without him. He lived off a diet of confidence and self-belief. When McCague went to Nudie at the start of the 1988 season and told him that he was looking for one last press of the shoulder to the wheel, the response was emphatic.

On the first night back training, Nudie had broken down in the third minute of a 15-minute run and McCague had sensed that he needed to address it.

'McCague cornered me and said we'd win nothing unless myself and Gerry McCarville got ourselves fit. So we trained unbelievably hard and got ourselves into the best shape possible. I'd be a real fattener for Christmas but, once the New Year came, I'd get down to serious business. Of all the years I was involved, I felt that in 1988 we could have won an All-Ireland title.'

In effect, that disappointing All-Ireland semi-final defeat by Cork brought a great era for Monaghan football to an end, a period which had its productive source in the promotion of a young McCague to the top job, at a time when the county had been hurting as a result of indiscipline, internal squabbling between clubs and an antiquated selection system.

'Before Seán McCague came, it was who you were in Monaghan, not what you were. You kicked the ball to someone you knew rather than engage in any great teamwork. There were clear club divisions,' recalls Nudie.

'But McCague changed all that. He was younger than some of the players, but he had an air of authority. He also made himself responsible for real decision-making. Before that, you could have a high-profile player taken off and when he went around each member of the selection committee, they'd all deny responsibility. That went on regularly. McCague smashed the system. He had respect in every one of the years he was in charge of us. As players, we were delighted when he came on board in 1978. We were delighted to have one man there who was willing to accept that the buck stopped with him. He was honest and he had a vision for us. He was from Scotstown. I was from Castleblayney and the rivalry was intense but the 'Blayney club backed him to the hilt.'

McCague bucked the trend by wearing a suit on match days in preference to the standard tracksuit look.

'It was another sign of authority for us but, to be quite honest, he could have worn nothing and it wouldn't have made a difference to us. We respected his word.'

Nudie was one of 14 children out of the Hughes' household on York Street and, despite little football pedigree, he displayed a prodigious talent from a young age, prospering in the football hotbed of Castleblayney, where tradition ran deep, in tandem with success.

'I was ambitious. I always set myself targets. Growing up, I watched Eamonn Tavey and Gerry Fitzpatrick in our town. They were the big names of the past in 'Blayney. The local postman, Christy Fisher, lived in York Street too, a great character who died about 20 years ago. But people spoke proudly of his football talents. I watched Fitzpatrick down in the local field practising free kicks, night after night, working on his kicking. I saw their dedication and made it my target to better those great men if I could.'

Such ambition took Nudie into the county minor team in 1974 and, within a year, he had graduated to an underachieving senior squad, primarily as a defender. For a few years, he drifted between attack and defence, but his propensity to push forward at every opportunity brought its own risks and, when Armagh's Jimmy Smyth destroyed him from centre forward in 1977, he was living on borrowed time as a defender. McCague kept him at right corner-back for the 1979 season, but his future lay as a forward and it was there that he would make his greatest impact.

Losing to a P.J. O'Hare-inspired Antrim in 1978, McCague's first year in charge was a huge setback, but it merely hardened Monaghan's resolve.

'Everyone united that year and there were big expectations so we were fierce disappointed after the Antrim game. But we kept it together for 1979 and when we beat Donegal in the Ulster final [1-15 to 0-11] the place went crazy.'

Inevitably, the county lost focus in the lead-up to that 1979 All-Ireland semi-final against Kerry.

'It was a case of "last out, switch off the lights". We were going around opening places after winning the Ulster final, the first for the county for 41 years. The national media came to Monaghan to talk to us. The whole county got ready to descend on Dublin. There was a story of a farmer in Scotstown who had sucklings and he placed an advertisement in the *Northern Standard* for someone to look after them because he was going up to Dublin for the weekend. He couldn't get anyone so he ended up selling them in Maggie Charlie's, a local pub, on the Saturday night.

We had a reputation building in the national media. One of the papers ran a headline after we beat Down in the first round that year with a reference to us being like something from outer space. There were supposed to be legs broken, left, right and centre but we had a motto at the time – we didn't mind what type of game it was as long as we won. The people of Monaghan were used to seeing Down teams going south for big championship games so it was unbelievable for us to be playing in an All-Ireland semi-final. The euphoria was incredible. Sure we were lambs to the slaughter.'

Kerry showed the newcomers no mercy, dishing out a 5-14 to 0-7 defeat that hit hard. However, Monaghan recovered quickly in the subsequent Ceannáras tournament, beating Dublin and Roscommon.

'Even though we had lost to Kerry so heavily, we knew we had been naive, so we went out in the Ceannáras tournament with a point to prove and won it.'

McCague stepped down a year later and Monaghan football edged towards the championship wilderness again, but they moved steadily through the tables in the National League, improving their status every season until they reached the top flight.

'In 1980 we were waiting for a result, which, if it had gone against us, would have sent us down to Division Four. However, we won our last game, avoided the drop and made steady progress through the Divisions after that.'

It was McCague's return for a second stint in 1983 which re-energised the county for another few memorable years in Ulster. In the meantime, Nudie began making a name for himself in Ulster, in the relaxed atmosphere of the Railway Cup. He won three medals with the province in 1980, 1983 and 1984 and was captain when they lost in 1986.

'I won my Railway Cup medals at right corner-back, right half-back and right corner-forward and, the year we lost to Leinster, I was at right half-forward, so it would have been a nice distinction to have won four medals on the four right flank positions.'

But even if he had never won a Railway Cup medal, he would have enjoyed the experiences, the laughs and the fun, not to mention treasuring the friends he made inside and outside Ulster.

'I could never forget some of the places we went to or indeed some of the places we stayed in. I remember being holed up in a room with Peter McGinnity somewhere in Skerries and it was so cold that we wore our tracksuits in bed. That great Down man, Seán O'Neill, was our manager at the time and he could never get the name "Nudie" right. He'd come out with something that sounded like "Ougie", giving the lads a great laugh altogether. The Railway Cup brought you into contact with really great players. I played in an Ulster forward line one year that had Peter McGinnity, Joe Kernan, Frank McGuigan, Greg Blaney and Martin McHugh, while Eugene McKenna and Liam Austin were at midfield. It was an honour to play on a team like that.

'The characters in the game at that time were unbelievable. I enjoyed the All Star trips immensely. It felt like a real reward for achievement and it was also a great chance to meet players from other counties. I remember in Chicago in 1980 being in a dressing-room with the All Star team getting ready to play Kerry and listening to Harry Keegan encouraging us to go out and play good football. He kept on about the need to give an exhibition of the best skills in Gaelic football. I said to myself, "This is a changed Harry". Sure enough, when we got out on the pitch and away from the earshot of the GAA officials on tour with us, his Roscommon colleague, Tom Heneghan, gathered us in and let fly, telling us to lay into the Kerry boys and that he didn't give a damn about them. He was a real character.

'Even on "away" League matches you could have your few pints because the pressure just wasn't the same. After our All-Ireland semi-final defeat to Kerry in 1985, we played them again in the League in Killarney and the whole of Monaghan went on the trip. It was a great occasion.'

Nudie spent time in America in the early 1980s, before returning for the second coming of McCague and a qualification for the Centenary Cup final against Meath in 1984, which they lost.

However, it sowed the seeds for a rich harvest and, a year later, Monaghan landed their first ever National Football League title, before returning to the winners' enclosure in Ulster with a new-look squad which had just six survivors from the 1979 team. Kerry lay ahead in the All-Ireland semi-final and Monaghan saw it as a real chance to make a big name for themselves.

This time the mood in the county was a lot more reserved. There were certainly no Scotstown sucklings being offered up to the cause the second time around. Monaghan drew the first game, thanks to a late, long-range point from a free by Eamonn McEneaney, but lost the replay by five points in a game that saw Ger Power pounce for a fortuitous goal that made a huge difference. Nudie recalls that fateful turning-point vividly.

'John Kennedy could hit a thousand balls the same as that day and they wouldn't bounce as kindly for Power. He was a great poacher, but we felt we were desperately unlucky with the way things went in both games.'

Luck didn't fall Monaghan's way in the 1988 All-Ireland semi-final either, when a controversial incident saw a challenge on Brendan Murray go unpunished. It led to a Cork goal by Dave Barry that effectively sealed Monaghan's fate, at a time when they were eating into a big lead with a strong wind at their backs.

'I have no doubt in my mind that we were closing in on Cork. But it's always the minnows that seem to suffer most from these controversial decisions. Brendan had his cheekbone broken that day and we felt a great sense of injustice. We never really recovered from that defeat.'

In truth, they still haven't and Nudie wonders now if they'll ever see a return to the good days.

'We always seemed to be one or two players short to complete the team. In my opinion, Eamonn Murphy was one of the best full forwards around, Ray McCarron and Eamonn McEneaney were two of the best free-takers. We had a lot going for us but I'm not sure if we ever had the proper belief to go all the way, although I had plenty of confidence in my own ability. McCague always encouraged the outfield lads to get the ball inside because he knew I could win it and I'd either be fouled or lay it off.'

At club level, Nudie was part of one the greatest rivalries between two clubs in any county, as Scotstown and Castleblayney locked horns with the utmost intensity.

Including replays, he played in 21 county finals, winning ten, and reserved some of his greatest displays for the Castleblayney jersey.

He recalls the 1985 final against Scotstown, which 'Blayney lost, as one of his finest performances because he scored four points from centre back. As for team performances, he doesn't recall a better one than when they held Scotstown scoreless (0-7 to 0-0) in a League match, just after Scotstown had been crowned Ulster club champions in 1979.

'I'll never forget it. Eamonn Tavey was on the "forty" for us that day and he came shouting at us near the end to pull the shutters down. We kept Scotstown out but it was very healthy competition, a great rivalry that benefited the county team.'

Being a flamboyant, cocky sort, Nudie appreciates that he was always a target for opponents willing to show a mean streak. He's had surgery to his face to repair fractured cheek and jaw bones on more than one occasion and acknowledged that some of the treatment dished out to him was severe. But he has never complained and never will.

'They might go out to hurt you but they would never go out to permanently damage you. A lot of it was intimidation.'

Nudie would like to see changes to the structures of the football League 'to make it a proper national competition. At the moment it's not a national competition because it's split into two 16s.'

And he would also encourage frees to be taken by the player, who is fouled to place more emphasis on better kicking and technique.

'I know not every free is awarded for a foul on a player, but I feel it would be a better way to promote kicking. How many teams can honestly say they have players who can kick points from within 40-yards' range?'

At some stage in the future, he would like to manage the Monaghan team and build on his record of coaching club teams in his own county, and in neighbouring Meath and Louth. If he ever did take over in Monaghan, he would have plenty of family connections on the panel. Paul Finlay's mother is his first cousin, midfielder Jason Hughes is a distant relation, Rory Woods is a nephew and, of course, there is the prospect of his son Ciarán, who was on the Monaghan minor team in 2004, following the path his father trod so regally.

Ciarán was born in 1986 and, to mark the fact that Nudie and his Monaghan colleague Ciarán Murray had been chosen on the 1985 All Stars, was christened Ciarán Eugene.

If Nudie doesn't get to manage Monaghan, it won't upset him unduly. He has enjoyed his life in football already and couldn't imagine how it would have been without it.

'I haven't changed. I am what I am. I was always the confident sort and I don't suppose I'll ever change. I'm still full of enthusiasm for the game that continues to play a major part in my life. It always will.'

---

* Nudie Hughes is the regional account manager with Interbrew Ireland in the northern half of the country and is married to Geraldine Hamill. They have two sons: Ciarán (17) and Conor (15).

When Galway Were Kings

Pete Finnerty (Galway)

ALL STAR WINNER: 1985, 1986, 1987, 1988, 1990

'It amuses me when I hear of teams training first thing in the morning and enduring various other hardships, as if it was something brand new. Galway were doing all that and more in the second half of the '80s.'

The great American athlete Carl Lewis was once asked to identify the most significant break he got during his formative years in sport. He paused for a second before surprising his young audience by declaring, 'that the 15 guys who were quicker than me in high school all gave up sprinting'.

It may have been a contrived answer, intended to convey the importance of persistence in any sphere of life but, if so, it hit the target. Pete Finnerty has a slightly different, but equally self-deprecating version of how good luck cleverly disguised itself as a burst blood vessel to come to his rescue in the summer of 1984.

The injury kept him out of Galway's All-Ireland semi-final clash with Offaly and, while he was very disappointed in the run-up to the game, he soon realised that the hurling gods move in mysterious ways. Offaly won by 14 points on a day when a young Joe Dooley prospered and Galway shrivelled. The embarrassing defeat led to a change of Galway management, with Cyril Farrell returning for his second stint, which he launched with a quick, ruthless cull. Having missed the Offaly debacle, Finnerty wasn't under scrutiny but it might have been different if he had been involved.

'I'd have been marking Joe Dooley, so who knows what would have happened. He could have cleaned me out and I might never have been heard of again.'

Somehow, it's unlikely that Finnerty would have spun out of orbit, but he still believes that the blood vessel did him a favour. By the time Galway reappeared for All-Ireland semi-final duty a year later, the whole landscape had changed. A new maroon-and-white model had been launched, one which proceeded to take Galway hurling onto the fastest circuits, where they reached speeds never previously seen by their supporters.

Between 1985 and 1991, Galway played in five All-Ireland finals (winning two), seven semi-finals (winning five), and three National Hurling League finals (winning two). And, in the guise of Connacht, they also qualified for six Railway Cup finals (winning four). Finnerty himself had the honour of captaining the 1991 side to a final victory over Munster. Truly, it was the golden age for Galway hurling, one that has never come close to being repeated.

Finnerty was involved in it all as a driven force in the No.5 jersey on a half-back line that could compare favourably with any outstanding trio the game has ever known. He fuelled his ambition to be the best with a power and determination that would have felled an elephant. Centre back Tony Keady had the feet of a dancer, the eyes of a hawk and the fetching capacity of a giraffe in the centre, while Gerry McInerney pressed the instinct button when he left the dressing-room and allowed that sense to be his guiding star.

Finnerty's excellence won him five All Stars in six seasons; Keady won two but McInerney was never chosen. That still rankles Finnerty, who believes that the failure to select McInerney remains one of the greatest oversights in the history of the All Star scheme.

'You ask people how many awards Mac got and most will automatically say two or three. It's impossible to believe that he turned in so many brilliant performances in All-Ireland semi-finals and finals without ever being selected. Maybe the fact that he spent much of the year in America came against him as he was only seen in August–September. Then again, he could have been a victim of positioning, in that Keady and myself were also vying for half-back places and since Mac was at left half-back, the selectors came to him last, which might have been a drawback. Whatever the reason, it was wrong that he didn't get an award.

'He was man-of-the-match in the 1988 All-Ireland final and came home from New York for the All Stars night because he looked certain to get an award. I was in New York at the time too, but I didn't travel back for the banquet. Instead, I was presented with my award outside St Patrick's Cathedral after 8 o'clock mass one morning. I thought Mac was an absolute certainty for an award, but he was overlooked again. Let's put it this way – the idea that I was entitled to five All Stars while he got none was absolutely daft.'

As always, plain speaking from Finnerty, but then that's no surprise since he was a hurler who always played the game in straight lines. His combination with Keady and McInerney was often alone worth the entrance fee, as they lined up to form the first line of security against ambitious raiders. Each had a distinct, yet very effective, style that perfectly complemented the others'.

'I was kept going by adrenaline rushes. If I got the ball and burst past a forward, I'd nearly want to go back and do it again. It was just the way I was. Keady had great feet and could turn on a sixpence, so it didn't matter how the opposition tried to frustrate him, he always seemed to have time and space to get in his clearance, while there wasn't a better centre back in the game when it came to catching a high ball. He was also a great striker. Some of his long-range frees knocked the heart out of the opposition, especially when they saw how casually he pointed them.

'And then you had Mac on the other side. Mac would run 50 yards with the ball and then pass it ten yards to a colleague. He loved running with the ball, but he could surprise you with his striking too, very often when we needed it most. In the 1988 All-Ireland final against Tipperary, he was marking Declan Ryan, who scored 0-4 from play. It was a good return from a right half-forward, but it didn't win the game for Tipp, whereas Mac's two points made all the difference for us. He hit two massive strikes into the wind in the second half, which were inspirational scores, while he also made some amazing catches when Tipp's pressure was at its highest. There really was only one Mac in the game.'

But then, that was a very special Galway team. Keady, Finnerty and McInerney had Sylvie Linnane, Conor Hayes, Ollie Kilkenny and John Commins behind them, while further afield Steve Mahon, Pat Malone, Michael Coleman, Joe Cooney, Martin Naughton, Eanna Ryan, Brendan Lynskey, Noel Lane, 'Hopper' McGrath, Anthony Cunningham and P.J. Molloy had star quality squeezed into every pore.

'Cooney and some of the other boys were so skilful that they could make the ball talk, but Lynskey never got the credit he deserved. He was as strong as an ox and had courage to match. Nobody took more belts than Lynskey, but he never let them get to him. He took the punishment and got on with it. The amount of ball he won and the number of passes he threw out to his colleagues was unbelievable. Galway have never been able to replace him.'

That applies to most of that team, which explains why they succeeded in exerting so much influence on the game during their peak years, which started out in the most amazing circumstances. If, at the start of the 1985 All-Ireland semi-final, Galway supporters had been told that Cork would score five goals, the general assumption would have been that it was going to be another miserable day in Croke Park.

Actually, it was miserable, but for different reasons. Sheets of driving rain swept relentlessly across Croke Park on that early August Sunday, rendering the pitch as close to unplayable as it has ever been. It looked bad for an experimental Galway team against reigning All-Ireland champions Cork but, despite conceding 5-5, they still made it to the final after scoring 4-12. The dreadful weather conditions, allied to the belief that Cork were absolute certainties to win, kept the crowd down to a disappointing 8205.

'It was by far the worst day I ever played hurling. There were two inches of water on parts of the pitch. It was absolutely unbelievable. I don't know how we hurled at all. Still, it turned out to be a massive day for Galway hurling as a new-look side had made a bold statement. Had we lost, half of us might never have been heard of again, but suddenly we were in an All-Ireland final,' recalls Finnerty, whose excellence earned him the man-of-the-match award.

They lost the final to Offaly, a jolt Galway would suffer again in 1986 when they were beaten by Cork. By the time they reached the 1987 All-Ireland final against Kilkenny, they were so desperate that they almost forgot to hurl.

'There wasn't five minutes of real action in the first quarter. It was all stoppages as both sides clattered into each other. We were hyper after losing the previous two All-Ireland finals and Kilkenny may have thought they could horse us out if it. We weren't taking it this time and the more we got, the more we gave back. We hurled better at times in the 1985 and 1986 finals, but didn't win. This time though, we just weren't going to be denied and while we only scored 1-12, we gave away just nine points.'

It was the launch of a glory era for Galway, one which derived much of its character and colour from their clashes with Tipperary, who had emerged from a 16-year Munster famine in 1987. Galway and Tipperary met in two All-Ireland semi-finals and one final, plus a National League final in the 1987–89 period, with Galway winning 3-1. It really was one of the most intense rivalries in the history of the game, reaching its peak in 1989, when Tipperary won a sulphurous All-Ireland semi-final in a season in which the suspension of Tony Keady (for playing illegally in the US) sparked a major controversy.

'It gave us a bit of a persecution complex. We thought the whole world was against us, especially the established powers of hurling, who felt we were winning too much. Rightly or wrongly, we believed the powers that be wanted us beaten and the suspension of Keady, who was the only big name hit by such a ban up to then, left us with a very sour taste in the mouth.

'Having said that, we should have handled it better. There was talk of Galway withdrawing from the All-Ireland semi-final and, amid all the controversy, we allowed ourselves to become distracted. If Keady had been injured, we would have had to cope anyway. That's the way we should have approached it. Galway had every reason to be sore over the way he was treated, but it should never have been allowed to get into the dressing-room. Keady was going to be a big loss but we had an excellent replacement in Seán Treacy, so we should simply have got on with the game and taken on the system afterwards.

'To make matters worse, a whole lot of questionable refereeing decisions went against us on the day and we eventually lost by three points. Ironically, Treacy hurled so well that he ended up with an All Star award.'

Finnerty and his colleagues still regard the 1989 championship as the one that got away. They were convinced that they were good enough to win the three-in-a-row, but circumstances conspired against them in the cruellest possible way. A year later, they reached another final but lost to Cork in a classic encounter. It was the defeat that hurt most of all.

'In 1985–86, we were learning. We were on top in 1987–88. Everything went against us in 1989, but 1990 should have been the redundancy package, the year we went out on a high. We hurled well enough, too, and opened up a seven-point lead in the second half, but then conceded some awful goals. Three years earlier, we conceded nine points against Kilkenny, but were hit for 5-15 by Cork in 1990. It was a massive disappointment because, whatever about the three-in-a-row, we felt we should have won three finals in that era. For all that, it had been a great period. The battles with Tipperary were something special and, while we didn't think it would happen at the time, it led to a whole lot of new friendships being forged. That rivalry was great for hurling. You would get crowds of 15,000–20,000 at Galway–Tipperary League games, while off the pitch Farrell and "Babs" Keating would go head-to-head regularly in the newspapers. Great stuff.'

The 1990 All-Ireland final was effectively the final flourish for that Galway team. By the time the 1991 All-Ireland semi-final came around, the team was breaking up. Finnerty was an uncomfortable and unhappy full back; cracks were appearing all over the place and Tipperary were at their prime. They easily beat Galway, a defeat which accelerated the breaking-up process.

The decision to use Finnerty at full back was symptomatic of the difficulties Galway were beginning to experience. The team had been so settled for so long that it virtually picked itself, so when the break-up began the replacements had very little experience. Nor were they as accomplished as their predecessors.

Finnerty recalls one particularly depressing outing during his days as an emergency full back, an occasion when it was forcibly brought home to him that a player really only is as good as his last game.

'We were playing Limerick in a League game in the Gaelic Grounds and I was marking Gary Kirby, who cleaned me out. Now Gary was one of the great gentlemen of the game and, by the time he had scored his third goal, he was almost apologising to me. I kept looking to the sideline muttering to myself, "Will ye write that bit of paper?" and, when they eventually did, I was glad to run off.

'Myself and Mac [Gerry McInerney] were having a few pints down in the hotel afterwards when this old fella came across to us. He started talking about hurling and how the match had gone. It wasn't a game I wanted to dwell on, but I reckoned the supporters saw it as just one of those days that wouldn't be repeated when he said, "Never mind, you and me will be up in Croke Park for the All-Ireland semi-final next August." And then came the punchline, low and hard across the shins: "But the two of us will be above in the Hogan Stand". I thought Mac would choke on his pint!'

A cruciate knee injury ruled Finnerty out in 1992 and, while he was back in 1993, he couldn't command a regular place on the team. Galway reached the All-Ireland final, where they lost to Kilkenny. Finnerty came on as a sub a few minutes from the end but, deep down, he knew it was nearly over for him. Still, he decided to make one last massive effort for 1994.

'I never worked as hard and I felt in tip-top shape for the All-Ireland semi-final against Offaly. I was as fit as I could be but, while my first touch was good, the legs were beginning to go. It's a strange feeling when that happens. The mind knows where it should direct you, experience shows you how to get there via the shortest route, but the legs say no. You arrive OK, but you're one-hundredth of a second too late. It's a horrible feeling because you know you will never get back to your peak. Offaly beat us and I took a long, lingering look around Croke Park because I knew that was the last time I would see it as a player.'

It was to be the start of a barren era for Galway – certainly, by comparison with the 1980s – and, while a slump might have been inevitable after so much success, Finnerty believes it was accelerated by changing managers and players too often. Galway were still doing well at underage level, so the natural tendency was to keep churning the panel in direct proportion to how they fared in the senior championship.

'Trouble was, we made too many changes. Managers usually lasted only two years; some players didn't even last that long because there was a feeling that Galway had so many good underage talents they should be winning senior titles. It doesn't always work like that. Sometimes, you're better off to stick with lads and work with them. Take Murty Killilea as an example. I always felt he was let go too quickly. Murty was a cold, case-hardened corner-back, who would do the same job for Carnmore in a League game in Athenry as he would for Galway in Croke Park. Christy Helebert was another who didn't last as long as he should have.'

Finnerty has no doubt that the Galway team of the 1985–90 period would have been just as successful in any era and also believes that their dedication and preparation compared favourably with anything today's game has to offer.

'It amuses me when I hear of teams training first thing in the morning and enduring various other hardships, as if it was something brand new. Galway were doing all that and more in the second half of the '80s. Morning sessions were quite common and I also remember one particular time when we thought Cyril Farrell was gone stone mad. He brought us out to Carraroe for a weekend get-together, starting on a Friday evening. We were allowed to stay up late that night but were down on the pitch the following morning at 7.30. Back up for breakfast and some rest two hours later, and out again for another gruelling session at 1.30. By evening time, we were all wrecked so Farrell announced that, because things had gone so well, we could all go home. "Ye deserve a break," he declared. A short pause. "But I'll see ye in Athenry at half-eight in the morning."

'Then, there was the day of Gerry McInerney's wedding. The reception was in Hayden's Hotel in Ballinasloe, so we thought we would have a day off training. Didn't happen. Farrell had us down on the pitch at 7p.m. with the promise that it would be a short session. Not so. It was nearly 11p.m. by the time we got back to the hotel. Farrell was obsessed by hurling during those years and so were we. So it didn't matter how tough the challenges were, we relished them. That whole Galway set-up was well ahead of its time.'

Galway's success ensured that they were high on the All Star hit parade (they won 30 awards between 1985 and 1990), with Finnerty winning five. He has fond memories of the tours to the US, which presented players with an opportunity to mix with their peers from other counties.

'The only time you came across opponents socially was on the night of the All Star banquet and on tour. That was a pity, but it certainly made the All Star scheme popular with those who got awards. I recall one trip to New York where the Galway lads were invited to a Connemara Man's Association function on a Saturday night. We didn't get back to the hotel until the following morning and met a few Offaly lads in the foyer. They thought we had been to mass and asked where the church was. "Out the front door, turn left, then right and head on for three blocks," declared a deadly serious Conor Hayes, as if he was an authority on New York churches. To the best of my knowledge, that wasn't the case! And we never heard if the Offaly lads got to mass.

'That was the thing about All Star tours. Lads could have a bit of crack and get to know each other. Galway–Tipperary rivalry was so intense at the time that we looked on each other as monsters. Certainly, we had built up Nicky English into a sort of hate figure, but we got to know him on tour and found he was as decent a man as you would ever meet. I'd like to think that some of the Tipp boys changed their views about Galway as well. Certainly, judging from the friendships that have built up since then, that must have been the case.'

Finnerty's involvement as an analyst with the *Sunday Independent* and on *The Sunday Game* has kept him closely involved with the hurling scene, a game that will never lose its attraction.

'Now that I can't play any more, I love going to games and talking about them. My philosophy is simple. I'll call it as I see it, but I try very hard to make sure I don't hurt players. I know what it's like from both ends of the spectrum. Whether you're playing or commenting, the important thing is to be honest and to never bring any hard feelings with you. As a player, I had some fierce battles with opponents but, at the end, it was always the same: shake hands and move on, irrespective of what has happened. Hurling is not a sport for carrying grudges.'

Nobody espoused that noble principle more than Finnerty in a glittering inter-county career, during which he set a record by becoming the first to win five All Star awards at right half-back.

Each was as well deserved as it was inevitable. The sheer force of will that he brought to his game reflected a personality that didn't accommodate second best. There was no more intimidating sight for opponents than Finnerty leaning back to gain possession, before powering his way forward to make the clearance.

'It was a good time to be a half-back for Galway because it didn't matter what sort of delivery you gave the forwards, they could make things happen. And very often they did.'

Of course, that creative attack had plenty of reasons to be thankful to Finnerty and Co., who were so accomplished at tying up rival forwards. Truly, an era when Galway were hurling kings.

---

*Pete Finnerty has business interests in property and catering, and is also involved in media work. He and his wife, Claire, have five children: Amy (13), Alan (10), Peter (8), Niall (4), Lisa (2).

Fuelling the Obsession

Gerry McEntee (Meath)

ALL STAR WINNER: 1987

'To me, the decline has come about because of a drop in standards of discipline and individual preparation, on and off the field. No one should ever put on a Meath jersey who doesn't want to die for it.'

Gerry McEntee avoids using the word 'sacrifice'. For him, playing for club or county could never be considered a sacrifice. You do what you have to do in whatever circumstances you find yourself and you expect the same from everyone around you.

He dared not fail them and they dared not fail him. That's the way it was in the Meath dressing-room for the latter half of the 17 years he spent here. If it wasn't sacrifice, then it had to be something else. Drive? Obsession? Madness, perhaps? To get a feel for what it meant to him, it's necessary to go back to 1989, when Meath were the reigning All-Ireland champions striving to win the three-in-a-row. For the fourth successive year, they had lined up in a Leinster final against Dublin. To Gerry and his Meath colleagues, the last Sunday in July was the barometer on which the whole season was judged.

But that year he had a dilemma. Towards the end of June he was accepted for a 12-month fellowship in the Mayo Clinic in Rochester, Minnesota, one of the most esteemed medical institutes in the world. It would be the most important stamp on his passport to a much cherished consultancy post in the Mater Hospital in Dublin.

Accepting the offer would obviously complicate his football career, but things were moving fast for the 34-year-old in the medical world and, as he saw it, 'an amazing experience' had presented itself. For a month, he settled into his new life in the US but, at the back of his mind, the last Sunday in July was coming into focus. He had always planned to return for the Leinster final and, when the late Noel Keating, the owner of Kepak and the Meath team's exceptionally generous benefactor, arranged to fly him home first class for the weekend, McEntee began making arrangements.

There were complications, however. The urge to break early from work on the Friday, to rush home across the Atlantic for a Gaelic football match, was something the Clinic directors could not understand. Time off was refused. So, without a day or even a few hours' leave to advance his travel plans, Gerry left Minneapolis at around 6p.m. local time (midnight in Ireland) on the Friday evening, flew to Gatwick and on to Dublin, arriving late on Saturday afternoon, less than 24 hours before the Leinster final throw-in.

The following day, Meath relinquished their Leinster and All-Ireland crowns after being caught by a late Dublin burst. A tired and cramping McEntee was hauled off with 15 minutes to go and, within 90 minutes, he was racing back through security and customs' checks in Gatwick airport to connect to Minneapolis, en route to the Mayo Clinic for an early Monday morning appointment. Some of his dejected colleagues had scarcely left the dressing-room as he soared high over the Irish sea.

'To this day, it remains the craziest and most stupid thing I ever did in football. But at the time I felt that anyone else on the panel would have done the same. The travel killed my legs and, with 15 minutes to go, I got cramp.'

The story is one of many that underline the obsession he had for playing with his county. How McEntee managed to walk the high wire for so long and balance the busiest and most prosperous part of his football journey with a burgeoning medical career that carried so much responsibility is not something to which he ever draws attention.

He spent two years in Stockton-on-Tees, near Middlesbrough in the north-east of England and returned to spend another year in Limerick, just as Meath's renaissance under Seán Boylan was cranking up in the mid-1980s.

It was ironic that just as McEntee could have been forgiven for backing off from the game he loved for professional reasons, he immersed himself more in it, cultivating a status as one of the most influential midfielders of his time.

His devotion to medicine and Gaelic football stemmed from childhood. He had uncles who were doctors on both sides of the family. His mother's brother, John O'Brien, was a Meath full back in the late 1940s and early 1950s. His father's brother, Lal, who had been a GP in Trim, made an early contribution to his enthusiastic nephew's growing love of football by presenting him with a Louth colleges' medal he won with St Mary's, Ardee in 1938.

As a young boy growing up in the rural hinterland of north Meath, just outside the village of Nobber, McEntee had two simple ambitions – to play for Meath in an All-Ireland final and to become a doctor. One of seven competitive boys in a family of eight, football was their lifeblood.

'There were a lot of McEntees and football meant a lot to them. It still does. We grew up with plenty of lads in our parish who shared the same interest in the game. The O'Reillys are a big family and, like most rural parishes, our teams depended on big families and regular transport. My own father, Tony, Mickey Smith, Eddie Eogan, Dudley Farrell Senior and many others drove us around. We piled into cars, played our game, and ate crisps and drank lemonade on the way home. That was our life and we enjoyed it.'

The pursuit of education brought Gerry to St Finian's College in Mullingar, although he suspects that football was the real reason he was despatched there. St Finian's didn't win any titles during his time there and it was only in UCD that he began to taste the trappings of success.

During his time in UCD, he came into contact with Eugene McGee who managed the college football team to seven Sigerson Cups, two Dublin county championships and two All-Ireland club titles. The perspective McGee gained there influenced what he would do in later years as manager of Offaly, who he led to three Leinster titles (1980, 1981, 1982) and an All-Ireland title in 1982.

McEntee won an All-Ireland club medal in 1975, the year he first joined the Meath squad, but it's not something he broadcasts loudly!

'I was a sub on the UCD team. I hadn't played in the Dublin championship and I only played in the All-Ireland semi-final against Roscommon Gaels because Kevin Kilmurray was injured.'

If UCD showed Gerry what could be achieved with proper organisation, the Meath team of that period was a perfect illustration of what could happen to good players when structures were poor. Meath beat Dublin in a National League final in 1975, went close in the 1976 and 1977 Leinster finals, and then headed into one of the worst periods in the county's history.

'The county scene was desperate and it wasn't helped by dominant clubs and players who gave more to their clubs than to the county. You had a situation where there were 11 or 12 players at Meath sessions while, at the same time, the others trained with their clubs. We had some great players, but I really resented the fact that we wasted so much time. It should have dawned on us much earlier that we were going to win nothing because the set-up was so appalling.'

Still, McEntee was enjoying his club football with Nobber, who were showing signs of progress even if silverware was evasive. They lost Division Two junior and intermediate county finals, before they finally made the breakthrough in 1980, around the same time as Gerry and Yvonne were planning their wedding.

Another illustration of the dedication they had for football in Nobber came on the weekend of the wedding in the Imperial Hotel, Cork. Nobber were due to play Kilmainhamwood in the Meath intermediate semi-final on the day after Gerry and Yvonne got married.

It was an age before players climbed on board helicopters to make dramatic dashes to games so, after a night of abstinence, the Nobber intermediate team were routed from their beds at around 8a.m. by Gerry's mother, put on a train to Dublin, collected and driven to the match.

'It was one of the best games that team ever played. Yvonne and myself drove back that morning. My brother Shane and I even went for a run in the Mardyke before the wedding. There was no question of missing a championship semi-final against the 'Wood. We eventually won the intermediate championship that year by beating Bohermeen Martry Harps in the final, which was undoubtedly one of the most satisfying moments of my career.'

Gerry's enthusiasm for Meath was wearing thin by the time Seán Boylan was put before them as their new manager in October 1982.

'We knew nothing about him, but he got fellas to commit themselves to the cause without ever having to actually drag it out of them. He treated players with respect and they returned it. Club rivalries were put aside.'

The influx of youngsters like Bob O'Malley and Bernard Flynn helped to invigorate some of the older players. Successive League semi-finals were reached and lost to Armagh and Galway respectively in 1983–84, but it showed that progress was being made. The upward graph continued when Meath won the Centenary Cup competition in 1984, beating Monaghan in the final.

However, the scourge of Dublin remained and the Leinster final defeat in 1984 hit hard. A year later Laois dumped Meath out of the Leinster championship, winning by ten points. Some saw it as an end, but McEntee sensed a 'blessing in disguise' as it led to an overhaul of the team.

By the summer of 1986, Gerry was back from a two-year stint in England and his midfield partnership with Liam Hayes was commanding huge respect. By his own admission, McEntee knew his limitations as a player but he worked hard at what he did well.

'I knew what I couldn't do. I couldn't solo, I scored very little and I wasn't fast. But I could read it well, I could defend and I wasn't afraid. I was much fitter towards the latter end of my career too. Seán had put us through some tough training programmes and I became more experienced and battle hardened.'

In his early years he had some great tussles with Dublin's Brian Mullins who, in McEntee's eyes, set the standard for midfield play in that era.

'I looked up to Mullins. For me, the Dubs of the 1970s changed Gaelic football. What Kerry subsequently did was a response to Dublin. Despite what people say, though, that brilliant Dublin team was dirty. We knew that if we didn't change, we weren't going to beat them. They essentially shaped the way we played.'

On a wet, windy, last Sunday of July 1986, that change finally yielded the result for which McEntee had yearned. Meath won their first Leinster title for 16 years and launched an era of dominance over their great rivals.

'If you weren't prepared for battle against Dublin, you could forget about it and, on that day, we were prepared. I remember diving to block a Tommy Conroy shot and there were two sets of

Meath hands there before me. That's how much we wanted that Leinster title.'

A year later, an All-Ireland crown followed with success over Cork, a season that would earn the 32-year-old his sole All Star award. But if 1987 was the zenith, the following year was the low point in his career, when he was sent off after just six minutes of the All-Ireland final replay against Cork for striking out at Niall Cahalane.

Despite being a man short for virtually the entire game, Meath won a much-maligned final by a point. McEntee still shudders at the consequences for him, had they failed.

'I wasn't proud of it then and I'm still not proud of it now. And if we hadn't won, I don't think I'd be able to have a conversation about football right now. Too much has been said and written about 1988 and the rivalry with Cork. I'd prefer to leave it. There were decent lads on that team, who were subsequently beset by tragedy. I holiday every year in west Cork and I like the people there, just as I like the people of Dublin, where I now live.'

McEntee has precise views about why that Meath team didn't add a third All-Ireland title to their list.

'I would say we were good enough to win three, but the players lost the 1990 final because we didn't treat Cork, who were the reigning All-Ireland champions, with enough respect.

'And in 1991 against Down, I thought that final was lost on the line. Tactically that game was lost by not playing Kevin Foley on James McCartan. People also didn't realise how significant the absence of Bob O'Malley, who had broken his leg earlier in the summer, really was.

'No disrespect to Brendan Reilly, who was a half-back if he was a defender at all, but it was a mistake to play him on a confidence player like McCartan. All the players wanted Foley on McCartan.'

And yet, McEntee looks at the 1991 season as perhaps the most enjoyable of all. Because of his increased responsibility as a surgical trainee in the Mater hospital, his football was restricted to the point where he had virtually retired after 1990.

But as the first 1991 Leinster championship game against Dublin approached, he began to appear more often at training.

'The training was going badly and it had almost got to the point where Colm O'Rourke and Mickey Lyons were going to be dropped. I always remember Noel Keating inviting us up to Kepak, feeding us with steaks and hosting a meeting that was frank in its exchanges. He told us that when things weren't going well in his business, they came into this particular room and didn't leave until there was blood on the walls and matters were sorted out. That's what we did that night. Noel kicked off the meeting by saying to Seán [Boylan] that he had taken his eye off the ball since he got married. Seán reacted as if he didn't like what he was hearing, but maybe he had put Noel up to it at the outset. We ended up having a healthy discussion and a great season.'

Sunday after Sunday, Meath filed through the doors of Croke Park on a remarkable ten-match run. McEntee believes that the four-week break between the All-Ireland semi-final against Roscommon and the final against Down was detrimental, as it broke the powerful momentum Meath had established.

Ironically, at the age of 36, it was one of his finest ever performances for Meath, even if it did end in disappointment.

'Of all the defeats, the 1991 final against Down gets me most. It should have been the pinnacle for us but then, there are no guarantees in sport.'

After 1991, he returned to Kings College in London and playing football finally began to drop down the list of priorities.

However, he has never faded too far away from the football scene, due to his successful development of Gilmore's Groin surgical procedure. Gilmore, a London-based surgeon, conducted research into athletes who had significant groin pain in the areas where hernias occur although there were no actual hernias there. He discovered disruption to the lower stomach muscles and pioneered a surgical technique to repair it.

When first approached by former Dublin player and sports injury specialist Noel McCaffrey about getting involved with this common athletic groin problem, McEntee saw it as a link to the football life he had enjoyed so much.

That link now stretches to having treated over 500 cases in what has become a minor epidemic of groin trouble for GAA and soccer players.

'The magnitude of the problem is incredible. I went to two Leinster semi-finals a few years ago and, between the two games, there were seven players who had had surgery for this type of groin problem. It's a very common injury in hurlers and footballers. It's an overuse injury that stems from too much twisting and turning, particularly from shuttle sprints. Some specialists don't agree with that. But the common thread among a lot of my patients is intense shuttle sprinting. Everyone does them because they are a form of torture and because they're a form of torture people think they must be good for you. But those movements are never replicated in a match. It's a daft exercise.'

McEntee has very definite views about the growing intensity and longevity of training programmes for amateur athletes.

'I tell players clearly about the dangers of over-training and the benefits of proper rest. The rising numbers of groin and knee injuries is, I'm sure, the legacy of over-training. With intense training programmes, teams are losing their appetite for competition. These training programmes make huge demands and are a form of stress on people. Rest is vastly under-appreciated.'

McEntee feels County chairmen, as much as managers, have to heed the warning signs soon: 'I was interested to hear that Tyrone only trained collectively twice a week at most when they won the All-Ireland in 2003. They looked the freshest team about.'

McEntee's own first steps into management have already been successful. With the experienced Paddy Clarke as coach, McEntee helped St Brigid's, a club which is based just a short drive from his Castleknock home, to win a first ever Dublin senior football championship in 2003. They followed up by winning a first ever Leinster title two months later.

However, he insists he won't graduate to inter-county management at present and has ruled out any involvement with Meath, despite consistently being linked with the position.

'It would be very attractive and, in different circumstances, I would like to get involved. But there is the travel and the huge time involved. One would have to be unemployed, have a private sponsor, or be independently wealthy to become involved and I don't figure in any of those categories.'

He wonders how Seán Boylan has continued for so long in Meath but while acknowledging his 'enormous contribution', he feels the time has come for the Meath manager to move on.

'The saddest possibility is that he would leave the team where he found it in 1982. That would be truly sad, but it's on the cards the way things are going. To me, the decline has come about because of a drop in standards of discipline and individual preparation, on and off the field. Seán has tolerated a number of players over the last few years who don't really care about playing for Meath. If they did, they wouldn't be in the shape they were and they wouldn't behave on and off the field the way they did. No one should ever put on a Meath jersey who doesn't want to die for it.'

Take it from one who knew.

*Gerry McEntee is a surgeon at the Mater Hospital, Dublin.
He and his wife, Yvonne, have a family of three:
Jennifer (20), Ciara (18) and Philip (14).

Through the Eyes of a Sniper

Pat Fox (Tipperary)

ALL STAR WINNER: 1987, 1989, 1991

'A pattern had developed: Tipperary would lose Munster championship games; players would be dropped off the panel, whether they deserved it or not; managers would change for much the same reason; and the whole depressing cycle continued.'

On the night before the 1991 All-Ireland hurling final, three battle-hardened warriors assembled in a room in the Burlington Hotel in Dublin.

Several floors below, the bar and foyer bustled with the typical fizz that prevails on the eve of an All-Ireland final. As Tipperary's base for the weekend, the hotel looked as if it had been hand-wrapped in blue and gold, as supporters from home and abroad congregated for the great occasion.

Two years earlier, Tipperary had won the All-Ireland title for the first time in 18 years but there was still a strange sense of unfulfilled ambition in the county and a fair degree of scepticism beyond it. Beating Antrim by 18 points in the 1989 final had achieved its main purpose, but doubts still persisted. For all their energy and effort, Antrim hadn't been up to the massive challenge and, despite the Ulster champions' stunning victory over Offaly in the semi-final, the only unanswered question going into the final was the margin of Tipperary's victory.

It would be different in 1991. Kilkenny were the opposition so there could be no assumptions, no comfort zones and, very definitely, no certainties. Tipperary were the narrow favourites but, as the full-forward line of Pat Fox, Cormac Bonnar and Nicky English stared out onto the packed Burlington Hotel car park on the night before the final, they could sense as many questions as answers.

All three had soldiered together since their U-21 days and, while the senior path had been strewn with landmines for years, the trio had finally made it through enemy fire to win the 1989 All-Ireland final. Now, Tipperary were desperate to prove that they were a team of genuine substance, rather than opportunists who, two years earlier, had availed of a kink in the form line.

Unfortunately, there was a problem. Actually, there were two problems. Both English and Bonnar were suffering from leg injuries that left them worrying more about their personal fitness than the Kilkenny defence.

English had visited Bonnar's room and was encouraged to hear that the 'Viking' was in a good mood. His leg was feeling better, although whether it would stand up to an afternoon of intense jousting with Kilkenny full back, Pat Dwyer, was a different matter.

English's spirits weren't as high. He felt that he couldn't possibly last the full 70 minutes, a fear he relayed to Fox when he walked into the room.

Fox's response was reassuring, if based on flimsy evidence. 'You'll be grand,' he declared with a smile. English would have loved to agree with him, but his damaged calf muscle was predicting a different scenario.

English would recall how Fox later stood up at a team meeting and made an astonishing promise to the team. Conscious that his full-forward colleagues were in trouble, he presented them and the rest of the team with a comforting proposition.

'Just give me the ball and I'll take the Kilkenny backs apart,' announced Fox in his quiet, matter-of-fact way.

He kept his word. He scored 0-5 from play in a man-of-the-match performance as Tipperary won by four points. Both Bonnar and English were forced to leave the action with a recurrence of their injuries, so it was absolutely imperative that Fox delivered.

'Those are the sort of days every kid dreams of, from the first time he picks up a hurl or kicks a football. He wants to play in an All-Ireland final and he wants to be man-of-the-match. It was just one of those days when things went right for me. And yes, it was very special to get the man-of-the-match award.'

But then, the 1991 championship had been a remarkable campaign for Fox and Tipperary. They had trailed Cork by seven points in the drawn Munster final at Páirc Uí Chaoímh, only to launch a defiant revival, which was accelerated by Fox's goal. They would later be denied an equalising point by a hotly disputed decision after English's booted effort was signalled wide, although it appeared to have been just inside the post. However, Fox saved the day with a typically opportunist point after wriggling clear of his marker.

The replay was even more dramatic and is very much embedded in Fox's mind as the best game in which he was ever involved. Twelve minutes into the second half, Cork were leading by 3-13 to 1-10 and even Tipperary's most devoted supporters were beginning to look towards the Semple Stadium exits.

Shortly afterwards, Fox found himself facing a decision.

'I had a chance of a goal but there was a bit of a risk involved, so I decided to take a point instead. I know people thought I should have gone for goal, but I took the view that a point might just stem the Cork flow, whereas if I went for goal and Ger Cunningham saved it, it might be the end of the line for us.'

Fox's gamble worked. Gradually, Tipperary increased momentum. John Leahy picked and drove to maximum effect, sub Aidan Ryan galloped into openings which weren't there earlier, while Fox's instinctive reactions and perfect touch began to unlock Cork's security system.

He scored a smashing goal that accelerated the recovery process and, as Tipperary grew in confidence, they powered their way to an amazing victory, 4-19 to 4-15. In a period of 24 extraordinary minutes, during which they had out-scored Cork by 3-7 to 0-2, they had turned a nine-point deficit into a five-point lead and ended up winning by four. Fox had scored 1-5.

'Our hurling during that comeback was as close to perfect as I had seen during my time with Tipperary. We were so full of confidence and so determined to make up for 1990 that nothing could stop us. It was an amazing feeling to be part of that team. I remember watching Kevin Hennessy jumping into the air after landing another Cork score and you could sense that he thought there was no way back for us. And who could blame him? But we refused to yield and I'll certainly remember that as a very special day. At the end of that campaign, we had beaten Limerick, Cork, Galway and Kilkenny, so nobody could say we weren't worthy champions.'

Fox had contributed 2-17 to the championship effort, guaranteeing himself every major honour on the awards circuit. Winning an All Star was a formality, but he also dominated the individual honours, having been chosen as the 'Hurler of the Year' and the 'Players' Player of the Year'. It was to be Fox's third, and last, All Star award and, while he won a further Munster title in 1993, there were to be no more All-Ireland successes either.

He hurled on until 1996, but his latter days were hampered by injury problems, although not linked to the knee damage that had come so very close to forcing him out of the game ten years earlier.

Fox had seemed destined to be one of Tipperary's great stars when he won three All-Ireland U-21 medals in a row in 1979, 1980 and 1981, the first as a midfielder, the latter two at left full back. When he injured a knee in an inter-firms game in 1982, he could have had no idea of the pain and frustration that would grow very close to despair over the coming years.

His cruciate ligament was three-quarters severed and, whereas nowadays that would result in immediate surgery, things weren't quite as advanced in the early 1980s. Various remedies were tried but none worked properly, leaving Fox trapped in a lonely world where sympathy was in short supply from all but his closest friends.

It's a memory that has made him very aware of the need to listen when a player complains.

'When a player has an ongoing injury, there is a tendency to be flippant about it: "Look at him, he's gone down again. Sure he couldn't be that bad." I know people were saying that about me, so it's something I'm very conscious of now when players are injured because I know what they're going through. It was hell for a few years. I should have had an operation, but it wasn't the done thing at the time, probably because the recovery period for ligament damage was so long. I missed 1983 and 1984 through recurring injuries and, while I came back in 1985, I wasn't right. We beat Clare in a Munster semi-final replay, but lost the final to Cork by six points, which was a savage disappointment, as Tipperary had been very unlucky against them in the previous year's final. The 1985 final certainly wasn't one of my better games. In fact, it wasn't a year I look back on with many – if, indeed, any – pleasant memories.'

With the knee problem still niggling away, Fox missed the 1986 season and, at the age of 25, looked to be finished with inter-county hurling. It was a time of great uncertainty in Tipperary, who hadn't won a Munster title since 1971. More often than not, they had been eliminated in the first round. It was an unstable environment, one where a player with a recurring knee problem tended to be well down the priority list.

'A pattern had developed: Tipperary would lose Munster championship games; players would be dropped off the panel, whether they deserved it or not; managers would change for much the same reason; and the whole depressing cycle continued. It was hard to keep interest going in such a disjointed set-up. Confidence levels were low because players felt that they could be discarded after one bad performance. It was no way to build a team.'

And then, the door opened and in walked one Michael 'Babs' Keating. While he didn't actually declare on the first night that Tipperary would win Munster and All-Ireland titles over the next few years, it was clear that he was going to do things differently. One of his early priorities was to convince Fox that his career was far from finished.

Fox did a huge amount of weight training during the winter of 1986, designed specifically to build up the muscles around the knee. By the spring of 1987, it was feeling a whole lot stronger, but Fox still had doubts about whether there was any point returning to the county scene. His first reaction was to ignore the new manager's overtures, but he eventually decided to take his chance.

He was invited to a trial game, only to be taken off at half-time. He thought it was a signal that the new management didn't want him, but afterwards Babs called him into training, convinced that he had found his right full forward. Fox's days as a defender were over. So, too, were the frustrating times when people looked at him as if he were exploiting his knee injury as a form of excuse.

'It was a whole new life for me. Babs was the first guy who really looked after me. To be honest, the rest didn't really want to know. But then that was Babs. He always did things his own way. He had set a target and would do anything to achieve it. He brought a whole new dimension to the scene. We got anything and everything we wanted. The Supporters' Club was a huge help too and, very quickly, the players were made to feel very good about themselves.

'Loads of boots would arrive in the dressing-room and you could take three or four pairs. Babs started talking about team holidays almost the minute he walked in the door. We were being well looked after on all fronts and we responded because we felt that there was a plan in place. We could achieve something if we put the work in. Players take all that for granted now, but it was very different back then, not just in Tipperary but right across the country.'

Tipperary captured their first Munster title for 16 years in 1987, after an extra-time replay success in an epic battle in Killarney. Fox had played a huge role in getting them the replay, having coolly slotted over two late frees in the drawn game. Despite that, Fox never liked the free-taking role and was quite happy to hand it over to English in 1988.

The 1987 Munster final success was the start of a glory period for Tipperary, during which they would win two All-Ireland titles and five Munster finals in seven seasons. Their battles with Galway in the late 1980s developed into one of the great rivalries of modern hurling.

Galway beat them in the 1987 All-Ireland semi-final, the 1988 All-Ireland final and the 1989 National League final, but lost the controversial 1989 All-Ireland semi-final. With Babs Keating and Cyril Farrell adding spice to the mix with their forthright views, and two excellent teams jousting for supremacy, it was a marketing dream for hurling. On the pitch, the individual battles were as intense as hurling has ever known, as the players grew to know every detail of each other's game.

Fox's personal nemesis was Ollie Kilkenny, an angle-grinding left full back who prided himself in making life hell for corner-forwards.

'Ollie was one hell of a marker. He gave me an awful hard time on a few occasions, but that was his style. Playing against Kilkenny and Sylvie Linnane was as tough as it got for corner-forwards. I had some great battles with Ollie in particular, and I suppose it ended up at about 50-50 over the years. Brendan Lynskey was another hard man on that Galway team. But then, they were all fierce competitors and there's no doubt that the Tipperary–Galway rivalry of that era was great for hurling. It's amazing the number of good friendships that still exist between those Tipperary and Galway teams. Ollie would call into the pub here in Cashel anytime he's passing and I'd see a fair bit of Brendan because we're in the same trade.'

Tipperary finally ended Galway's glory run in a rancorous All-Ireland semi-final in 1989. Two years later, Tipperary hammered Galway in the 1991 semi-final but, in 1993, Galway reasserted themselves on a day when Fox couldn't play due to a foot problem.

By then, he was beginning to pick up irritating injuries which were unrelated to the original knee problem and, while he struggled on until the 1996 Munster final defeat by Limerick, he was no longer the instinctive menace that had tormented so many defences.

Despite losing some of his best years through injury in the early 1980s, he retired with no major regrets, having reached peaks he had never thought possible. He would, of course, have loved to be part of a team that won successive All-Ireland titles, an ambition that he believes could have been achieved in 1990.

'That was definitely the one that got away. Cork beat us well in the Munster final. Maybe we thought we had the measure of them but, for whatever reason, it didn't happen for us that season. Cork went on to win the All-Ireland but to be honest, it wasn't one of their better teams. Had we won the 1990 All-Ireland, I feel we would have completed the three-in-a-row in 1991. But it's not a big deal. We did a whole lot better than anybody would have thought possible at the start of 1987.'

Cork turned out to be Tipperary's tormentors again in 1992, beating them by a goal in the Munster semi-final, on a day when

Fox discovered that, however well you play in an All-Ireland final, you never know what lies ahead next year.

In 1992, he found himself being marked by a tall, powerful teenager, who answered to the name of Brian Corcoran. It was a chastening experience for Fox after the previous year's glory trail.

'I had never heard of Brian Corcoran before the game but, boy, did I know about him afterwards. He gave me a complete trouncing and it didn't matter what I did, I couldn't get my game going. You would expect problems against the likes of Ollie Kilkenny or Martin Hanamy, but here was a kid hardly giving me a ball. It was a tough day, but then Corcoran went on to be some player afterwards. Unfortunately for me, I was the first to feel the brunt of his amazing powers.'

Given that he suffered so many injury problems in his early days, it might be expected that once the glory days were over, Fox would decommission his hurley and spend his time coaching and talking about the game with the constant flow of customers that pass through his pub in Cashel.

Far from it. He won two All-Ireland Masters (over 40) with Tipperary and is still playing junior 'B' hurling with his club, Annacarty, as well as managing the intermediate side. The golf handicap is at 12 and under threat, while, when things are quiet, he takes off for a day's deep-sea fishing.

However, for all the attractions of the golf course and the open sea, nothing sparks the light in Fox's eye like hurling, which is why he finds it difficult to understand how some players can walk away from the game when their playing careers are over.

'I'd know lads who wouldn't go to a game anymore. I could never see a day when that would happen to me. I'll play for as long as I can and, after that, I'm sure I'll still be involved in the game in whatever way I can. Being in the pub trade in Tipperary means you're never far away from hurling anyway, because there isn't a night goes by when lads aren't talking about the game while they're having a drink.'

Despite some of the gloom being peddled about the direction hurling is taking, Fox is convinced that it has a bright future. He also believes that the level of skill is as high now as at any time in the past, while the pace is increasing all the time.

He applauds the change in the championship system, which gives counties extra games, but is adamant that no attempt should ever be made to scrap the Munster or Leinster championships as part of a radical overhaul.

'I know what the Munster final means to players and supporters. It's something special and must always be part of hurling. I'm sure Leinster people feel the same about their championship. I'd like to think that the new system has the best of both worlds, in that it retains the provincial championships while also giving teams a second chance to win the All-Ireland.'

Fox would love to be starting out again on a career which took him into a world he never thought possible. Babs Keating has always maintained that right corner-forward is the most difficult position to fill in hurling, yet, when he took over the Tipperary team, he knew instinctively that, with Fox around, No.13 wouldn't be a problem for him. Nor was it, but it sure created some serious difficulties for the opposition.

---

*Pat Fox runs a pub in Cashel. He and his wife, Marita, have two daughters: Rianne (19) and Tracey (14).

Wicklow's First and Only

Kevin O'Brien (Wicklow)

ALL STAR WINNER: 1990

*'I often wonder, if we changed the names of counties and jersey colours
and started all over again, would it make a difference?'*

Kevin O'Brien thumbed through his match programme,
stopped at the Kildare team and wondered. What if he had
ignored his homing instincts and accepted the invitation to leave
Baltinglass and Wicklow and move across the border to Kildare?

Would he now be out there on the Croke Park pitch, limbering
up for the All-Ireland final? Would Mick O'Dwyer be whispering
in his ear, telling him that this was his day, his stage, his destiny?

He glanced at the Galway line-up and recognised several
names from the team which Wicklow had beaten by three points
in a Division Three National League game at Aughrim, less than
two years previously. Wicklow had even finished three points

ahead of Galway on the table at the end of that season. How had Galway progressed so much in the interim while Wicklow remained stagnant?

As O'Brien stared down from the Hogan Stand prior to the 1998 All-Ireland football final, his thoughts flicked back over a 12-year senior inter-county career, in which pain and frustration had seemed like permanent companions. Still, they could never destroy an indomitable spirit or rob him of the sheer joy of playing football.

He had captained Wicklow to victory in the 1992 All-Ireland 'B' title, but a win over Antrim in Navan wasn't quite the same as winning the 'real' All-Ireland final.

Even Wicklow's moments of relative glory had included an embarrassing incident on the Páirc Tailteann presentation podium.

'When I hoisted the cup over my head, one of the handles fell off. Maybe in my excitement I pulled too hard, but anyway the handle broke off. Somehow, you couldn't see it happening with the Sam Maguire Cup.'

In many ways, it defined a weaker county's existence. Winning the unimaginatively titled 'B' final on a dreary December afternoon represented a peak of sorts for Wicklow, but it was never enough to satisfy a player like O'Brien.

Yet, he knew that he could never leave Wicklow, although the opportunity had presented itself with Kildare and Dublin. Both approaches had been of an informal nature but O'Brien has no doubts that, had he entertained either, arrangements would have been made to smooth his exit from Wicklow.

'I was asked by a Dublin contact if I would consider leaving Wicklow. It was suggested to me that I had little chance of ever winning anything with Wicklow, whereas Dublin were serious Leinster and All-Ireland contenders every year. A job would be sorted out for me if I moved to a specified club in the city and I could then declare for Dublin. It was much the same with Kildare. Move across the border, join a Kildare club and I'd be eligible for their county panel. Again, there was to be a job involved. I have no doubt that, had I shown any interest in either approach, things would have been organised for me. It was flattering to be asked by two counties who were going well, but I couldn't move. For a start, I'd be run out of Baltinglass as a traitor! Besides, I have always been a Baltinglass man and my loyalty to this area and this club was something I couldn't walk away from. Sure, I would have loved to play in an All-Ireland final, but it would have had to be with Wicklow. That's the way I'm made and nothing could ever change me.'

Still, as O'Brien watched the Kildare forwards allow themselves to be gradually rounded up and herded into a pen by the Galway defence in the 1998 All-Ireland final, he wondered if he would have made any difference. The answer is almost assuredly yes, since he was an incredibly gifted player.

Former Dublin star goalkeeper, John O'Leary, who played with O'Brien on various Leinster Railway Cup and International Rules teams, insists that he was one of the greatest forwards of his generation. He even rated him ahead of Pat Spillane, a quite remarkable tribute, which O'Leary explained in his autobiography, *Back to the Hill*.

'People might think I'm mad to put him ahead of Spillane, but I'll stand by my judgement on this one. Let's put it this way – O'Brien would have been a resounding success with the great Kerry team of the 1970s and 1980s – how good would Spillane have been with Wicklow?' he wrote.

O'Leary had never heard of Wicklow's new star, when a shy 20-year-old was brought into the Leinster squad for training in 1986. O'Brien hadn't even played senior championship football for Wicklow, but he was called for Leinster trials anyway. O'Brien believes he has fellow Wicklow man, Jack Boothman, to thank for that.

'Jack was a Leinster selector and was keen to have a Wicklow involvement on the team. I never thought I'd be the one, but I was chosen at centre forward for the semi-final against Ulster in

Breffni Park. It was an amazing experience. I hadn't even played championship football for Wicklow and here I was in the same dressing-room as several All-Ireland winners.

'It was a fierce cold day and my feet were freezing. So much so that after about ten minutes I caught a ball and tried to kick for a point. But my feet were so cold that the ball dropped short, but somehow looped into the net over Brian McAlinden's head. It was a pure fluke, but it must have looked good from the sidelines because the following day's papers credited me with chipping the goalkeeper. If only!

'Anyway, I must have done reasonably well because I was retained for the final in Ballinasloe on St Patrick's Day. I was named at centre forward, but just before we went out, the manager Bobby Millar told me to switch to full forward. I remember Connacht full back Harry Keegan eyeing me as I came in. Harry had been one of the top Roscommon stars for many years and I really didn't know what to expect, so I decided to play my own game and hope things went well.'

They did. O'Brien scored two points while also contributing so much to general play that he was named as man-of-the-match. To crown a memorable day, Leinster won.

As O'Brien returned home to Baltinglass that evening, having joined an élite band of Wicklow players who had won Railway Cup medals, he would have been forgiven for thinking that the good times were set to roll. All the more so when, three months later, Wicklow delivered one of the championship shocks of the decade, beating a Laois side that had won the National League title a few weeks earlier.

The game has gone down in history as the 'Battle of Aughrim', a fractious occasion that saw four players dismissed – three from Laois. O'Brien scored 2-2, including a goal which resulted from what he describes as 'the worst penalty I ever kicked'.

'It came back off the goalkeeper but, luckily for me, bounced into my path and I managed to force the ball over the line. We went on to win by four points. Laois had a really good team and were bursting with confidence after winning the League, but we always felt we had a chance in Aughrim.'

Meath awaited Wicklow in the Leinster semi-final and, just as quickly as Wicklow had inflated their air tanks, they were mercilessly deflated in a nine-point thrashing.

Wicklow managed to reach three Leinster semi-finals over the next four years and were desperately unlucky not to have beaten Meath in the 1991 quarter-final. Meath had been involved in four epic battles with Dublin and, having survived those, they may have felt that beating Wicklow would be a routine exercise. It wasn't. The first game finished level and, while Meath won the replay, Wicklow had again done enough to give them a tantalising peek into the exclusive club. Sadly, they never got any closer.

O'Brien believes that not enough was done to build on the solid base which had been put down in the 1986–91 period. He believes too few people in Wicklow actually believed in the county team, an attitude that infuriated him. There were times, too, when a lack of ambition permeated through to players, with the result that some didn't always show enough commitment to the cause.

O'Brien was different. The greater the disappointment, the greater the challenge; the bigger the problem, the bigger the need for a solution.

'I always believed Wicklow had a chance every year. I'd think: *This is it. This is the year we'll do something in the championship.* We'd play challenge games and win them. God, that would do your head in. If we could perform against good teams in challenge games, why couldn't we step it up on the big day?

'To be honest, I think it was an attitude thing within the county. I'd call it the maintenance approach. I often felt that the County Board were happy to keep things ticking over, fulfil the competitions and close the books. Great if we won a few games, but there was no analysis or soul-searching as to why we never progressed beyond a certain stage. I'm not sure it's any different now. We have some great football people in this county, but we need to think differently. The problem in counties like Wicklow is that not enough people believe. We don't have a tradition of winning, so each generation of footballers is starting from scratch. I still believe the breakthrough can be made if, instead of simply keeping things ticking over, we force them. Too many people in Wicklow look for excuses. Even the geography of the county is blamed for our lack of success, on the basis that we're effectively two counties, who don't really get on because the mountains separate us. There are mountains in Kerry too, but they don't seem to have interfered with their football.

'Sadly, there are times when Wicklow seem content to act out the weaker county role without looking for ways of improving. I'd analyse every match I ever lost and wonder if there was anything I might have done differently. Lots of other players would do the same, but you would always have a few whose commitment was questionable. I remember going to Punchestown races one year and meeting several of the lads. We had a training session that evening and, while most of us were there in good time, a few stayed behind and we heard later that they had spent the evening drinking over in Ballymore.

'Small things like that eat you up. I would readily admit that, when it came to football, I always had a mad streak so I had to keep pushing myself all the time, however badly things might be going. Limerick beat us in a League game one year, which really was a bad result because they weren't anywhere nearly as good then as they are now. I arrived home that Sunday night, threw my gear in the back kitchen and announced that I wasn't playing with Wicklow anymore. The following night, I was working out in the gym and looking forward to the next game. One guy came up to me and said, "You're mad. Limerick are after hammering the daylights out of you lot and you're down here pumping iron. Would you ever get a bit of sense?" Maybe he was right, but, when it came to football, I'd do anything to improve.'

While O'Brien didn't enjoy much success with Wicklow (although he did win an All-Ireland junior medal late in his career), he achieved the ultimate honour with Baltinglass, who became the first (and, so far, the only) club in the county to win the All-Ireland title. He won 13 county senior titles, but the highest peak was reached in 1990, when Baltinglass plotted their way to success in the All-Ireland championship.

Wins over Longford Slashers, Ferbane (Offaly) and Thomas Davis (Dublin) won them the Leinster title, a target which many assumed to be the highest achievable for Baltinglass. They saw it differently.

'It was our opportunity to really make a statement for ourselves and Wicklow football. The club had always been a huge focal point for me. Even when things were going badly with Wicklow, I always knew that we had a good chance of winning the county title, which helped keep me going. When we won the Leinster final in 1989, we began to realise how close we were to achieving something really big. Cork champions Castlehaven had to come to Aughrim for the All-Ireland semi-final and, to be honest, it was a huge help to us. It rained all morning and the place was so wet that water had to be scooped off the surface before the game. The whole of Baltinglass turned out and created a great atmosphere, which shook the Castlehaven boys out of their stride in the first half. Larry Tompkins was Castlehaven's main man, but there was only so much he could do on his own. A fierce competitor, he was always one of the players I admired most, but on this particular day we managed to keep him from doing too much damage.

'We played Clann na nGael [Roscommon] in the final and beat them by two goals. It was their fourth successive final defeat, which must have been unbearable. I felt sorry for Tony McManus, who had done so much for them, but we needed the title just as much as they did. It was an unbelievable feeling to win the club final. I know it's special for every club, but when you're from a weaker county, it's even more memorable.'

The year got even better for O'Brien, who was selected on the Irish International Rules team for the tour to Australia, an experience he greatly enjoyed.

'I absolutely loved it. It was fantastic to be part of an international set-up, which was run so professionally. Eugene McGee was team manager and I found him great, even if he did give out to me after a warm-up game. The Australians weren't used to goal-scoring, so our plan was to concentrate on point-taking in the warm-up game and then hit them for goals in the Test matches. I got a few goal chances in the practice game and couldn't resist lashing them into the net, which didn't please Eugene!'

Ironically, it was while O'Brien was in Australia that the subject of the All Stars came up. He enjoyed a good year, but thought it most unlikely that he would be selected.

'Jim Stynes and myself spent one night begging Dermot Power, who was then with Bank of Ireland, to send us two invitations. Jim was going home for Christmas and wanted to meet all the lads again. I told Dermot that I'd sit outside the door if I had to. A few weeks later, I got the biggest shock of my life when I was driving to work one morning and I heard the All Stars being announced on the radio. I was on the team! At full forward, no less. I couldn't believe it. I'd be getting an invitation in my own right. I nearly crashed the car. An All Star award is a great honour for any player, but it was extra special for me because nobody from Wicklow had ever won one before.'

While it was a huge personal triumph for O'Brien, it also brought some embarrassing moments as he was now seen in a different light.

'I walked into a pub one night and this guy at the bar declares, "Here comes the All Star." He kept at it and, to be honest, I found it embarrassing. I don't know if he was pleased for me or having a go, but I bought him a drink anyway, just to shut him up. His opinion didn't count, unlike that of Jack of O'Shea, who came to me some time later and told me to stick my chest out and enjoy my All Star because I deserved it. I really appreciated that. I found Jacko a great International Rules captain and a lovely guy. He thought like a winner, but then, he had the advantage of coming from a successful county. I often wonder, if we changed the names of counties and jersey colours and started all over again, would it make a difference? As things stand, tradition – both bad and good – seems to be deep-rooted in every county.'

Given his determination to drive himself as hard as possible, it was almost inevitable that O'Brien would suffer some serious injuries. His knees bothered him regularly, including cruciate, ligament and cartilage trouble plus, as he puts it so graphically, 'bits flying around here and there'. He has had no fewer than nine operations and may need more.

O'Brien is still addicted to football and is heavily involved with Baltinglass. His eldest son Seán was on the Wicklow minor team this year, at the age of 16, and looks certain to develop into a star of the future.

'He's bigger than me already and he loves the game. The one thing I want for him and his generation is that they don't have to struggle for everything the way we had to. Wicklow have to start thinking more ambitiously and then set about achieving their goals. And that includes looking after young lads properly. They're the future – in fact, they're the only real asset we've got.'

O'Brien saw the world through his football exploits, with Chicago and New York as favoured summer destinations once Wicklow were out of the championship. He played with the Wolfe Tones club in Chicago and the Leitrim club in New York and still speaks fondly of the people who looked after him so well in both cities. They were experiences that he greatly enjoyed and which exposed him to a different way of life. Still, Baltinglass was home and the attraction of the US, Kildare or Dublin, for that matter, could never change that.

He may not have had much big time success with Wicklow, but he enjoyed his long career, including those training sessions on cold, dreary nights, even if they did provide the occasional unplanned hazard.

'We were coming home from Laragh one foggy, winter night when we hit a deer somewhere up the mountains. Raymond

Danne, David Whelan, Mick Fitzpatrick and myself got out of the van and stood in a huddle around the deer, but there wasn't a move out of him. Still, we wanted to give him every chance, so we lifted him into the back of the van with the intention of bringing him back to Tommy Murphy [the local vet and Baltinglass teammate]. Mick went into the back to keep an eye on the deer but, about five minutes down the road, all hell broke loose. The deer had revived and wasn't happy to find himself caged in. He was kicking and bucking, Mick was yelling, the van was swaying – it was absolute bedlam. We screeched to a halt, dashed around and opened the door and the deer bounded over the Wicklow Gap and into the night. It took Mick several days to get over the shock, but we presume the deer was none the worst for his ordeal.'

It's one memory from a cast of thousands for a man who played senior inter-county championship football between 1986 and 2000. His trophy cabinet may not be as burdened as those of players from the more successful counties, but his contribution to Gaelic football is just as sizeable. Probably even more so, since it took a very special talent to maintain such high standards of performance and dedication in an environment where the highest peaks were hidden by circumstances and tradition.

---

*Kevin O'Brien is an official with Wicklow County Council.
He and his wife, Catherine, have three children:
Seán (17), Áine (4) and Niamh (1).

King Who Waited for His Crown

George O'Connor (Wexford)

ALL STAR WINNER: 1981, 1988

'The weaker counties may in a sense be lost sheep, but we must always keep looking out for them, because I feel very strongly that the right to play hurling is a cultural thing that must be respected.'

George O'Connor couldn't understand why not all of his colleagues had climbed the steps of the Hogan Stand. Some had stayed down on the pitch, waiting almost impatiently for the presentation to be over, but O'Connor didn't want it to end.

He had climbed the stairway towards heaven for the first time and was acquiring a taste for this new and enriching land he assumed would be his on several occasions in future years. Even his more experienced teammates would have thought that bountiful harvests lay ahead.

Late September 1979, and Wexford had beaten Offaly by three points in the Oireachtas final at Croke Park. George O'Connor, a tall, lean teenager had made his senior debut and was marking its successful conclusion by skipping up to the presentation podium. His older colleagues, who had won Leinster titles but lost All-Ireland finals in 1976–7, would have regarded the Oireachtas final as little more than a competitive warm-up for the National League, itself a tuning exercise for another All-Ireland push.

'I was 19 years old, full of hope, full of confidence and completely convinced that bigger days were on their way. That was the Wexford scene I came into. We had been All-Ireland champions in 1968, won three Leinster titles and reached three All-Ireland finals in the 1970s, so there was no reason for a young lad to believe that the McCarthy Cup wouldn't be visiting us again soon. I was certain that it was only a matter of time before I'd be on the Hogan Stand again, after winning an All-Ireland final.'

He was right. It was only a matter of time – a very long time. A whole 17 years actually, a period in which Wexford hurling was trapped in the bleakest desert, intermittently dotted by an oasis, which usually turned out to be a mirage.

Between 1981 and 1994, Wexford lost six Leinster and five National League finals in a hideous run that even had incurable optimists being treated for despair. Wexford's repeated failures were reflected in the All Star selections, which saw them win just seven awards in that period.

O'Connor accounted for two of those in 1981 and 1988; Liam Dunne also won two in 1990 and 1993, while John Conran (1987), Eamonn Cleary (1989) and Martin Storey (1993) were the other recipients.

'Not very many for a county like Wexford, but then, All Star awards follow success and we didn't deliver through all those years. Events overtook us and Offaly very definitely overtook us. I could never have thought, after we beat them in the Oireachtas final in 1979, that Offaly would become such a powerful force so early in the 1980s. But they did and they stayed there.'

Wexford have tried to rationalise how Offaly replaced them as Kilkenny's biggest rivals during the 1980s and most of the 1990s, but it hasn't been easy to find a coherent answer. Bad luck was often cited as a seriously corrosive agent in Wexford, but O'Connor believes that that's an over-simplification.

'Certainly, there were days that if we backed both horses in a two-horse race, they would trip each other up, but you can't blame bad luck all the time. Offaly came along with a combination of fine hurlers, a simple game plan and huge determination. They took less out of the ball than anybody else and it worked. But, most importantly of all, they played like a team whereas we didn't. We're a very proud people in Wexford and, unfortunately, that manifested itself in a sense of individuality that wasn't good for the team. We all seemed to think that we could win a game on our own. Our psyche was self, not team. There was no shortage of commitment or effort but we didn't play as a unit. Passing the ball was the last thing on some lads' minds. It wasn't that they were being selfish, but it was the culture of the time in Wexford. A player who was used to being the star for his club felt obliged to be the same for the county. Put a squad like that together and, however talented they may be as individuals, they won't beat a team that plays for each other.'

By the end of 1994, O'Connor had endured enough. Offaly had beaten Wexford for the fourth time since 1981 in a Leinster final and, at the age of 34, he saw little point in prolonging the anguish. As he pondered life without Wexford hurling, he didn't know that deep in the administrative undergrowth, a hugely significant call was about to be made.

His cousin Liam Griffin, a man whose entire system would seize up immediately if words were ever to be rationed, was about to talk his way into the Wexford manager's job. News of Griffin's appointment had barely broken around the county when he contacted O'Connor.

'Retiring? No, you're not. And here's why.' Griffin, who dubbed O'Connor 'The Uncrowned King of Wexford', outlined his plans at great length and even greater speed. They sounded impressive and the aspect O'Connor liked most of all was the promise that, whatever happened, Wexford would play as a unit. Team first, individual second, ego nowhere. 'Let's do it for Wexford. Are you with me, George?'

'In the end, I felt we were like two oul' fools dreaming the same dream. We were definitely talking the same language. Liam's philosophy with underage teams, with football teams, in fact with any squad, was always the same: team first, individual second. That was the single biggest difference between 1996 and other years. It was also there for the 1997 Leinster campaign but we went back to the old ways a bit after that. Maybe the fact that lads had won an All-Ireland title made them feel they could do everything on their own again.'

Griffin's arrival was not followed by an instant turnaround. Quite the opposite in fact, as 1995 was another troubled year for Wexford and ended with a group of supporters calling for Griffin's removal. Their attempted heave failed, but there was still a huge degree of scepticism hanging over the Slaney at the start of 1996.

'Griffin had a fierce hard first year, which was probably inevitable. There were lads who thought they didn't need him and others who wanted to test him out. He was getting to know us and we him, which was always going to take time. At the end of it all, he knew who was weak and who was strong, who looked strong but was actually weak and vice versa. That would stand to us over the following year.'

O'Connor recalls how the spirit which would prove so important later in the year became apparent from very early in 1996. He could sense a different mood among his colleagues and even surprised himself, albeit painfully, with a reaction to a particularly good gym session in January.

'I had finished doing chin-ups and I jumped down from the bar, but I felt so pumped up that I punched the wall in front of me. I wrecked my knuckles and had to wrap them in ice while the rest of the lads slagged me. In its own way, I suppose, it showed how fired up I was for the year ahead.'

The 1996 summer/autumn passed in a kaleidoscopic blur for Wexford, who won their first Leinster title since 1977 and their first All-Ireland crown since 1968. O'Connor took a nasty blow to the hand in the semi-final win over Dublin, which ruled him out of the final against Offaly, except for a late cameo contribution. Still, he could always say he had played on a winning Leinster final side.

It was at this stage that the gods decided that they had special plans for 'The Uncrowned King'. He didn't get a place on the starting line-up for the All-Ireland semi-final against Galway but came on after 28 minutes, when his brother John had to retire after taking a bang on the head.

John was fit for the final but Seán Flood wasn't, so George joined Adrian Fenlon at midfield. Seventeen years after making his debut, the All-Ireland chance had arrived, one which O'Connor and Wexford gratefully seized as they beat Limerick by two points.

The sight of O'Connor kneeling on Croke Park after the final whistle, hands joined in silent prayer, remains one of the most powerful images from this, or probably, any generation. It didn't last long as the stampeding hordes whizzed in from all sides.

'This guy nearly broke my neck as he grabbed me. It was an incredible feeling. We had done it. We were All-Ireland champions. It was the day I'd waited for all my life.'

It was also his last competitive game for Wexford. He played a club game for his club, St Martin's, a week later, but he knew that it was time to sign off. He was asked to go back as a sub a few years later when St Martin's were challenging (successfully as it happens) for a Wexford title, but he declined. He was happy to be a fan instead, dashing onto the pitch afterwards to congratulate his friends and neighbours.

It's over eight years since George's hurling career ended, but he still lives the game as much as ever. He has helped out with Wexford minors and remains fiercely passionate about a sport which he feels needs far more nourishment and encouragement than it currently receives.

'There are 136 separate skills in hurling, so it stands to reason that you can't be good at the game unless you start young and practise constantly. It will always be very difficult to expand beyond the traditional counties, but we can never stop trying. The weaker counties may in a sense be lost sheep, but we must always keep looking out for them, because I feel very strongly that the right to play hurling is a cultural thing that must be respected. It doesn't matter at what level or what age group, the important thing is that the opportunity to play the game is not denied to anybody.

'You meet lads in any part of the world who have played hurling and there's a bond there. That's the type of game it is. Unless you've played it, you have no appreciation of how beautiful, yet difficult, it is. It's a bit like art. Most people who dabble in art will never become great painters, but it gives them an appreciation of those who are.

'Here's a rough test to show the difference in skill levels between hurling and football, soccer or rugby. A drunk is walking down the street late at night. Hand him a football or a rugby ball and ask him to kick it. Chances are that he'll make some sort of contact, even if he has never played any sport. Hand him a hurley and a sliotar and he could be there until dawn and he would still be more likely to strangle himself than hit the ball. We have a unique and special game in hurling and we must do whatever it takes to develop it as the great national asset that it is.'

He believes that the only way to spread the hurling gospel is to devote a lot more resources to coaching. That involves putting a paid coach into every club, who can act as the central anchor for the various teams.

'The old days are gone. Years ago, most families would have had three or four brothers, so there were plenty of opportunities to practise but, with smaller families and a more materialistic lifestyle, it's more important to have a formal coaching structure in place nowadays.

'In most cases, certainly in urban areas, both parents are working away from the home during the day so they can't put much effort into sport during the week. Sunday is family day, which leaves Saturday for sport. With a game like hurling, you need to be at it all the time and I believe that the only way to organise it is to have a coach in every club to coordinate things. The GAA is only giving token support to full-time coaching. If you want the best, you have to invest and, while it might be costly, it's the only way forward. Wouldn't it be a good idea to use the money which could be earned from renting Croke Park to other sports to promote hurling?'

For all that, O'Connor is concerned that a small, élite band of counties will continue to dominate. He compares it with world rugby, where first New Zealand, then Australia, then South Africa and finally, England continued to raise the target bar. Because of their structures and their numbers, Kilkenny, Cork, Tipperary and Galway could become the equivalent in hurling, with others making an occasional raid on the titles.

As a dual county, Wexford has a specific problem and advantage, depending on your viewpoint. O'Connor played for both the senior hurlers and footballers until 1984, but believes that the day of the dual inter-county player is over.

'Forget about it. If you want to play both at county level, prepare to win in neither. Do what you like with your club. You're a man of your community with the club but, once you move onto the county scene, you're an amateur training as a professional. The dual issue has always been a problem in Wexford. People ask me how things are going in Wexford and I reply "great" because sport in general is very healthy in the county, but is hurling? Now that's a different matter.'

O'Connor enjoyed his own days as a dual inter-county star, particularly in the 1981 championship, when Wexford beat Meath by a point in the Leinster football quarter-final. O'Connor was at centre back on that memorable afternoon in Croke Park, when Wexford stunned a Royal outfit which included Gerry McEntee, Liam Hayes, Colm O'Rourke and Joe Cassells, a quartet who later proved so influential in Meath's dominance of the second half of the 1980s.

Wexford lost the semi-final to Offaly by five points, but O'Connor has no doubt that had greater emphasis been placed on football in Wexford at that stage, they could have made huge progress.

'I was one of the smaller guys on that team, which shows you how big some of them were. They had more than size, though. They were also very good footballers but, back then, there was a feeling that once the hurling started, there was no real interest or commitment from the county towards football.'

His football instincts prompted him to live a very dangerous existence in hurling, where he never properly protected his hand when he soared into the air to make one of those spectacular catches. The swish of whirling ash quite often ended with a painful thud, as yet another of his fingers buckled. He broke them all at one stage or another and now jokes that when he is sitting at home, one of his fingers points towards Wales and another towards Kilkenny. Only they're on the same hand!

'I had a footballer's catch. I never seemed to learn to protect my hand properly, so every 19 or 20 times I'd put my hand up, I'd get a belt of a hurl, so if you multiply that by all the years I spent in the game, it's a fair bit of thumping. But in those days, you didn't worry about it. The magic bottle took care of everything and you got to fix the breaks later.'

He accepts that it's a different world nowadays, one where players are better looked after, but the demands are also greater. Skill levels may not have risen over the years, but the pace and intensity of the game certainly has, which makes it much more difficult to execute the touches. Training regimes are more severe too, but the rewards are far greater.

'Players head for the four corners of the globe on paid holidays nowadays. In my time, all we knew about holidays came from the advertisements that appeared on the TV just after Christmas. But it's right that the players are well looked after. And I hope it gets better, but it does need to be controlled. I have no doubt that the GAA is heading towards some form of professionalism. The dam has been cracking slowly over recent years and, while it has been repaired, it can never be as strong again. The GAA authorities may think that the Gaelic Players' Association are pretty militant, but they're actually moderate by comparison with what will follow in future years. The amateur dam will eventually burst. Will it be good for the game? I honestly don't know, but I would certainly like to see the GAA setting the agenda in this area rather than reacting to it all the time.

'We don't seem to be very good at marketing in the GAA. Take Setanta Ó hAilpín. We had to wait more than 100 years for a guy by the name of Setanta to come along. He's a great hurler, who certainly increased interest in the game in 2003, but what happens? He should be a marketing dream, but instead he's allowed to head off to Australia. Cork should have kept him, whatever it took. I'm certain that if he were from Kilkenny, he would never have been let go. He wasn't just hurling's loss; he was a huge loss to the GAA in general.'

While O'Connor believes that the GAA may be edging ever nearer to a professional era, he has absolutely no regrets that there wasn't more material gain to be had during his career.

'Not a bit of it. Hurling cost me money over the years, but I never thought of that. Money can't buy you a good night's sleep. Peace of mind is everything in whatever walk of life. Anyway, I had some fantastic experiences, especially in America with All Star tours and various weekend trips. It was quite common to head over to New York, Chicago or some other city on a Friday morning and return on Monday and, because Wexford were often out of the championship a lot earlier than we should have been, I travelled to the US quite often. The All Star trips were great too, as you met lads from other counties, whom you never got a chance to talk to back home.'

Still closely involved with his club, St Martin's, where his son, Barry, is taking his first sporting steps, O'Connor believes deeply in the philosophy of exposing all youngsters to sport, without ever pushing them too hard. Barry is being brought up in a GAA environment, but if he wants to try other sports, he will be encouraged.

'Naturally, I would love to see him playing hurling. Apart from being a superb game, it represents Irishness at its best. It's an important part of our culture and we've got to hang on to it. It's far too precious to be neglected. And, even if you never won a medal, it's a game well worth playing.'

George's 1996 All-Ireland medal is on top of a dresser in the O'Connor kitchen, but its significance continues to live with him every day.

'The medal itself is not all that important, but what it represents is. The sense of achievement in finally winning it is still unbelievable. I won an Oireachtas medal in Croke Park in my first game and an All-Ireland medal in my last game, 17 years later. So what happened in between? Enough to give me a load of memories that will last me as long as I live.'

George O'Connor is a farmer. He and his wife, Ellen, have three children: Katie (8), Barry (6) and Ella (4).

Journey into Folklore

Willie Joe Padden (Mayo)

ALL STAR WINNER: 1985, 1989

'The biggest sense of regret I would have is that we were so badly organised when I first came on to the county team.'

In song, the legend has grown larger than the Connacht titles, the high catches or the flamboyance.

Not even a striking resemblance to one of England's best-known cricketers, Ian Botham, a likeness which even led to him being approached on the streets of London, has created the notoriety that those few catchy lines succeeded in creating.

When Leo Moran, a member of The Sawdoctors, sat down in 1991 to pen a song recalling life growing up in Tuam and the phrases he associated with days saving the hay, a No.1 hit was born. It also ensured that the legacy of a great Mayo footballer was enshrined.

As long as Tuam's finest are belting out 'Hay Wrap' as the encore to their shows, the lines 'Will Galway bate Mayo? Not if they have Willie Joe!' will inevitably raise the roof at venues at home and abroad.

Willie Joe was one of Mayo's greatest ever Gaelic footballers. That he should be remembered in verse by such a popular Irish band as The Sawdoctors is a tribute to the esteem in which he was held.

Padden could never have imagined that ten simple words would make such an impact.

'I had Americans coming into the pub I used to be involved with in Castlebar asking me, "Are you the guy in the song?" And you'll always have someone singing it in front of me and thinking they're the first to do it! But no, it hasn't made me a rich man,' he said.

The warmth of the words helped preserve the legacy of one of the greatest fielders the modern game has known. There may be humour in what Leo Moran wrote, but there was also a deep sense of respect from Galway people peering over the border at one of the giants of the game.

Once Willie Joe was playing, there was always a doubt whether Galway would 'bate' Mayo.

His aerial ability was a phenomenon in the game he adorned so splendidly. He had a unique 'spring' that allowed him to climb higher than taller opponents and stay airborne for long enough to win possession. In basketball, it's referred to as 'hang time'.

In a career spanning 15 seasons with his county's senior football team, Willie Joe enjoyed some of his greatest battles with Galway.

But beyond the western province the roads were strewn with heartbreak. One All-Ireland final appearance (1989) from five Connacht titles is a poor return for a footballer of his stature. Each one of those Connacht title successes had its own subsequent tale of despair, prolonging the famine that has lasted since 1951.

Any regrets are tempered by the knowledge that he is in very good company. 'Any time I think of what might have been, I console myself that there are others in the same position. Mickey Kearins [Sligo] and Dermot Earley [Roscommon] were fantastic players who never won an All-Ireland medal. There are several players from other provinces, too, in the same boat.'

To this day Willie Joe Padden remains one of Mayo's most popular footballers. Few GAA stars of past or present vintage are addressed by their Christian names so often and so casually. It's as much a term of endearment as convenience.

A child prodigy of great strength and athleticism, he made the Belmullet minor team at the age of 13 and, two years later, he joined a senior team that was rising through the ranks on the back of junior and intermediate championship successes in 1974 and 1975.

Belmullet, in the northwest tip of Mayo is splendid in its isolation and beauty. The Paddens had a farm overlooking Erris peninsula, near the village of Ballyglass, about six miles from the town. For every young man in the area, fishing and football were stitched into the tapestry of life from an early age.

The young Padden excelled at football and, at the local Convent of Mercy, under the watchful eye of Fr Killeen, his talent was nurtured.

'He had a huge influence on my career. He played for Knockmore and later Belmullet and really fuelled great enthusiasm in us to play football.'

The school team had no more than 100 boys playing football at the time, but they made impressive strides by winning a couple of Connacht 'C' championships, before eventually graduating to 'B' status, winning another provincial crown and losing an All-Ireland final.

'We had a very small selection to choose from, but Fr Killeen still managed to develop some very good footballers. There were three of us on a Mayo minor team one year and, at another stage in the early 1980s, there were four of us on the Mayo panel:

myself, John Gallagher, Michael O'Toole and Liam Donoghue,' he recalled.

Willie Joe himself spent three years with the Mayo minors, eventually captaining the side in his last year, 1977, when they lost an All-Ireland semi-final to a Down team inspired by current senior team manager, Paddy O'Rourke.

By then, Padden's natural strength and athleticism was ready for exposure at a higher level and, within a few weeks of the 1977 minor semi-final, he made his senior debut against Cavan in a National League game.

'I'll never forget it. I was 18 at the time and found myself travelling as a sub to my very first senior inter-county game. Seán Kilbride was picked to play at midfield, but had to withdraw for some reason, so I was drafted in and marked Steve Duggan.'

Mayo went on to enjoy a good League campaign, eventually reaching a final which they lost to Dublin, in a game where Willie Joe played at full forward, marked by vastly experienced Hill 16 hero Seán Doherty.

Dublin won by five points on another disappointing day in what was a bleak period for Mayo football. They went through the entire 1970s without winning a single senior provincial title, which left Padden struggling to develop his wide range of skills at the highest level.

'The biggest sense of regret I would have is that we were so badly organised when I first came on to the county team. When Kerry and Dublin were forcing the rest of the country to examine their preparation, we stood still. There was a tradition of training twice a week and that was it. Others had moved much further ahead of us.

'The management structures weren't right. The environment in which you might better yourself didn't exist. I would have trained as hard as I was asked to train, like the other lads but I suppose, on reflection, we could have done more to organise ourselves.'

Emigration was a problem too and few counties were hit harder than Mayo. Good footballers were lost and never retrieved.

'I have friends in New York who left Mayo and never came back. Others went to London and Dublin and lost interest in the game. A large number of talented 19- and 20-year-olds were lost to Mayo at that time. For example, Ger Geraghty from Ballintubber, a brilliant U-21 player, went to Chicago. He would have made a huge difference to us around that time. My own north Mayo area was hit harder than anywhere.'

The dominant Roscommon team of that era was another significant barrier to Mayo. Connacht final defeats in 1979 and 1980 were as predictable as they were heavy.

Four years into his senior career, Willie Joe finally tasted success in Connacht, when Mayo beat Sligo by 0-12 to 0-4 in the 1981 final to end a 12-year famine.

'It was a big thing at the time because we had gone right through the 1970s without winning a Connacht final. But we got a real eye-opener in the All-Ireland semi-final against Kerry. We were only two points behind at half-time, but they went on to beat us by 16 points. It was a complete wipe-out.

'We didn't score in the second half. Michael Webb was our goalkeeper and the big question was whether or not he could get back to his line after a kick-out, before the next ball came in! It was a definite wake-up call for Mayo football but, even then, I still didn't think that we were heading in the right direction. But there was a regime change at the end of the next year and the arrival of former Galway footballer Liam O'Neill as manager gave us some impetus.'

From 1982 to 1984 Mayo lived in Galway's shadow, losing all three provincial finals to their arch rivals.

'They hammered us by 16 points in 1982, but in the following years we could sense that the team was coming together.'

By 1985, Mayo were a strong force and the midfield partnership of Willie Joe and T.J. Kilgallon had gained a reputation as one of the best in the game.

'I always enjoyed playing with T.J. He would have been my preferred midfield partner. But the problem with Mayo around then was that we were top heavy with natural midfielders and short on forwards. That meant that T.J. and myself didn't always get to play midfield together. Liam McHale and Pádraig Brogan had come onto the scene; Seán Maher was also there and later his brother Greg arrived too. Sometimes I'd end up at centre forward, which I didn't mind, but I felt I was at my best at midfield.'

Mayo's win over Roscommon in the 1985 Connacht final signalled the end of a great career, when Dermot Earley announced his retirement. It also ended a fascinating rivalry between Earley and Willie Joe.

'It was a fantastic era for midfielders. In my early days, Galway's Willie Joyce was the man; obviously Brian Mullins and Jack O'Shea were two of the greats, but I also had a big rivalry with Dermot and John O'Gara.'

The 1985 All-Ireland semi-final against Dublin still brings a sense of regret to Padden. It's one he believes Mayo should have won, but Dublin triumphed in a replay.

'There was an All-Ireland in us that year. Kerry beat Dublin in the final and I felt that, good and all as Kerry were, they would have been vulnerable against us. They might not have treated us with the same respect as they showed Dublin.'

Willie Joe's midfield partnership with Kilgallon reached its zenith in the drawn game when they outplayed the Mullins–Jim Roynane pairing.

But he felt they lost the initiative when Seán Lowry, a former Offaly star who had transferred to Mayo, was dropped for the replay.

'Seán had come to Mayo and was working as a technician in the power station in Bellacorick, about 20 minutes from Belmullet. As a linesman at the time, I had regular contact with him and I would have felt he was the type of player Mayo needed, an experienced head in the full-forward line.

'Tom Beirne was picked instead of him, but Tom sustained a hand injury early in the game and struggled on. Tom was a good servant but I would have felt Lowry was a better option. He knew how to win big games from his days with Offaly and, crucially, he knew how to win games against Dublin.'

Willie Joe was arguably at his peak in the mid-1980s, cultivating a reputation for spectacular catches.

'I always had a good jump and it probably improved the more I played against taller opponents. I was only 5' 11" and conceding four and five inches to opponents forced me to adapt. It was a question of timing.'

He picked up his first All Star award in 1985 and the following summer delivered what he considers his finest ever individual display.

Mayo carried five injuries into a Connacht semi-final against Roscommon and lost by two points, despite a Herculean effort by Padden.

'I could do nothing wrong that day against Paul Earley. Our backs were to the wall because of all the injuries. As far as I recall, John Maughan's knee troubles started around then and he was one of the players who couldn't line out. It was a big setback to lose that game and no consolation to me to have played well.'

By the end of 1987, Liam O'Neill was gone as manager and a young John O'Mahony had taken over. Again Willie Joe sensed an injection of enthusiasm.

'Martin Carney and I often discussed the years from 1985 to 1990. Mayo should definitely have won an All-Ireland title in that period and under John O'Mahony we came closest.

'John is a very organised man, but it was simple things that he enforced most. Training started on time and was better structured than before. I often regret that he didn't arrive in 1979 instead of 1988 because the better days were starting to become less frequent for a few of us.'

Willie Joe's third and fourth Connacht titles were won during O'Mahony's reign and he also made his only All-Ireland final appearance in that period.

'Meath beat us in the 1988 semi-final when we had a perfectly legitimate goal by Liam McHale disallowed. It came at a crucial time and we lost by five points in the end, but it might have been very different had that goal been allowed.'

The following year Willie Joe was sure Mayo were ready to make the breakthrough. Kerry, Dublin and Meath were out of the way, leaving Cork as their main rivals.

'We won a great Connacht final replay against Roscommon after extra time, one of the most memorable games I played in. We beat Tyrone in the All-Ireland semi-final and, going into the final, we certainly weren't afraid of Cork. We thought that, after losing the previous two All-Ireland finals to Meath, there would be doubts in their mind. Unfortunately, it didn't work out for us. The chance for a goal that Anthony Finnerty missed is always seen as the turning point of that final, but I felt an injury to Greg Maher was hugely disruptive too. We were two points up at the time, made a few switches when he went off and couldn't get it together again.

'In other years a Connacht title would have been a consolation and maybe reaching an All-Ireland final was something for some of the lads at the time. But to me it was a lost chance and the last chance I would have.'

He won his second All Star in 1989 but, by the early 1990s, Willie Joe's career was in decline and football was no longer the priority in his life.

His fifth and last Connacht medal in 1992 carries the fewest memories for him as he sat on the bench for much of the season. A subsequent All-Ireland semi-final defeat by Donegal signalled his last involvement with a Mayo team.

'I felt I was still playing well enough in 1992 to make the team. Anthony Molloy was dominant against us in that Donegal game and I felt I could have handled him. But Pádraig Brogan was brought on instead. Pádraig had played for a spell with Donegal and when he was introduced it was just what Donegal needed. I felt that was a bad call and another missed opportunity.'

He was in America when, later in the year, the controversial players' revolt helped bring an end to Brian McDonald's term as manager. A letter signed by most of the panel had called for McDonald's removal and bitter acrimony ensued.

'Personally I felt some of the stories about Brian's training were exaggerated. He was a good selector with Liam O'Neill, but he wasn't the most communicative figure. I was out of the picture at that stage anyway,' recalled Willie Joe.

Advice from Dr Pat O'Neill on a troublesome knee brought the curtains down on his career and he's been left to reflect on what might have been.

His involvement in a Castlebar public house occupied him for most of the 1990s and recently he has become immersed in an estate agents, with emphasis on foreign properties. One particular Portuguese scheme has international footballer Rui Costa as one of the investors.

On the football front, he got enjoyment from being a selector with the Mayo minors in 2004, even if they did lose to Galway in the Connacht championship.

His eldest son, Billy Joe, is a member of the Mayo squad that lost to Kerry in the 2004 All-Ireland final and a player with a big future, while his second son, David, is a promising goalkeeper.

'Hopefully the two lads can reach their potential. As for myself, I don't know if I could commit myself 100 per cent to being involved with an inter-county team. I'd have great admiration for the way John Maughan came back as Mayo manager in 2002. That took a lot of guts.'

---

*Willie Joe is a partner in Aran Property and Financial Services in Castlebar. He has three children, Billy Joe, David and Ashling from his first marriage and two, Carla and Ryan, from his relationship with Mary Walsh Padden.

Rocking to the Hill 16 Beat

Barney Rock (Dublin)

ALL STAR WINNER: 1983, 1984, 1985

'The influx of country players to Dublin clubs isn't good for the game in the county. I genuinely believe it should be controlled by whatever means are necessary.'

Even the name evoked magic. Barney Rock: Hill 16 hero; swashbuckling half-forward; steely-eyed assassin, who could shoot the opposition dead from 50 yards and walk away with a smile, as the blue flags fluttered in the summer breeze around Croke Park.

This was his territory, a place where he felt at home among his own people as they looked on with respect and reverence at one of the great natural talents of his era. A product of the 1970s, growing up amid Kevin Heffernan's Dublin revolution, destiny dealt him a very strong hand.

First, it gifted him an expansive array of skills, before carefully placing him in an environment where he could express and cultivate them. Then, it watched proudly as he grew from child to boy to man, improving all the way until he reached a stage where he became a virtual automatic choice for an All Star award.

Unlucky to lose out in 1982, he won three successive All Star awards in 1983, 1984 and 1985, all at right half-forward. At the age of 24, there seemed no limit to the heights he could achieve. No frontier seemed too intimidating for the golden boy of Dublin football, as he racked up big scores from frees and general play for club (Ballymun Kickhams) and county.

And then the gods mocked him. He sustained a serious shoulder injury against Meath in the 1986 Leinster final and wrecked ligaments in his knee the following year. Both injuries took a heavy toll and, while he played on until 1991, he was no longer the awesome presence of the 1982–86 period. He still made a huge contribution to Dublin, but he had set such high standards in his earlier years that he didn't seem quite as menacing to opponents anymore.

Eventually, his inter-county career petered out in 1991, playing his final game in the third of the epic four-match Leinster championship saga with Meath. For reasons that still baffle him to this day, he was left on the bench for all of the fourth game, which Dublin lost by a point. They had a late chance to level the tie and send it into extra-time again, but Jack Sheedy's long-range free drifted wide of the Meath posts.

Had Rock been on the pitch, he would have taken the kick and, given his remarkable record from frees throughout his career, the odds suggest that he would have pointed it. As it was, he looked on sadly from the bench, unaware that it was the last time he would be on the Dublin panel.

'I never retired. It was a case of not being picked anymore which, to be honest, I found very frustrating. I had only turned 30 in 1991 and felt that I still had a few more years to go with Dublin. But when the squad went back training in the autumn,

Paddy Cullen [the then Dublin manager] told me they were going to try out some new players and fresh ideas but that they might come back to me. I never got the call and my days with Dublin were over.'

Dublin lost the 1992 and 1994 All-Ireland finals, plus the 1993 semi-final, defeats that cut deep into the county's soul, prompting many of the supporters to query if Rock's presence might have made the crucial difference.

'I was still playing well with the club in those years, scoring an average of seven or eight points a game, but the Dublin selectors had obviously made up their minds that I wasn't fit for inter-county football anymore. I disagreed then and I disagree now. Even if I weren't on the starting 15, there were days when I know I could have made an impact as a sub. I was still able to kick the frees well and I had a good record with penalties too, something that Dublin definitely didn't have in that period. But, it's all history now. It was the team management's call and I had to live with it.'

It frustrated Rock so much that he even thought of leaving his beloved Dublin and declaring for Louth. In 1994, he was coaching Louth club Stabannon Parnells and got to know the Louth scene so well that he contemplated making the big move. However, the idea was quickly banished when he realised that he would have to join a Louth club to become eligible for their county team. Leaving Ballymun Kickhams was not an option he considered for very long, so the prospect of re-launching his inter-county career faded away.

The thought of Barney Rock, a true-blue Hill 16 favourite, playing for another county would have filled the Dublin supporters with dismay, especially since many of them felt that he should still have been part of the set-up in the early 1990s, a period when the team fell tantalisingly short with the finish line in sight. Playing for another county wasn't something that Rock could ever have countenanced in his earlier days but, fuelled by a desire to prove that he was still good enough for the inter-county scene in his early thirties, the prospect of joining Louth was attractive, albeit temporarily.

In the end, it never materialised and Rock will always be remembered as the quintessential personification of Dublin and Hill 16, a combination which locked so many opponents in a psychological trance. Having won an All-Ireland minor medal in 1979, alongside John O'Leary and Ciarán Duff, two others who would go on to enjoy prolonged and successful senior careers, Rock was immediately promoted to the senior squad at a time when Dublin football had enjoyed six memorable seasons.

The All-Ireland breakthrough in 1974 had changed the whole perception of Dublin, inside and outside the county. Three All-Ireland titles (1974, 1976, 1977) and six successive Leinster titles (1974–79) had hoisted Dublin into a successful world that before this had only been occupied by Kerry. Granted, Kerry had moved to an even higher peak but Dublin had maintained a relentless chase and, when they won the 1979 minor title, it looked as if they were poised to launch a whole new era.

It didn't happen, not immediately anyway. In fact, Dublin wouldn't win another Leinster senior title until 1983, having been supplanted by Offaly, who proved themselves to be an excellent team by destroying Kerry's five-in-a-row dreams in 1982.

'That was a fine Offaly side and I suppose Dublin were going through a transition period. Having said that, I always felt that the absence of Brian Mullins was a huge loss to us in 1980–81. He had been in a bad car accident, which ruled him out for nearly two seasons and we really did miss him. We lost the 1980 Leinster final to Offaly by two points, but you wonder would it have been different if Mullins were playing.'

By the time Dublin reasserted themselves in 1983, Mullins was back at midfield, while Rock had established himself as a prolific right half-forward. Victory over Meath in a Leinster first-round replay was the launch pad for a productive season that ended with an All-Ireland title, after one of the most controversial finals of all time.

Dublin had Mullins, Ray Hazley and Duff sent off by Antrim referee John Gough, while Galway's Tomás Tierney was also dismissed in a sulphurous game in which tempers frequently boiled out of control. The unsavoury aspects tended to overshadow Dublin's amazing achievement in holding out against the wind and a team with two extra players for most of the second half. It was the ultimate in defensive defiance to which every Dublin player contributed. However, it would have counted for nothing, only for their first-half scoring burst, which included a brilliantly taken opportunist's goal by Rock.

Five years earlier, Kerry's Mike Sheehy had stunned Dublin in the All-Ireland final by cheekily chipping a 21-yard free to the net over Paddy Cullen's head, but Rock's goal against Galway in 1983 was equally remarkable. Galway goalkeeper Pádraig Coyne kicked a free into the strong wind. Rock fetched the ball and calmly lobbed it over Coyne's head and into the Galway net from all of 50 yards.

'I had this habit of making a run when a kick-out or free was being taken. Very often, the ball wouldn't even come my way but, on that particular day, it sailed right into my hands. I looked up, spotted that the keeper was off his line and took a gamble. The ball seemed to take an age to drop into the net but it finally made it. It was just one of those spur-of-the-moment things. The chance was there and I took it.

'I have always regretted one thing about that All-Ireland final. I'm convinced that if it had been played in good weather conditions, none of the nasty incidents would have taken place. It was a horrible day with high wind and blustery showers. Players were slipping in all directions, it was hard to control the ball and frustration set in. Unfortunately, tempers frayed on a few occasions and four players were sent off.

'There was absolutely no history of animosity between Dublin and Galway, so I can only put it down to the influence of the weather. People might still talk about that final for the wrong reasons, but the record books show that Dublin won it which, from our viewpoint, is all that matters.'

At the age of 22, Rock was now the proud holder of both All-Ireland senior and minor medals and seemed certain to add substantially to his collection over the next ten years. He picked up three more Leinster medals, but another All-Ireland title continued to elude him all the way to the end of his career.

Meath's re-emergence as Leinster champions in 1986 moved the power base away from Dublin, restricting them to just one provincial crown (1989) in the next six years. Significantly, an incident involving Rock in the 1986 Leinster final may have changed the course of the history of that period.

He sustained a serious shoulder injury just before half-time, leaving Dublin without a reliable free-taker, which seriously reduced their prospects of retaining the Leinster title. Dublin missed some crucial frees in the second half and Meath went on to win by two points, launching a whole new era under Seán Boylan.

'I can still remember how I sustained the injury. I flicked the ball on to Dully [Ciarán Duff], leaving myself open as I did so. Liam Harnan kept coming and charged into me. The shoulder snapped and I went down. The referee [Seámus Aldridge] obviously didn't spot how serious it was and kept telling me to get up. He obviously thought I was faking the injury, but I most certainly wasn't and I still have the lump on my shoulder to prove it!

'Oddly enough, I almost came back on in the second half. Brian Mullins [joint manager] asked me if I was able to go back out, even if I could only kick frees. I told him I wouldn't be able to do anything else and, in the end, the switch wasn't made, which was probably just as well because the shoulder was badly broken, even if I didn't quite realise it at the time. If I hadn't got that injury, I would probably have pointed a few frees in the second half and we might well have won that game. I often wonder what impact that would have had on Meath. We had beaten them in 1983 and 1984 and Laois had hammered them in 1985, so if they had been beaten again in the 1986 Leinster final, it might have put serious doubts in their minds. Seán Boylan might have even been replaced as manager. Instead, Meath won and went on to dominate in Leinster for a few years.'

Dublin beat Meath in the 1989 Leinster final, but lost to Cork in the All-Ireland semi-final, a defeat which effectively ended Rock's prospects of playing in another final as they didn't win the provincial crown again until 1992, by which time he was no longer on the panel.

Despite the downturn against Meath, Dublin football didn't lose confidence and gradually forced its way back up the rankings, until eventually reclaiming the No.1 spot by winning the 1995 All-Ireland final. However, since then, it has shed much of its stature and no longer carries the intimidating aura which froze so many opponents, especially in Croke Park.

'When I came into the team we had a history of winning behind us. The Heffo [Kevin Heffernan] era was still in full swing and we thought like winners. We always believed we could win the Leinster title at the very least and, while Offaly came along and dominated for three years in the early 1980s, we felt confident that we would be back. And so we were, but it's all changed now. Nowadays, four or five Leinster teams believe that they can beat Dublin. What's gone wrong with Dublin? For a start, there isn't enough football being played in the county. You have young lads going for weeks in the summer months without getting a game, which just doesn't make sense. Look at the *Evening Herald* any week and you will find an awful lot more soccer fixtures than GAA fixtures. There is a better defined system in soccer. Lads know when they are playing, from week to week, and can look forward to 30–40 games in a year. The average club footballer can expect 18–20 games a year, which isn't anywhere near enough.

'I'm not a fan of the style of football which has crept into Dublin's game over the years either. In my time – and before it – we were always good at getting goals, but that's not the case anymore. We don't move the ball quickly enough, which limits the chances of creating goal opportunities. I believe we should go back to the style which served Dublin so well. We also need to bring a bit more class and refinement to our county teams.

'The problems extend beyond the county team. Dublin hardly make any impact on the colleges' scene, which is very worrying. I really do think that the Dublin County Board and the GAA should look very seriously at the problems in the county because they won't go away unless action is taken.'

Among the radical steps advocated by Rock is a ban on players from the country signing for Dublin clubs, unless they agree to play for Dublin. It's not that he wants to pack the Dublin team with imports, but he strongly believes that if a country player were obliged to switch county allegiance once he joined a city club, there would be a lot less movement.

'The influx of country players to Dublin clubs isn't good for the game in the county. I genuinely believe it should be controlled by whatever means are necessary. Having said that, I still believe we have the nucleus of a good side in Dublin, but it needs to be brought on quite quickly. I would be very concerned that if Dublin don't win an All-Ireland in the next two or three seasons, we could go ten years without one. That's not a nice prospect.'

He also believes that there is far too much emphasis on fitness levels, at the expense of skill and tactics. Physical training is an integral part of every sport but Rock fears that it's being taken to extremes in Gaelic football.

'It's a problem inside and outside Dublin. Fitness is important, but it has reached crazy levels when you have club players being put on special diets and told how to live their lives. In my day you were told not to have a drink on the night before a game, but nobody was too concerned whether you had fish and chips on the way home. I'm not suggesting that players stuff themselves with chips but I think the balance has gone too far the other way now. Give me a player who can stick the ball in the net ahead of the guy who can run 40 laps of the pitch in record time.'

Rock has always kept himself in fine physical shape and even resurrected his Dublin career with the county's over-40s team in recent seasons. He continues to be involved in club management and, of course, had a spell as Westmeath manager in 1996–97. He enjoyed it immensely, especially the second season when Westmeath played Wexford twice, winning the replay before drawing with an Offaly team managed by Tommy Lyons.

'Westmeath were two points up with about ten minutes to go and very nearly held on for a win, but Vinny Claffey kicked the equaliser for Offaly in injury time. They won the replay fairly easily and went on to win the Leinster title. I often wonder what would have happened if we had beaten them the first day. Still, it was the first time in a long time that Westmeath had played four championship matches in the one season.'

Although he would like to try his hand at inter-county management again, Rock doesn't have the time for such a demanding job these days. He has seen the pressure grow on managers to such a degree that the fun seems to have been sucked from a role which, for all its profile, is still supposed to be enjoyed.

'Some of the treatment that Dublin managers in particular have had to endure is absolutely scandalous. After all, it's an amateur game and these guys are putting in a huge effort purely for the good of football in Dublin. Admittedly, it's only a small minority of supporters who try to make the manager's life hell when things go wrong, but they give everybody a bad name.'

It was all so different when Rock started out as a player with Dublin, under the expert tutelage of Kevin Heffernan, a man who presided over one of the greatest eras ever enjoyed by the county. He encouraged his teams to play with a swagger and to assert themselves as proud sons of Dublin on a determined mission.

That was the world into which Rock arrived in the late 1970s and it is one that he yearns to see returning.

'There can't be a better feeling in the world for a Dublin player than seeing Hill 16 alive with blue flags when things are going well in a big championship game. I had plenty of disappointments, but I also enjoyed lots of great days, which have left me with enough memories to last me a lifetime. I just hope now that the new generation of Dublin players get a chance to experience the good times. They – and indeed the entire Dublin GAA scene – badly need another All-Ireland title because the longer we go without winning one, the more damage that will be done. That would be bad news for Dublin and, indeed, the GAA in general.'

Ironically, what Dublin probably lack most of all these days are players like Rock, men who saw the big stage as their natural environment and who were at their best when the pressure was at its most intense. He enjoyed some great times in Croke Park and beyond, in a senior championship career that lasted from 1980 to 1991 and will always be fondly remembered by Dublin supporters as a star act who helped make Hill 16 rock so often to a winning beat.

---

*Barney Rock is a sales executive with Bryan S. Ryan Office Equipment in Tallaght. He and his wife, Kathleen, have a family of five: Hazel (21), Jacinta (16), Dean (14), Laura (12) and Shannon (7).

Court Jester in the Square

Joe Brolly (Derry)

ALL STAR WINNER: 1996, 1997

*'There were grown men trying to get through the wire. I didn't enjoy it,
but I did it to make a statement, to put the two fingers up at them.'*

J oe Brolly hadn't planned it. Down, the 1991 All-Ireland
champions, had travelled to Celtic Park for a National League
match against a Derry side that had dragged them right down to
the wire in two absorbing Ulster championship games the
previous year.

At the time, Derry were involved in a fascinating Ulster power
struggle with Down and Donegal, so margins were very tight.
With less than five minutes remaining in the League game, Derry
were trailing by a point when their midfielder, Anthony Tohill,
got possession inside his own half and drove the ball 60 metres in
the direction of the Down goal.

Brolly read the flight and direction of the kick perfectly, gained possession and as Down goalkeeper Neil Collins advanced off his line, Brolly sent a curling left-foot shot high into the net. The crowd went wild. Sensing the upbeat mood, he raised his arms high above his head and gravitated towards the Derry supporters. As he got closer, the acclaim grew louder. Brolly lapped it up, laughed incessantly and charged down the field, his arms still raised above his head.

For a Gaelic footballer, such flamboyant celebrations represented alien territory and even some hardened Derry supporters recoiled at his reaction.

But Joe Brolly was never one for convention. He couldn't buy into the stereotype because it wasn't natural to him. Football was too much fun for that. Brolly insists he was a very serious footballer. But the man who was met with a hail of missiles and abuse when he blew kisses to the Tyrone crowd in the 1997 Ulster semi-final, after scoring another brilliant goal, will always be remembered for the smile he wore on his face, even in the most tense games.

That Brolly prospered in the demanding world of Ulster football in the 1990s is a testament to his natural ability and engaging personality. He hated the gym but loved the football. He was fast, very fast, and he had a deadly left foot, making him a natural right-sided forward and an integral part of the most successful team in Derry history.

A barrister by profession, he's a raconteur in spirit. These days, *The Sunday Game* on RTÉ is the main stage for his wit and wisdom.

He now looks back on those goal-scoring, kiss-blowing days and notes that not once did his exuberant celebrations invite defeat.

'The kisses were only blown when I felt the goal was a killer blow. There was a time and place for it. It would always be in the last quarter when I sensed a team was there to be finished off. Before playing Tyrone in 1997, one of my brothers asked me to do it, whether I felt like it or not. I walked around the goals that afternoon, blew kisses and just about everything was thrown at me. There were grown men trying to get through the wire. I didn't enjoy it, but I did it to make a statement, to put the two fingers up at them.'

For Brolly, the whole act was about demoralising opponents. Heads dropped when the showman raised his hands in celebration. Tyrone's Fergal Logan tells of how, before that semi-final in 1997, he gathered his co-defenders in training and they agreed that whatever happened, 'the bastard' was not to score a goal. Players from other counties disliked Brolly's antics too and there were recriminations in a National League match against Meath and a Railway Cup match against Munster, when he had his nose broken.

But that was Brolly's way. It was entertainment, a pause in the intensity of the day. But then Brolly's family were heavily involved in the entertainment business. His father, Francie, and mother, Ann, now deeply immersed in politics, were a well-known folk-singing double act in the 1970s. They met on the BBC programme *As I Roved Out* and enjoyed success with a few albums.

Joe's original Christian name was Pádraig but when his grandfather, Joseph, died after a tunnel collapsed on him in Dungiven, the one-year-old was given his second name in honour of his grandfather.

His grandfather was a learned man, who filled in various forms for local farmers, and when he passed away his son Francie took up the reins in a tight-knit community.

Today Francie Brolly, having retired from his teaching job, is the Sinn Féin MLA for the area, but in 1973 he was one of hundreds of Catholics interned by the British.

A Latin scholar and contemporary of the poet Séamus Heaney at St Colm's in Derry, Francie spent over two years in Long Kesh without parole, until one day Don Semple from the shop next door to Brolly's came in and told Ann it was time to collect her husband.

'I remember it well,' recalls Joe. 'Don knocked on the door and said, "Ann, you have to collect Francie. He's waiting at the front gate." That was it! It was a regular occurrence for us to have soldiers coming through the front door and tossing up beds. They lifted two school teachers from Dungiven in 1973. They even took in the local blacksmith, but released him after four weeks and said it was a mistake. I remember me and my two infant brothers visiting Long Kesh at Christmas time, wearing our cowboy outfits.'

When life on the outside resumed for Francie it was consumed by family, music and football. As his popularity soared and late nights on the circuit became a way of life, Joe ended up boarding at St Patrick's in Armagh. But Sundays were sacrosanct and father and son rarely missed a Derry game.

St Patrick's shaped the independence in him. 'I was never homesick. I took to this new life from the first moment. It was an enlightened school with a strong emphasis on drama and sport and I flourished in that environment.'

Brolly developed a reputation as a point guard in basketball, won two Irish titles with the St Patrick's team and also represented Ireland. In 1986, his team headed for Israel for the European Championships and he saw what basketball was really about.

'We played Israel and most of their team had already secured scholarships to America. The game was only a few seconds old when one of their players dribbled towards me. "I have him," I shouted, as he slam-dunked the ball over my head. I looked towards the coach and we burst out laughing. We had to take a time-out to compose ourselves. Then, back out we went to the inevitable slaughter.'

Within days of progressing to Trinity College in Dublin, he met his future wife, Emma Rose McCann from Ballymena, daughter of well-known solicitor and raconteur Jack McCann, and cousin of the actor Liam Neeson.

At Trinity, Brolly also played for one of the best Sigerson Cup teams ever to represent the college. 'I don't think I ever played on such a stylish, ball-playing team. I worked on the skills every spare minute. I got up early and kicked point after point on the old rugby pitch. Eventually, I kicked them with my eyes closed, which was great not only for balance and technique, but also confidence. The time spent on this was invaluable, since after college, spare time tends to disappear.'

His exploits in Sigerson Cups brought recognition in Derry and manager Eamonn Coleman eventually gave him a start with the county team. Brolly liked Coleman; in fact everyone in the squad enjoyed their colourful manager.

'He's impossible to dislike. Essentially he is a man's man. Like, for example, Mick O'Dwyer and Páidí Ó Sé, he was a charismatic leader. Coleman's style was to buoy everyone up. He'd often say to us, "You are without doubt the greatest Gaelic footballers I have ever seen and you will win the All-Ireland."

'He'd say to Brian McGilligan, "You are the greatest midfielder this game has ever seen." He said to me once in 1994, "I just cannot believe how good you are. You're flying. No one is going to be able to mark you."

'Now we obviously had talent, but winning an All-Ireland was something others did. However, Coleman made it sound real. He made us believe it could happen. He wasn't terribly scientific, but he had a bunch of quality players around him and he knew how to get the best out of them.'

Derry won a National League title in 1992, beating Tyrone in the final, but lost by two points to Donegal in the Ulster final. Still, they were an improving team and Brolly believed Derry couldn't really lose the 1993 All-Ireland championship. He only became a fixed asset on the team for the All-Ireland semi-final against Dublin, the game that really defined them.

'It was the crucial game for us, perhaps one of the greatest Gaelic football games ever, certainly the most exhilarating occasion I have been part of. The final was an anti-climax. Cork went a goal up and led by five points early on, but we reeled them in quickly. At the start of the second half, John O'Driscoll scored a brilliant goal but again we reeled them in. We won by three points, but should have beaten them by seven or eight points. You ask anyone in Derry and they'll tell you there was a feeling of inevitability about that game. A touch of complacency set in a year later and Down took us in that great Ulster championship game in Celtic Park. If there were back doors then, we would have galvanized ourselves and could well have gone on to retain the All-Ireland.'

Internal problems erupted in the wake of that defeat. Coleman headed for America, lined up work and football for some of the players, and discovered later in the summer that he had lost the Derry job. Mickey Moran replaced him, civil war broke out and, in truth, that Derry team never recovered.

Many theories abound as to why Coleman was effectively sacked. Brolly feels it was partly because Coleman was an outspoken players' man. After a challenge match in Meath before the All-Ireland semi-final in 1993, a post-match meal in a local hotel erupted into a row over playing gear between the captain, Henry Downey, and the then County Board treasurer, Jim McGuigan, which led to the Gardaí being called.

'The upshot of it was that the cold war between the players and the Board became an open war. We said we didn't want Jim in the changing-room again and he wasn't there for the All-Ireland semi-final or final, which I know would have been a big blow to him, since he had been the kit-man for 30 years.

'Then, for our first league game as All-Ireland champions, we were playing Mayo "away". There was a carnival atmosphere within the squad and the night before was spent drinking and carousing in Castlebar. Coleman just sat back and let it flow.

'The following day, we arrived in the dressing-room and started to tog out. There was a terrific buzz, with the Sam Maguire Cup sitting casually in the corner. We were putting out the All-Ireland 15. The next thing, Jim made his way in with the jerseys and everything stopped. It was like pressing pause on the video. Jim continued to fold and lay out jerseys and no one said anything, we just started putting our clothes back on.

'Jim finally asked if there was a problem. Coleman said, "You're the problem Jim." Jim left and, if I recall correctly, we gave him a rousing cheer on the way out. We were as thick as thieves with Coleman, but I think that was probably the beginning of the end for him.

'When Coleman was formally sacked, Mickey Moran called a players' meeting prior to the commencement of the 1994 NFL and told us he had been offered the post, but that he would only take it with the players' blessing. Henry asked him to leave the room so we could discuss it. Mickey had been stressing to us that the business with Coleman had nothing to do with him. When he came back in, we told him that we didn't want him to take the job. He said how disappointed he was and walked out. The next thing we heard, training was called for the following Tuesday night and Mickey was the new manager.'

With some players opting to stay aboard the panel while others stayed away, Derry's league campaign started with defeats by Laois and Donegal and it looked as if they were on a serious downward spiral. However, Coleman met the players in Ballymaguigan and told them that since they were Derry men first and foremost, they had to return.

A fractured peace was restored and Derry turned the League season around, but the atmosphere in the camp was never the same. 'We won a league title in 1995, but we were on autopilot,' recalled Brolly. 'I broke my wrist in the final against Donegal and missed the championship.'

'We played Tyrone in the Ulster championship and were winning by three points at half-time. Tyrone had two men sent off, so we should have won quite comfortably, but our mood was all wrong. Tyrone began to fight towards the end of the first half because they could see the way it was going. Damien Barton had his nose busted badly and the blood was pouring from it, but he hadn't struck back.

'We went out in the second half, went through the motions and Tyrone got their dander up. Then Fergal McCusker was sent off.

It was the worst, most limp surrender you will ever see. It was rotten. It just wouldn't have happened in the old days. The scene was never the same again after that.'

Moran departed following that defeat and a new manager was sought. On the way out of Croke Park after the All-Ireland final in 1995, Brolly met former Dublin star Brian Mullins. They chatted and Brolly jokingly asked him if he was interested in the Derry job, now that he had taken up a school principal's job in Carndonagh.

'He told me he would be interested. I asked him if he was serious. He gave me that Mullins' glare and said, "I'm always serious." He was exactly what we needed to lift the team, to get the heads up again.'

Within weeks, Mullins was the new Derry manager and another League title was secured the following spring.

'Mullins is a legendary figure and a huge man in the flesh. He met the squad and instantly lifted morale. We left the first meeting excited.'

They blazed through the early rounds in Ulster in 1997, but lost the final to Cavan because, according to Brolly, they didn't pay them enough respect. Dungiven won Derry and Ulster club titles that autumn, before losing an All-Ireland semi-final to Corofin in the spring of 1998. The Galway champions put two players on Brolly and the tactic worked.

'I scored four points. I had been getting 1-6 or 1-7, but they "double teamed" me. Ray Silke told me afterwards that a barrister from Donegal who was living in Corofin had come up with the idea. Typical smartass barrister. It made it very difficult to get the ball, with a man standing ten yards in front and another beside me. We had a man sent off after ten minutes and ended up losing by a point. Corofin strolled the final.'

Brolly rejoined Derry for the start of the 1998 championship and the team again powered through Ulster, this time beating Donegal in the final.

'After that Ulster final, we went to Roscommon to watch Galway and Roscommon in their provincial final replay. It was an awful match. Galway were terrible, winning against the run of play with an extra-time goal after a fumble by the goalie. We came away laughing. We were euphoric. On the way home, we stopped off in Sligo for the night. It was a wild night with drinking and carousing in what, for the previous two years, had been an extremely well-disciplined camp. I was one of the worst offenders and big Brian was genuinely very angry with me, particularly since at that stage I was the forward leader and one of the veterans.'

Derry lost the All-Ireland semi-final to Galway and Brolly recalls an irate Mullins roaring at him during the half-time interval.

'There was chaos everywhere. We were behind, but I still felt that with a bit of order we could have won the game. Not long into the second half Brian took me off. The Galway lads still poke fun at me about that. My only consolation is that I held Tomás Mannion [Galway corner-back] scoreless!'

Within two seasons, Brolly had lost his appetite for inter-county football and retired, restricting his involvement to Dungiven.

'I always had a good, varied life. As I grew older I became less obsessive about Gaelic football. By the time I quit, I only felt relief. I had a great adventure, but it was over.'

In Dungiven he found himself getting serious again. 'The longer I played, the less tolerant I became on the field. I was fit to be tied after some of the matches. One great thing about club football is that you get to play in all those tournaments that you missed out on during your inter-county career. It also gives you a chance to work on your skills again. In the last five years, I have been working flat out on my right foot. Soon I will be able to kick with it.'

His 13 years as a barrister have been varied and interesting. The Belfast Crown Court invariably is.

'The life suits me, even though it does mean exploring the darker side of human beings. In any civilized society a strong criminal defence system is a vital protection for people and a very important bulwark against the excesses of the police and government. *Rumpole of the Bailey* and *Columbo* first attracted me to the criminal bar. Columbo's "my wife just loves your work" trick of drawing somebody in by flattery, before flooring him with the classic, "just one last thing sir..." still delights me.

'The art of persuasion is a very mysterious one. Sometimes a full frontal attack on a witness is necessary, other times a gentle, sympathetic approach is required. The crossing of swords with a witness always brings a stimulating contest. I am argumentative. I always side with the underdog. I view the police and establishment with scepticism. I think these are the right tools to do what I do and I am privileged to defend people who have had very few advantages in life.'

He'd like to be remembered as a player who got people sitting on the edge of their seats.

'The happiest place I played in was Celtic Park. The intimacy of the crowd and the vibe you got there was something special. Causing 10,000 people to jump to their feet and laugh and cheer. Where else would you get it?'

---

* *Joe Brolly is a barrister and lives in Belfast with his wife,*
Emma McCann, and their three children:
Rory (4), Toirealach (2) and Meabh (1).

The Power and the Poise

Brian Lohan (Clare)

ALL STAR WINNER: 1995, 1996, 1997, 2002

'There was no feigning injury and manufacturing frees like there is now. I'd like to think that, as a group of defenders, we'd be remembered as being honest and forceful.'

I n his first few years as a professional golfer, it was customary for Tiger Woods to wear a red shirt on the final day of competition. The colour sent out a clear message to his rivals, suggesting danger and competitiveness and giving him a sense of the untouchable that others understood.

However, in order to create a softer image, Woods heeded advice to tone down to a more reserved wine shade. His handlers wanted to present a more human face to their product and it worked.

Brian Lohan could never contemplate such a makeover. For ten years, his striking red helmet has been the most recognised piece of equipment in hurling. Former great Kilkenny centre-back Ger Henderson wore a gold helmet for many years as a symbol of the imperious authority he brought to his game, while Galway's Gerry McInerney wore fetching white boots that portrayed athleticism and nimble feet.

Lohan's red helmet sent out a different, yet clear message. Quite simply, it warned of danger. Most opponents of the fearsome Clare full-back interpreted it that way too. On bad, frustrating days like the 2002 All-Ireland final against Kilkenny, he'd discard the helmet and opponents would take it as a sign that the fortress he guarded so zealously was, in some way, being breached.

Once, in the aftermath of Clare's 1997 All-Ireland success, Ger Loughnane organised an auction on Clare FM to raise finance for a team holiday and promised that the famous red helmet would go under the hammer. Loughnane made the promise without consulting Lohan, however. When he finally made contact, he was told where to go! Lohan would sacrifice just about anything for Clare hurling, but never his prized red helmet.

Instead, Ger 'Sparrow' O'Loughlin's helmet and Seanie McMahon's boots were put on offer. Loughnane got the message.

'I told him no way,' recalled Lohan. 'I've had the same helmet for years. It's in bits now and barely stays on my head. But I wouldn't change it.'

Such loyalty is a virtue that Lohan always carried into the dressing-room and through some of the most ferocious hurling battles the modern era has seen. Beneath the helmet is a mind with an iron will and a frame so hard that it might have been hewn from rock.

His importance to the Clare team that lit up the game in the mid-1990s with two All-Ireland titles and three Munster crowns can never be overstated. For a few years he was virtually unbeatable on the edge of the Clare square, a nemesis for a range of full forwards and rival managers who attempted to devise ways of outsmarting him.

He was comfortable with those around him in those glorious days. On one side was younger brother Frank; on the other, his great school friend Michael O'Halloran. In front, were men whose force of personality matched his own: Liam Doyle, Seánie McMahon and Anthony Daly, the components of one of the most accomplished half-back lines ever assembled.

Lohan knew he could depend on all of them. 'There was great unity there, a feeling that if anything started to go wrong, there were good guys beside and in front of you. I always felt that, as defenders, we were manly. There was no feigning injury and manufacturing frees like there is now. I'd like to think that, as a group of defenders, we'd be remembered as being honest and forceful.'

If Lohan felt he could depend on those around him, the feeling was entirely mutual. The All Star awards came easily in 1995, 1996 and 1997 and were a tribute to the power of his character and the force of his will, which was overwhelming in those years.

Many observers and current hurlers credit that Clare team with setting new levels of intensity in the manner in which they went about their business. By extension, Lohan himself was regarded as the barometer for good preparation within the Clare set-up.

Almost religiously, he has cultivated a routine of training six days a week, using Wednesday as his day of rest. A few years ago, when he sensed that his 'yard of speed' was deserting him, he employed a personal trainer to help him retrieve it. In the Clare dressing-room, Lohan's mood would often set the tone for the day. He wore a stone face and rarely spoke before games. Anything different was a source of anxiety for the Clare management.

His story is one of perseverance and self-development, rather than outstanding natural talent. As a young man, he was a better than average club hurler, not quite good enough to make it on to the stronger teams, however.

Shannon is home to the Lohans, where father, Gus and mother, Brede, settled when Gus, a Garda, was transferred to the county in 1971, the year Brian was born. Gus was a noted hurler and footballer from Cappataggle in Galway. He played hurling with his native county and had a short spell with the Monaghan footballers when he was stationed on the border, but it was with Clare that he made his mark as a hurler, winning a National League title in 1977 and 11 county titles with Newmarket-on-Fergus.

In the environs of the Tullyglass estate, which gets its name from the hill where Loughnane's Clare team did much of their famed stamina training, the love of hurling and sport was nurtured among the young Lohans. They played rugby, soccer, Gaelic football and hurling, but the influence of several primary school teachers in the expanding town made hurling the dominant game.

'The main factor in the growth of hurling in the Shannon area was the primary schools. You had men like Loughnane, Seán Cleary, Brendan Vaughan, who was a former County Board chairman in Clare, Joe Walsh and Brian Torpey either running the schools or involved in some capacity.'

From an early stage in his life, a desire to don the saffron and blue of Clare burned deep within Lohan. He recalls his father, dressed in a Garda tunic, visiting the school with the National League trophy after the 1977 triumph. Seán Stack, another key member of that team, was a teacher in the local Comprehensive School; Loughnane lived nearby and regularly peered over his wall to watch the kids exhaust their energy on the local green. All around, there were icons of Clare hurling.

It was in this environment that Lohan's thirst for competition grew. When he failed to make the Clare minor team that reached the All-Ireland final in 1989, or the Shannon Comprehensive team that played in the all-Clare Harty Cup final against St Flannan's earlier in the year, he took it in his stride.

'I wasn't bothered by it that much. I always saw myself as a good club player. Sure, it was a disappointment. But whenever I'd wonder about why I wasn't making the team, I'd put it down to the intelligence of the selectors!'

One of the selectors was his father, the other was the manager, Mike McNamara, who would later fill an important role as Clare's diamond-edged physical trainer in the 1995–99 period. He was a man for whom Lohan developed enormous respect.

'My father always blamed Mike Mac for leaving me out. Mike Mac said my father didn't want me there,' he chuckled in the knowledge that one of them, or perhaps both, got it wrong.

He shared the bench with O'Halloran for the Harty Cup final defeat to a Jamesie O'Connor-powered St Flannan's in 1989.

'After the final we had a meeting in one of the rooms, a sort of debriefing session. Stack, who was manager, addressed us and I remember him saying that we could take it as a learning experience. He said that fellas on the team could expect to have good hurling careers ahead of them, but those who didn't make the team could have even better careers. He mentioned me in that regard. "Hally" [Michael O'Halloran] says he mentioned him too, but I don't remember that!'

'Those words stuck with me because I knew I was more committed than most. Myself and "Hally" were very serious about hurling, even though we weren't on the team.'

Three years later, Lohan finally made a Clare U-21 team for the first time, but when they lost the 1992 Munster final to Waterford, he figured it could blight his future. Better days lay ahead, however, and as a student of business at the University of Limerick, he found another hurling avenue to consume him. 'The biggest thing about college to my mind was the Fitzgibbon Cup,' he recalled.

In the process of trying and eventually succeeding in 1994, when he was considered 'Player of the Tournament' as UL won the Fitzgibbon Cup, he became a much better hurler.

By then, the routine of visits to the gym, the ball alleys in St Flannan's and Shannon and the long runs was established. He was a Clare senior in 1993 and the established full back 12 months later. Loughnane was assistant manager to Len Gaynor, but was already making plans for his succession.

'Loughnane had it in his head who would be full back and centre back, long before I got to know McMahon. He knew who could stand the pressure. I remember him saying he would allow a player to fail once on a big day but, if it happened on two big occasions, that was the last jersey they would get from him.'

Clare lost the 1994 Munster final to Limerick, a defeat that stunned Lohan.

'Going down to the game, I just couldn't see us being beaten. I felt any of our backs would handle their forwards one to one. It didn't work out that way.'

Within days of Offaly's All-Ireland final success over Limerick two months later, Clare were preparing for the 1995 championship under the Loughnane/McNamara/Considine triumvirate.

'All the talk at the time was that we were training for an All-Ireland final almost 12 months later. Now for that to be directed at a group of Clare players might have seemed a little misguided, given the record over the years. But that was Mike Mac. It was all psychological.'

Lohan missed most of the grinding punishment that Loughnane and McNamara put the squad through that winter as he was banking in London at the time.

'They flew me over for League matches but I missed much of the training,' he recalled.

He knew enough to realise what he was missing. 'Loughnane was a brute. He was ruthless, a rough man on the training field. But he always did it with the aim of improving the team. It was the same with Mike Mac. They did what they had to do to improve players and consequently the team.'

Clare lost the 1995 National League final to Kilkenny, but less than three months later, they were celebrating a first Munster title for 81 years. The hard work had paid off.

'The whole occasion passed over the players' heads a little because we always felt we were training for an All-Ireland final.'

His own preparations for the final against Offaly were interrupted by a hamstring injury picked up late in the semi-final win over Galway. It's a measure of the man that he survived in Joe Cooney's exalted company on the day he first sustained the hamstring injury. But, when the hamstring snapped again five minutes into the second half of the final, he knew he was in trouble.

He gestured to the sideline but was told he *had* to stay on. He did and survived again.

'Croke Park was a much smaller, tighter field back then and an All-Ireland final was more intense than it is now. It was a more physical game. I didn't want to come off that day so I played smart. Offaly were three points up at one stage and John Troy had two opportunities to put them four clear. He didn't know my hamstring was gone when he beat me for two balls out near the sideline and pushed past me. I couldn't get back to him, but he didn't have the legs to pull clear away from me, either. He shot wide twice, much to my relief. If Offaly had pulled four points clear that day, they would have won the match.'

He had a broadly similar experience in the 1997 final against Tipperary, when a blow to the hip before half-time left him in a distressed state during the interval.

'I was going to come off and I said to the management, "If I'm letting the team down, take me off." They didn't and, as it transpired, I got away with it. In fairness to Eugene O'Neill, he played well on me, but probably could have played much better. I think he was probably happy with what he was doing.'

Despite the historic dimension of the 1995 All-Ireland breakthrough, Lohan regards the 1997 success as a greater achievement.

'Beating Tipperary in a Munster final and then repeating it in an All-Ireland final a few months later made it very special. We were gunning for them that year. Earlier in the season, Tipp had beaten us by a point in a League game that turned into a real war. Frank [Lohan] was sent off, tensions were running high and it probably set the tone for the season.

'It was a serious rivalry between the counties at that stage. Maybe Tipp felt we had no right to beat them, but I don't know why because Clare beat them regularly in the 1980s. In fairness, though, there was no real badness in it. A few clips alright but never any bad strokes.'

In between winning All-Ireland titles, Clare were dislodged by Limerick in the Gaelic Grounds in the 1996 Munster semi-final, on one of the warmest days he ever recalls.

'We weren't right that day. Frank and Seánie were doing final exams the week of the game. As a team, we hadn't the work done.'

However, Lohan was in prime condition and it showed in a performance that was possibly the most accomplished of his career. That performance earned him his second All Star award in a year in which his club, Wolfe Tones, claimed Clare and Munster club titles for the first time. Another All-Ireland title beckoned for Lohan, but while Wolfe Tones reached the final, they were beaten by a Eugene Cloonan-inspired Athenry on St Patrick's Day 1997.

The focus returned to the county team again and more big days in Croke Park. He prefers to forget about 1998 and the controversies that dogged the summer. He was sent off together with Waterford's Micheál White, after an angry flashpoint between the pair in the opening minutes of a combustible Munster final replay. Despite retaining the Munster title, Clare's summer spiralled into chaos from there on, in the controversial aftermath of that clash with Waterford. Eventually, Clare relinquished their All-Ireland title to Offaly in the third game of a high-profile semi-final saga. The first game finished level, the second ended too early after a time-keeping error by the referee, while Offaly proved too good third time out.

'We weren't a united team. We could have got away with it but we just weren't together,' Lohan recalled.

By then, he had detected cracks in the management structure that had held them together for four great years.

'You had two really powerful individuals [Loughnane and McNamara] involved. There was talk of Loughnane giving it up after 1998. It was obvious they weren't getting on as well as they used to. The dynamic between them wasn't the same. I would have noticed it at times in 1998, but mostly in 1999. The lads were getting cute too. If they knew Mike Mac was taking a session, they'd be on to Loughnane to excuse themselves. If Loughnane was taking one, then Mike Mac would get the call.'

In the end, Loughnane stayed and Mike Mac and Tony Considine moved on. Lohan missed Mike Mac's bark and big personality. When Loughnane went 12 months later, he missed him too.

Tipperary hammered Clare in Páirc Uí Chaoímh in 2000, on a day when Lohan was at his lightest ever for a championship game.

'My normal weight was about 14 stone. For the Tipp game I was $12^1/_2$ stone. We were supposed to be the fittest Clare team ever, but we had trained too hard. We didn't train smart. We just trained for the sake of training. It was stupid stuff. There was an awful lot of strength in a stone and a half. "Hally" said to me afterwards that as he was walking up the steps, he looked out on the field and saw Seánie McMahon pucking beside Alan Markham. Markham looked a bigger man than Seánie. He knew straight away we were in trouble.'

Cyril Lyons took the managerial baton from Loughnane for 2001 but by then Lohan had begun to feel that that 'yard of pace' was missing.

'I told Loughnane before he left that if I didn't get it back, I was quitting. To me, hurling is about speed and strength. Your striking will always improve because you are doing so much hurling anyway. A bit of hard work will sort that out. But if you don't have the basics of speed and strength, you're at nothing. So I got in touch with a power lifter from Limerick, Eoin Franklin, and he devised a programme for me. It worked.'

By 2002, the Lohan of old was back and he captained Clare as they stormed through the All-Ireland qualifiers, after an early season Munster championship defeat by Tipperary. A fourth All Star award, a record in Clare, was assured for Lohan. Preparations for the All-Ireland final, however, weren't smooth. Clare's sponsors, Vodafone, kindly dispatched mobile phone gift packs to the squad and management a couple of weeks beforehand.

'Some guys took two, some took three, but who were they taking them from? Five days before an All-Ireland final, we were asking lads to hand back phones they had taken from their own teammates.

'We gave that game to Kilkenny. Clare is not like Kilkenny and Cork. In our approach, we have to be united to get the best out of ourselves. But we didn't deserve to win an All-Ireland title after that phone episode.'

These days, the hamstrings continue to bother him. His style of running is the main reason they trouble him so much.

'I've been told I'll always have the problems as long as I play. The bend on my back is putting a lot of pressure on the hamstrings.'

The players with whom he won All-Ireland medals are still close, but some things have changed. Daly is now Clare manager and Loughnane has turned media analyst. Not everyone in Clare warms to his critical and honest comments, but Lohan could never doubt his loyalty.

'When Ger was manager he was always fiercely loyal to his players. He looked after people on and off the field.'

But then it worked both ways, since Lohan and Co. brought an honesty and loyalty to the Clare cause that has guaranteed them a permanent place in the county's affections and in its hurling folklore.

*Brian Lohan lives in Ennis and has recently opened his own auctioneering and real estate business in the town.

In Search of Perfection

Cormac McAnallen, 1980–2004 (Tyrone)

ALL STAR WINNER: **2003**

'If ever God needed an example of how we should use our talents, then Cormac epitomised exactly that.'

Stored away in a drawer at his home in the secluded corner of south Tyrone known as The Brantry, close to the villages of Eglish and Benburb, are a few sheets of foolscap pages that carry a personal account of every game in which Cormac McAnallen played during the four seasons before his untimely death on Tuesday, 2 March 2004.

The pages serve as monuments to the meticulous nature of a young man for whom perfection in every aspect of life was an abiding objective. Each handwritten line of every sheet lists the game, date, teams, venue and competition, before he gives himself a mark under the headings – 'offensive', 'defensive', 'head', 'body' and 'legs'.

Club, county, university, province and country all feature in his self-assessment portfolio, providing a fascinating insight into how Cormac looked upon himself as a player and how he compartmentalised the game into the sections that he felt were important.

A glance reveals some critical self-analysis and, to underline the precision of his assessments, he introduced a series of half-marks in some sections. Very few nines are awarded and, significantly, there's not one full mark on any page. To bestow a perfect ten would have been to acknowledge a sense of completeness and, for Cormac, would have interfered with the pursuit of improvement that he regarded as essential. His search for perfection always had to be ongoing.

Significantly though, the more recent entries show a steady rise in marks. At the time of his tragic passing, it was clear that he was feeling good about his football.

Cormac McAnallen's death was one of those JFK moments that instantly trigger the question – where were you when you heard it first?

Few events have stunned the wider GAA community more than the passing of one of the finest young players of his generation. It was a week when the Association stood still, a time when the quiet rural hinterland of south Tyrone became the focus of mourning, respect and disbelief at the passing of an instantly recognisable figure.

Some of the greatest names in the game streamed through the McAnallen household to sympathise with his parents, Brendan and Bridget, and his brothers, Donal and Fergus.

Messages of condolence arrived from all across the land. Few deaths have transcended the North's ideological divide in quite the same way. The dignity of the funeral struck a chord. So too did the hushed silence, the fiddle solo played by his 87-year-old grandfather, Charlie O'Neill, and the guards of honour that lined the route of the cortège.

Supporters of Linfield FC sent messages of sympathy through UTV sports editor Adrian Logan; members of the Dungannon Swifts soccer club arrived at the house; hockey and rugby clubs sent cards and letters, while Jim Boyce, Chief Executive of the Irish Football Association, was present at the funeral.

Perhaps the most unusual source of a message of sympathy was the headquarters of the Royal Black Preceptory, an organisation with strong links to the Orange Order, who sent a letter to the McAnallen family, further illustrating just how much his death had touched an entire community.

The popularity that he enjoyed was typified by the fact that he was generally known by his Christian name only. He didn't crave popularity but, as Tyrone manager Mickey Harte acknowledged, the crowd was inevitably attracted to him.

Cormac had everything going for him before that fateful Tuesday morning. Just six weeks earlier, he had been appointed the Tyrone senior football captain, replacing Peter Canavan, whose future was clouded by doubt at the time because of the nature of his ankle injury.

Cormac's promotion seemed a natural progression for the player and for the team that had swept all before them in 2003. He had been captain to many of those players for three All-Ireland underage titles, so he was the logical choice when Canavan indicated that the armband would be more appropriately placed elsewhere for 2004.

Within weeks of his appointment, Cormac was raising the Dr McKenna Cup aloft after an impressive Tyrone victory over Donegal, completing the sweep of senior titles in a nine-month spell that included National League, Ulster championship and All-Ireland successes. With his instinct for the No.3 shirt sharpening with every game, he seemed destined for a long and brilliant future. In the days after Cormac's death, Canavan would comment on the growing maturity in his game, so evident in a League encounter against Longford and in that McKenna Cup final in Ballybofey.

On a personal level, Cormac had announced his engagement to his fiancée and great friend, Ashlene Moore, and they were in the planning stages for a future wedding and the building of a new house near the McAnallen homestead.

The sudden nature of his passing left people confused and bewildered. There was scarcely a GAA player, or indeed a sportsperson in any discipline, who didn't question his or her own mortality in the days and weeks afterwards.

The immediate post mortem declared that Cormac had died from a viral infection of the heart, but that now appears to have been a term of convenience.

In their desire to establish exactly what happened to their son and brother, the McAnallens made contact with a London professor, Bill McKenna, who has provided greater insight into the cause of death. But still, they are not totally sure and the sense of mystery remains.

The term 'Sudden Death Syndrome' is too general and Professor McKenna himself has referred to what he calls 'Long QT (Quiet Time) Syndrome' as a better explanatory term.

'Long QT syndrome is the heart condition, which Professor McKenna has identified as the most likely cause of Cormac's death. There are several different types of LQT syndrome including LQT 3, which is genetically inherited and which he thinks Cormac died from. Sudden Adult Death Syndrome is a very general term to explain a complex issue,' said Cormac's mother, Bridget.

For the McAnallens, the desire to establish more precise details of how their middle son died and to discover whether or not his death could have been prevented through better awareness and testing procedures, will continue.

In time, they hope that the awareness of cardiac risk in the young will become greater, and that the GAA can seize the initiative on an issue that has grown in importance throughout a calamitous year for young sportsmen.

In his passing, however, Cormac leaves quite a legacy. In the seven years since he first donned the Tyrone shirt competitively as a minor, 14 inter-county titles were claimed by teams he influenced heavily. It's no coincidence that the most productive era in the county's GAA history is proportionately indexed to his arrival.

The list of achievements makes for quite a portfolio: two Ulster minor championships, one All-Ireland minor championship, two Ulster and All-Ireland U-21 championships, two NFL titles, two Ulster senior titles, the coveted All-Ireland senior title and, for good measure, a Hastings (U-21) Cup and Dr McKenna Cup.

Mickey Harte never hid his admiration for Cormac, which was reflected in the decision to appoint him captain for 2004. Harte believed that a training session was always the better for his presence. If the manager ever felt a session needed a boost, it was to Cormac he looked to provide it.

Cormac's meticulous approach to planning and preparation carried over into other aspects of his life. When he took on a politics class at St Catherine's, Armagh, where he taught up to the time of his death, family members recalled how he would sit in front of the television at night, taking notes on discussion programmes relevant to the subject.

Tyrone colleagues recall how Cormac, on hearing that a player had suffered dental problems because of his intake of energy drinks, took to brushing his teeth in the shower after every training session and game. And, of course, there was his characteristic application and flexibility in the face of every challenge that presented itself.

Arguably the boldest move by Harte in 2003 was deciding to switch Cormac to full back for the Ulster final replay against Down. The towering Dan Gordon had pinched two of Down's four goals in an epic drawn encounter so, sensing the need for increased security on the edge of the square, Harte turned to the reassuring presence on whom he knew he could depend.

When he called Cormac aside at a training session, prior to the replay, and told him he had a new job for him, the response was as Harte would have expected. It was a move that the manager was determined would remain a secret until match day, with only a handful of players aware of what was to unfold. Cormac's brother Donal recalls how even their father, Brendan, didn't know about his son's switch to the full-back line.

'Daddy went to the game that afternoon and there were people coming up to him, saying Cormac was in at full back. He was a bit surprised because Cormac hadn't said anything about it.'

Down scored just 1-5 that day and, the following evening as the McAnallens sat down to tea, Donal congratulated his brother but reminded him that his prospect of an All Star award was gone.

'I made the point to him that the transfer from one position to another in mid-season would probably damage his prospects of an All Star. It might have been different had he switched from one part of the defence to another. But we felt it was too much a change going from midfield to full back. Typically, he proved me wrong.'

Three matches later, Tyrone were All-Ireland champions, without conceding a further goal and Cormac McAnallen, already shaping like the best full-back around, was virtually an automatic choice for an All Star award.

In just four matches, he had convinced the selection committee of his worth in his new position. It more than made up for the disappointment of missing out in 2001, when he had been challenging for a midfield position, but lost out to Galway's Kevin Walsh and Westmeath's Rory O'Connell. There had been a consolation, however, as he had picked up the 'Young Player of the Year' award, which had felt like a 16th All Star at the time.

To the people of Eglish, where his love of football was nurtured, Cormac's versatility was accepted as being an entirely natural virtue and it was no great surprise to them that he mastered full back so quickly. He had grown up admiring the skills of his uncle Peter O'Neill from the Moy, who lived a short distance down the lane from Seán Cavanagh's home. Seán would later grow up to become a key member of the Tyrone side alongside Cormac.

When Eglish won the Tyrone minor championship in 1996, 16-year-old Cormac was man-of-the-match in the final, with the No.3 shirt on his back. A year later they retained the title, propelling the rising star on to the county minor team.

By common consensus, he never stood out from the crowd as a juvenile player. But he made striking improvements around the age of 16 and, as Harte would acknowledge, he had the drive to 'be the best he could be'. Harte's recollection of the first time he ever met the young McAnallen is still vivid. Harte was one of a number of coaches chosen by the Tyrone County Board as part of an initiative to tour clubs and he was assigned Eglish.

He noted how at least four of Cormac's teammates appeared more talented, but none were more enthusiastic. Within a year, Harte had him on his minor team and the graph was still rising last March.

'Cormac always seemed to be a year to 18 months younger than the teams he played on and I think that was of benefit to him,' explained his brother Donal.

'He was still a bit chubby when he was 15 or 16; he wasn't particularly fast or skilful, but he just improved in all of those areas because he was so driven.

'One of the things that helped him was basketball. At one stage in St Patrick's, Armagh, he played on a team alongside five other future All-Ireland medal winners – Philip Jordan, Ryan Mellon [Tyrone], Paddy McKeever, Paul McCormack and Kevin McElvanna [Armagh]. He represented Ulster at U-15 level and was on the stand-by panel for an international team,' Donal recalled.

In one of the many written tributes to Cormac after his death, Harte detailed what he saw in the young man in those early years.

'In the narrowest of senses of the term "talent", Cormac did not immediately stand out from the crowd. From a more discerning perspective, however, if ever God needed an example of how we should use our talents, then Cormac epitomised exactly that. In a sporting context, his dedication to being the best he could should serve as an inspiration to all athletes. I believe his example is particularly encouraging to those who apparently don't "make it" at a young age.'

While at St Patrick's, Armagh, McRory Cup success eluded Cormac as they lost to St Patrick's, Dungannon, in the 1997 Ulster final, but his strike rate at third level was better. He was awarded a Queen's University Blues award for outstanding contribution to sport, at the renowned Belfast seat of learning in 2000 and he won a Sigerson Cup medal a year later.

Together with his Tyrone minor colleagues, he had to learn to cope with the tragedy of Paul McGirr's death in 1997. It was a numbing experience but, in the longer term, it helped foster Cormac's leadership qualities, just as the shocking Omagh bombing did a year later.

Tyrone selector Fr Gerard McAleer noted how, when they split the players into small groups for discussion, Cormac's groups inevitably made the most vibrant contributions. He had those 'Pied Piper' qualities.

By the end of 2000, he had added Ulster and All-Ireland U-21 medals to his growing collection, captaining the team in both finals. Donal recalls his brother's second-half performance in a Sigerson Cup semi-final that year as one of his most outstanding.

The following year was a huge personal success, with Ulster senior and All-Ireland U-21 titles, a first Ulster senior medal and a host of individual awards, from BBC 'Player of the Ulster championship' to the Ulster GAA writers' 'Footballer of the Year' award. The set was complete with the All Star 'Young Player of the Year' award and recognition by the International Rules management, who brought him to Australia where he emerged as one of the star performers.

All the time, Cormac was improving and yet, his willingness to learn never ebbed. By that stage, he had completed four years of studies at Queen's, where he got a degree in History and a diploma in computer-based learning. He then elected to take a H. Dip. at UCD, in preparation for a career as a teacher. While at UCD he won a Dublin football championship medal with the college, to add to a first NFL medal with Tyrone.

Harte's arrival as senior manager in late 2002 brought most of the players back into contact with the man who had been their guide through the glorious underage years. By the time Cormac had switched to full-back in 2003, he had scored 1-10 from 16 senior championship appearances for Tyrone, an impressive contribution by any midfield standards.

In his last four championship games of 2003, he gave exceptional performances against Down's Dan Gordon, Fermanagh's Stephen Maguire, and Kerry's rising star, Declan O'Sullivan, before finally getting to grips with Armagh's Steven McDonnell in the All-Ireland final.

'Looking back on it, I think he was more uptight about facing Declan O'Sullivan than anyone else. At least he knew what to expect from Steven McDonnell. Kerry had a habit, over the years, of producing very good championship youngsters like Colm Cooper and Mike Frank Russell, so he was concerned about O'Sullivan because he was an unknown quantity. But I think he was pleased with how it worked out,' said Donal.

Away from football, general knowledge quizzes were among Cormac's other great interests and, in 1997, he captained the St Patrick's team to victory in the final of RTE's *Blackboard Jungle*, for which the college won a minibus. In tandem with Donal, they delivered several Scór (the GAA's talent competition) titles to Eglish and Tyrone, winning three county Scór na nÓg and three Scór na Sinsear titles, with an All-Ireland Scór na nÓg crown in 1995 thrown in for good measure.

University Challenge also became a priority in the McAnallen household and the armchair battles were intense.

'He got to the stage where he was correctly answering some of the ridiculously hard questions. He developed the art of logical answers with educated guesses. He thought quickly and delivered snappy answers and I suppose that mirrored how he was able to read a game of football so effectively. There was a huge appetite for knowledge and learning in the house. Our parents always encouraged it,' said Donal.

'There was always a competitive edge in that regard. Not many people know this, but Cormac almost appeared on *The Weakest Link*. They rang the house looking for him one day and I gave the researcher a phone number for the school. Through some mix-up, they failed to make contact with him and the chance was missed.'

In many ways, Cormac lived his life ahead of his time. He was only 10 when he entered Grammar School and by the time he lifted the Tom Markham Cup, after Tyrone won the 1998 All-Ireland minor championship, he was already in his second year at Queen's. By the age of 24, he had won every team honour in the game and collected almost all of the individual accolades that could be bestowed on a player.

It was fitting that Cormac chose 'Gold', the Spandau Ballet hit of the 1980s, as his contributory song to the Tyrone team tape that was played on match days. It typified his life in so many ways.

---

*Cormac McAnallen (1980–2004) was a school teacher. He is survived by his parents, Brendan and Bridget, his brothers, Donal and Fergus, and fiancée, Ashlene Moore.

All Star Facts & Figures (1971–2003)

ALL STAR FAMILY WINNERS

BROTHERS (HURLING)

Bonnar (Tipperary) – Colm: 1988; Conal: 1989, 1991; Cormac: 1989, 1991; Total: 5

Cashman (Cork) – Tom: 1977, 1978, 1983; Jim: 1990, 1991; Total: 5

Comerford (Kilkenny) – Andy: 1999, 2000; Martin: 2002, 2003; Total: 4

Connolly (Galway) – John: 1971, 1979; Joe: 1980; Total: 3

Cooney (Galway) – Jimmy: 1980, 1981; Joe: 1985, 1986, 1987, 1989, 1990; Total: 7

Dooley (Offaly) – Johnny: 1994, 1995, 2000; Billy: 1994, 1995; Joe: 1998; Total: 6

Doran (Wexford) – Colm: 1973; Tony: 1976; Total: 2

Fennelly (Kilkenny) – Liam: 1983, 1985, 1987, 1992; Ger: 1983; Total: 5

Henderson (Kilkenny) – Pat: 1973, 1974; Ger: 1978, 1979, 1982, 1983, 1987; John: 1983; Total: 8

Kelly (Tipperary) – Eoin: 2001, 2002; Paul: 2002; Total: 3

Lohan (Clare) – Brian: 1995, 1996, 1997, 2002; Frank: 1999; Total: 5

O'Connor (Kilkenny) – Willie: 1992, 1997, 1998, 2000; Eddie: 1993; Total: 5

Ó hAilpín (Cork) – Seán Óg: 2003; Setanta: 2003; Total: 2

Ryan (Tipperary) – Aidan: 1987; Bobby: 1988, 1989; Total: 3

Quigley (Wexford) – Martin: 1973, 1974, 1975, 1976; John: 1974; Total: 5

BROTHERS (FOOTBALL)

Connor (Offaly) – Matt: 1980, 1982, 1983; Richie: 1981; Total: 4

Connor (Offaly) – Tomás: 1978; Liam: 1982; Total: 2

Earley (Roscommon) – Dermot: 1974, 1979; Paul: 1985; Total: 3

Lowry (Offaly) – Seán: 1979, 1982; Brendan: 1981; Total: 3

McHugh (Donegal) – Martin: 1983, 1992; James: 1992; Total: 3

Spillane (Kerry) – Pat: 1976, 1977, 1978, 1979, 1980, 1981, 1984, 1985, 1986; Tom: 1984, 1986, 1987; Mick: 1985; Total: 13

BROTHERS (HURLING & FOOTBALL)

Carr (Dublin & Tipperary) – Tom (Football, Dublin, 1991); Declan (Hurling, Tipperary, 1989); Total: 2

FATHER & SON (HURLING)

Larkin (Kilkenny) – Phil 'Fan': 1973, 1974, 1976, 1978; Philip: 2002; Total: 5

FATHER & SON (FOOTBALL)

O'Neill (Galway) – Liam: 1973; Kevin: (Mayo), 1993; Total: 2

Reynolds (Meath) – Pat: 1971; Paddy: 1996; Total: 2

Earley (Roscommon) – Dermot Snr: 1974, 1979;

Dermot Jnr: (Kildare), 1998; Total: 3

McGuigan (Tyrone) – Frank: 1984; Brian: 2003; Total: 2

BACKS & FORWARDS (HURLING)

Brian Whelahan (Offaly) – right half-back, 1992, 1995, 1999; full forward, 1998; Total: 4

BACKS & FORWARDS (FOOTBALL)

Anthony McGurk (Derry) – left full forward, 1973; centre half-back, 1975; Total: 2

Paddy Moriarty (Armagh) – left full forward, 1972; centre half-back, 1977; Total: 2

'Nudie' Hughes (Monaghan) – right full-back, 1979; left full forward, 1985, 1988; Total: 3

Ger Power (Kerry) – left half-back, 1975, 1976; right half forward 1978, 1979, 1980; left full forward, 1986; Total: 6

Seán Lowry (Offaly) – full forward, 1979; centre half-back, 1982; Total: 2

Graham Geraghty (Meath) – right half-back, 1994; full forward, 2001; Total: 2

LEADING AWARD WINNERS (HURLING)

9 – D.J. Carey (Kilkenny): 1991, 1992, 1993, 1994, 1995, 1997, 1999, 2000, 2002

7 – Noel Skehan (Kilkenny): 1972, 1973, 1974, 1975, 1976, 1982, 1983

6 – Nicky English (Tipperary): 1983, 1984, 1985, 1987, 1988, 1989

6 – Joe McKenna (Limerick): 1974, 1975, 1978, 1979, 1980, 1981

5 – Jimmy Barry-Murphy (Cork): 1976, 1977, 1978, 1983, 1986

5 – Joe Cooney (Galway): 1985, 1986, 1987, 1989, 1990

5 – John Fenton (Cork): 1983, 1984, 1985, 1986, 1987

5 – Pete Finnerty (Galway): 1985, 1986, 1987, 1988, 1990

5 – Pat Hartigan (Limerick): 1971, 1972, 1973, 1974, 1975

5 – Ger Henderson (Kilkenny): 1978, 1979, 1982, 1983, 1987

5 – Joe Hennessy (Kilkenny): 1978, 1979, 1983, 1984, 1987

5 – Eddie Keher (Kilkenny): 1971, 1972, 1973, 1974, 1975

5 – Tony O'Sullivan (Cork): 1982, 1986, 1988, 1990, 1992

LEADING AWARD WINNERS (FOOTBALL)

9 – Pat Spillane (Kerry): 1976, 1977, 1978, 1979, 1980, 1981, 1984, 1985, 1986

7 – Mike Sheehy (Kerry): 1976, 1978, 1979, 1981, 1982, 1984, 1986

6 – Jack O'Shea (Kerry): 1980, 1981, 1982, 1983, 1984, 1985

6 – Ger Power (Kerry): 1975, 1976, 1978, 1979, 1980, 1986

5 – Peter Canavan (Tyrone): 1994, 1995, 1996, 2002, 2003

5 – John O'Keefe (Kerry): 1973, 1975, 1976, 1978, 1979

5 – John O'Leary (Dublin): 1984, 1985, 1993, 1994, 1995

5 – Páidí Ó Sé (Kerry): 1981, 1982, 1983, 1984, 1985

4 – John Egan (Kerry): 1975, 1977, 1978, 1982

4 – Eoin Liston (Kerry): 1980, 1981, 1982, 1984

4 – Tommy Drumm (Dublin): 1977, 1978, 1979, 1983

4 – Paddy Cullen (Dublin): 1974, 1976, 1977, 1979

4 – Robbie Kelleher (Dublin): 1974, 1975, 1977, 1978

4 – Tommy Dowd (Meath): 1991, 1994, 1995, 1996

4 – Martin O'Connell (Meath): 1988, 1990, 1991, 1996

4 – Anthony Tohill (Derry): 1992, 1993, 1995, 2000

4 – Tony Scullion (Derry): 1987, 1992, 1993, 1995

DUAL ALL STARS

Jimmy Barry-Murphy (Cork): Football (1973, 1974, right full forward); Hurling (1976, left half forward; 1977, centre half forward; 1978, right half forward; 1983, 1986, full forward); Total: 7

Ray Cummins (Cork): Football (1971, centre half forward; 1973, full forward); Hurling (1971, 1972, 1977, full forward); Total: 5

Brian Murphy (Cork): Football (1973, 1976, left full back); Hurling (1979, 1981, right full back); Total: 4

Liam Currams (Offaly): Hurling (1981, midfield); Football (1982, left half back); Total: 2

PROVINCIAL ALL STAR TOTALS (1971–2003)

Football		Hurling		Combined Totals	
Leinster	168	Munster	232	Munster	374
Munster	142	Leinster	192	Leinster	360
Ulster	108	Connacht	65	Connacht	142
Connacht	77	Ulster	6	Ulster	114

A total of 25 counties have won football All Star awards, while 14 have won hurling awards. Only Carlow, Longford and Louth have failed to win an award in either code. Period: 1971–2003.

COUNTY ALL STAR TOTALS (1971–2003)

Football		Hurling		Combined Totals	
Kerry	89	Kilkenny	116	Cork	134
Dublin	72	Cork	84	Kilkenny	116
Cork	50	Galway	65	Galway	102
Meath	48	Tipperary	59	Kerry	89
Galway	37	Offaly	42	Dublin	74
Offaly	30	Limerick	41	Offaly	72
Derry	24	Clare	39	Tipperary	61
Tyrone	22	Wexford	30	Meath	48
Mayo	20	Waterford	9	Limerick	41
Armagh	19	Antrim	5	Clare	40
Down	19	Dublin	2	Wexford	30
Roscommon	15	Down	1	Derry	24
Donegal	14	Laois	1	Tyrone	22
Kildare	11	Westmeath	1	Down	20
Monaghan	6	Armagh	0	Mayo	20
Laois	5	Donegal	0	Armagh	19
Sligo	3	Tyrone	0	Roscommon	15
Cavan	2	Fermanagh	0	Donegal	14
Leitrim	2	Derry	0	Kildare	11
Tipperary	2	Cavan	0	Waterford	9
Antrim	1	Monaghan	0	Antrim	6
Fermanagh	1	Mayo	0	Laois	6
Clare	1	Roscommon	0	Monaghan	6
Westmeath	1	Sligo	0	Sligo	3
Wicklow	1	Leitrim	0	Cavan	2
Carlow	0	Carlow	0	Leitrim	2
Limerick	0	Kerry	0	Westmeath	2
Longford	0	Longford	0	Fermanagh	1
Louth	0	Louth	0	Wicklow	1
Waterford	0	Kildare	0	Carlow	0
Wexford	0	Wicklow	0	Longford	0
Kilkenny	0	Meath	0	Louth	0

ALL STAR FOOTBALL TEAMS (1971–2003)

1971

P.J. Smyth
(Galway)

Johnny Carey	Jack Cosgrove	Donie O'Sullivan
(Mayo)	(Galway)	(Kerry)

Eugene Mulligan	Nicholas Clavin	Pat Reynolds
(Offaly)	(Offaly)	(Meath)

Liam Sammon   Willie Bryan
(Galway)   (Offaly)

Tony McTague	Ray Cummins	Mickey Kearins
(Offaly)	(Cork)	(Sligo)

Andy McCallin	Seán O'Neill	Séamus Leydon
(Antrim)	(Down)	(Galway)

Nine counties were represented on the inaugural team. It was a spread that would not continue over the years.

Offaly (4), Galway (4), Antrim (1), Cork (1), Down (1), Kerry (1), Mayo (1), Meath (1), Sligo (1)

1972

Martin Furlong
(Offaly)

Mick Ryan	Paddy McCormack	Donie O'Sullivan
(Offaly)	(Offaly)	(Kerry)

Brian McEniff	T.J. Gilmore	Kevin Jer O'Sullivan
(Donegal)	(Galway)	(Cork)

Willie Bryan   Mick O'Connell
(Offaly)   (Kerry)

Johnny Cooney	Kevin Kilmurray	Tony McTague
(Offaly)	(Offaly)	(Offaly)

Mickey Freyne	Seán O'Neill	Paddy Moriarty
(Roscommon)	(Down)	(Armagh)

The legendary Mick O'Connell won an award after making his last appearance in an All-Ireland final.

Offaly (7), Kerry (2), Armagh (1), Cork (1), Donegal (1), Down (1), Galway (1), Roscommon (1)

1973

Billy Morgan
(Cork)

Frank Cogan	Mick Ryan	Brian Murphy
(Cork)	(Offaly)	(Cork)

Liam O'Neill	T.J. Gilmore	Kevin Jer O'Sullivan
(Galway)	(Galway)	(Cork)

John O'Keeffe   Denis Long
(Kerry)   (Cork)

Johnny Cooney	Kevin Kilmurray	Liam Sammon
(Offaly)	(Offaly)	(Galway)

Jimmy Barry-Murphy	Ray Cummins	Anthony McGurk
(Cork)	(Cork)	(Derry)

John O'Keeffe, who would later win four awards at full back in 1975, 1976, 1978 and 1979, picked up his first All Star at midfield.

Cork (7), Galway (3), Offaly (3), Derry (1), Kerry (1)

1974

Paddy Cullen
(Dublin)

Donal Monaghan	Seán Doherty	Robbie Kelleher
(Donegal)	(Dublin)	(Dublin)

Paddy Reilly	Barnes Murphy	Johnny Hughes
(Dublin)	(Sligo)	(Galway)

Dermot Earley   Paudie Lynch
(Roscommon)   (Kerry)

Tom Naughton	Declan Barron	David Hickey
(Galway)	(Cork)	(Dublin)

Jimmy Barry-Murphy	Jimmy Keaveney	John Tobin
(Cork)	(Dublin)	(Galway)

Dermot Earley became the first Roscommon man to win an All Star.

Dublin (6), Galway (3), Cork (2), Donegal (1), Kerry (1), Roscommon (1), Sligo (1)

1975

Paudie O'Mahony
(Kerry)

Gay O'Driscoll	John O'Keeffe	Robbie Kelleher
(Dublin)	(Kerry)	(Dublin)

Peter Stevenson	Anthony McGurk	Ger Power
(Derry)	(Derry)	(Kerry)

Denis Long   Colm McAlarney
(Cork)   (Down)

Gerry McElhinney	Ken Rennicks	Mickey O'Sullivan
(Derry)	(Meath)	(Kerry)

John Egan	Mattie Kerrigan	Anton O'Toole
(Kerry)	(Meath)	(Dublin)

Anthony McGurk, chosen at left full forward two years earlier, became the first to win an award as a forward and a defender.

Kerry (5), Derry (3), Dublin (3), Meath (2), Cork (1), Down (1)

1976

Paddy Cullen
(Dublin)

Ger O'Keeffe	John O'Keeffe	Brian Murphy
(Kerry)	(Kerry)	(Cork)

Johnny Hughes	Kevin Moran	Ger Power
(Galway)	(Dublin)	(Kerry)

Brian Mullins   Dave McCarthy
(Dublin)   (Cork)

Anton O'Toole	Tony Hanahoe	David Hickey
(Dublin)	(Dublin)	(Dublin)

Bobby Doyle	Mike Sheehy	Pat Spillane
(Dublin)	(Kerry)	(Kerry)

Pat Spillane won the first of his nine awards on a Dublin-dominated selection that included Kevin Moran, who went on to become a soccer star with Manchester United and the Republic of Ireland.

Dublin (7), Kerry (5), Cork (2), Galway (1)

1977

Paddy Cullen
(Dublin)

Gay O'Driscoll	Pat Lindsay	Robbie Kelleher
(Dublin)	(Roscommon)	(Dublin)

Tommy Drumm	Paddy Moriarty	Pat O'Neill
(Dublin)	(Armagh)	(Dublin)

Brian Mullins   Joe Kernan
(Dublin)   (Armagh)

Anton O'Toole	Jimmy Smyth	Pat Spillane
(Dublin)	(Armagh)	(Kerry)

Bobby Doyle	Jimmy Keaveney	John Egan
(Dublin)	(Dublin)	(Kerry)

Paddy Moriarty followed Anthony McGurk's versatile example by winning an award in defence, having been chosen in attack five years earlier. Dublin won nine awards, the highest number by any county up to then.

Dublin (9), Armagh (3), Kerry (2), Roscommon (1)

1978

Ollie Crinnigan
(Kildare)

Harry Keegan	John O'Keeffe	Robbie Kelleher
(Roscommon)	(Kerry)	(Dublin)

Tommy Drumm	Ollie Brady	Paudie Lynch
(Dublin)	(Cavan)	(Kerry)

Colm McAlarney   Tomás Connor
(Down)   (Offaly)

Ger Power	Declan Barron	Pat Spillane
(Kerry)	(Cork)	(Kerry)

Mike Sheehy	Jimmy Keaveney	John Egan
(Kerry)	(Dublin)	(Kerry)

Ollie Crinnigan became the first Kildare All Star, while Ollie Brady brought similar honour to Cavan.

Kerry (6), Dublin (3), Cavan (1), Cork (1), Down (1), Kildare (1), Offaly (1), Roscommon (1)

1979

Paddy Cullen
(Dublin)

'Nudie' Hughes	John O'Keeffe	Tom Heneghan
(Monaghan)	(Kerry)	(Roscommon)
Tommy Drumm	Tim Kennelly	Danny Murray
(Dublin)	(Kerry)	(Roscommon)

Dermot Earley   Bernard Brogan
(Roscommon)   (Dublin)

Ger Power	Seán Walsh	Pat Spillane
(Kerry)	(Kerry)	(Kerry)
Mike Sheehy	Seán Lowry	Joe McGrath
(Kerry)	(Offaly)	(Mayo)

Eugene 'Nudie' Hughes became the first Monaghan All Star; Seán Lowry was chosen at full forward and would win a second award at centre back three years later.

Kerry (6), Dublin (3), Roscommon (3), Mayo (1), Monaghan (1), Offaly (1)

1980

Charlie Nelligan
(Kerry)

Harry Keegan	Kevin Kehilly	Gerry Connellan
(Roscommon)	(Cork)	(Roscommon)
Kevin McCabe	Tim Kennelly	Danny Murray
(Tyrone)	(Kerry)	(Roscommon)

Jack O'Shea   Colm McKinstry
(Kerry)   (Armagh)

Ger Power	Dinny Allen	Pat Spillane
(Kerry)	(Cork)	(Kerry)
Matt Connor	Eoin Liston	John Egan
(Offaly)	(Kerry)	(Kerry)

Jack O'Shea won the first of six successive awards at midfield; Kevin McCabe became the first Tyrone All Star.

Kerry (7), Roscommon (3), Cork (2), Armagh (1), Offaly (1), Tyrone (1)

1981

Martin Furlong
(Offaly)

| Jimmy Deenihan | Paddy Kennedy | Paudie Lynch |
| (Kerry) | (Down) | (Kerry) |

| Páidí Ó Sé | Richie Connor | Seámus McHugh |
| (Kerry) | (Offaly) | (Galway) |

Jack O'Shea   Seán Walsh
(Kerry)   (Kerry)

| Barry Brennan | 'Ogie' Moran | Pat Spillane |
| (Galway) | (Kerry) | (Kerry) |

| Mike Sheehy | Eoin Liston | Brendan Lowry |
| (Kerry) | (Kerry) | (Offaly) |

The midfield pairing was provided by the same county for the first time. Only four counties were honoured.

Kerry (9), Offaly (3), Galway (2), Down (1)

1982

Martin Furlong
(Offaly)

| Mick Fitzgerald | Liam Connor | Kevin Kehilly |
| (Offaly) | (Offaly) | (Cork) |

| Páidí Ó Sé | Seán Lowry | Liam Currams |
| (Kerry) | (Offaly) | (Offaly) |

Jack O'Shea   Pádraig Dunne
(Kerry)   (Offaly)

| Peter McGinnity | Joe Kernan | Matt Connor |
| (Fermanagh) | (Armagh) | (Offaly) |

| Mike Sheehy | Eoin Liston | John Egan |
| (Kerry) | (Kerry) | (Kerry) |

Peter McGinnity became Fermanagh's first All Star. Offaly broke Kerry's dominance, picking up seven awards after their dramatic All-Ireland success.

Offaly (7), Kerry (5), Armagh (1), Cork (1), Fermanagh (1)

1983

Martin Furlong
(Offaly)

Páidí Ó Sé	Stephen Kinneavy	John Evans
(Kerry)	(Galway)	(Cork)

Pat Canavan	Tommy Drumm	Jimmy Kerrigan
(Dublin)	(Dublin)	(Cork)

Jack O'Shea   Liam Austin
(Kerry)   (Down)

Barney Rock	Matt Connor	Greg Blaney
(Dublin)	(Offaly)	(Down)

Martin McHugh	Colm O'Rourke	Joe McNally
(Donegal)	(Meath)	(Dublin)

Dublin won four awards, which was unusually low for All-Ireland champions while runners-up Galway had just one player honoured. Eight counties won awards, the widest spread for many years.

Dublin (4), Cork (2), Down (2), Offaly (2), Kerry (2), Galway (1), Donegal (1), Meath (1)

1984

John O'Leary
(Dublin)

Páidí Ó Sé	Mick Lyons	Seámus McHugh
(Kerry)	(Meath)	(Galway)

Tommy Doyle	Tom Spillane	P.J. Buckley
(Kerry)	(Kerry)	(Dublin)

Jack O'Shea   Eugene McKenna
(Kerry)   (Tyrone)

Barney Rock	Eoin Liston	Pat Spillane
(Dublin)	(Kerry)	(Kerry)

Mike Sheehy	Frank McGuigan	Dermot McNicholl
(Kerry)	(Tyrone)	(Derry)

Dublin goalkeeper John O'Leary won the first of five awards; Dermot McNicholl became the first Derry All Star winner since 1975.

Kerry (7), Dublin (3), Tyrone (2), Derry (1), Galway (1), Meath (1)

1985

John O'Leary
(Dublin)

Páidí Ó Sé   Gerry Hargan   Mick Spillane
(Kerry)   (Dublin)   (Kerry)

Tommy Doyle   Ciarán Murray   Dermot Flanagan
(Kerry)   (Monaghan)   (Mayo)

Jack O'Shea   Willie Joe Padden
(Kerry)   (Mayo)

Barney Rock   Tommy Conroy   Pat Spillane
(Dublin)   (Dublin)   (Kerry)

Kevin McStay   Paul Earley   'Nudie' Hughes
(Mayo)   (Roscommon)   (Monaghan)

Mick Spillane joined brothers, Pat and Tom, in the All Star club; Paul Earley followed older brother, Dermot, into the exclusive club; 'Nudie' Hughes was chosen in attack six years after being honoured in defence.

Kerry (5), Dublin (4), Mayo (3), Monaghan (2), Roscommon (1)

1986

Charlie Nelligan
(Kerry)

Harry Keegan   Mick Lyons   John Lynch
(Roscommon)   (Meath)   (Tyrone)

Tommy Doyle   Tom Spillane   Colm Browne
(Kerry)   (Kerry)   (Laois)

Plunkett Donaghy   Liam Irwin
(Tyrone)   (Laois)

Ray McCarron   Eugene McKenna   Pat Spillane
(Monaghan)   (Tyrone)   (Kerry)

Mike Sheehy   Damien O'Hagan   Ger Power
(Kerry)   (Tyrone)   (Kerry)

Colm Browne and Liam Irwin became the first Laois football All Stars; Ger Power was honoured for the sixth – and last – time.

Kerry (6), Tyrone (4), Laois (2), Meath (1), Monaghan (1), Roscommon (1)

1987

John Kerins
(Cork)

Bobby O'Malley	Colman Kerrigan	Tony Scullion
(Meath)	(Cork)	(Derry)

Niall Cahalane	Tom Spillane	Ger Lynch
(Cork)	(Kerry)	(Kerry)

Gerry McEntee   Brian McGilligan
(Meath)   (Derry)

David Beggy	Larry Tompkins	Ciarán Duff
(Meath)	(Cork)	(Dublin)

Val Daly	Brian Stafford	Bernard Flynn
(Galway)	(Meath)	(Meath)

Meath's arrival on the All-Ireland podium earned them five awards for the first time while Cork won four, their highest since 1973.

Meath (5), Cork (4), Derry (2), Kerry (2), Galway (1), Dublin (1)

1988

Paddy Linden
(Monaghan)

Bobby O'Malley	Colman Corrigan	Mick Kennedy
(Meath)	(Cork)	(Dublin)

Niall Cahalane	Noel McCaffrey	Martin O'Connell
(Cork)	(Dublin)	(Meath)

Shea Fahy   Liam Hayes
(Cork)   (Meath)

Maurice Fitzgerald	Larry Tompkins	Ciarán Duff
(Kerry)	(Cork)	(Dublin)

Colm O'Rourke	Brian Stafford	'Nudie' Hughes
(Meath)	(Meath)	(Monaghan)

No representation for Connacht in a year when only five counties won awards. A third award for 'Nudie' Hughes and a first for 18-year-old Maurice Fitzgerald.

Meath (5), Cork (4), Dublin (3), Monaghan (2), Kerry (1)

1989

Gabriel Irwin
(Mayo)

Jimmy Browne	Gerry Hargan	Dermot Flanagan
(Mayo)	(Dublin)	(Mayo)

Connie Murphy	Conor Counihan	Tony Davis
(Kerry)	(Cork)	(Cork)

Teddy McCarthy   Willie Joe Padden
(Cork)   (Mayo)

Dave Barry	Larry Tompkins	Noel Durkin
(Cork)	(Cork)	(Mayo)

Paul McGrath	Eugene McKenna	Tony McManus
(Cork)	(Tyrone)	(Roscommon)

A third successive award for Larry Tompkins, one of six Cork recipients. Tony McManus ended a long wait to join the All Stars.

Cork (6), Mayo (5), Dublin (1), Kerry (1), Roscommon (1), Tyrone (1)

1990

John Kerins
(Cork)

Bobby O'Malley	Steven O'Brien	Terry Ferguson
(Meath)	(Cork)	(Meath)

Michael Slocum	Conor Counihan	Martin O'Connell
(Cork)	(Cork)	(Meath)

Shea Fahy   Mickey Quinn
(Cork)   (Leitrim)

David Beggy	Val Daly	Joyce McMullan
(Meath)	(Galway)	(Donegal)

Paul McGrath	Kevin O'Brien	James McCartan
(Cork)	(Wicklow)	(Down)

First All Star award for Wicklow and Leitrim; Kerry failed to win an award for the first time; a third award for Bobby O'Malley.

Cork (6), Meath (4), Donegal, (1), Down (1), Galway (1), Leitrim (1), Wicklow (1)

1991

Michael McQuillan
(Meath)

Mick Deegan	Conor Deegan	Enon Gavin
(Dublin)	(Down)	(Roscommon)

Tommy Carr	Keith Barr	Martin O'Connell
(Dublin)	(Dublin)	(Meath)

Barry Breen   Martin Lynch
(Down)   (Kildare)

Ross Carr	Greg Blaney	Tommy Dowd
(Down)	(Down)	(Meath)

Colm O'Rourke	Brian Stafford	Bernard Flynn
(Meath)	(Meath)	(Meath)

All-Ireland runners-up Meath won six awards, two ahead of champions Down; Martin Lynch became the first Kildare All Star since 1978.

Meath (6), Down (4), Dublin (3), Kildare (1), Roscommon (1)

1992

Gary Walsh
(Donegal)

Seámus Clancy	Matt Gallagher	Tony Scullion
(Clare)	(Donegal)	(Derry)

Paul Curran	Martin Gavigan	Eamonn Heery
(Dublin)	(Donegal)	(Dublin)

T.J. Kilgallon   Anthony Molloy
(Mayo)   (Donegal)

Anthony Tohill	Martin McHugh	James McHugh
(Derry)	(Donegal)	(Donegal)

Tony Boyle	Vinny Murphy	Enda Gormley
(Donegal)	(Dublin)	(Derry)

Donegal's first All-Ireland win helped them win seven All Stars, including two for the McHugh brothers; Séamus Clancy became Clare's first football All Star.

Donegal (7), Dublin (3), Derry (3), Clare (1), Mayo (1)

1993

John O'Leary
(Dublin)

J.J. Doherty   Dermot Deasy   Tony Scullion
(Donegal)   (Dublin)   (Derry)

Johnny McGurk   Henry Downey   Gary Coleman
(Derry)   (Derry)   (Derry)

Anthony Tohill   Brian McGilligan
(Derry)   (Derry)

Kevin O'Neill   Joe Kavanagh   Charlie Redmond
(Mayo)   (Cork)   (Dublin)

Colin Corkery   Ger Houlahan   Enda Gormley
(Cork)   (Armagh)   (Derry)

Mayo's Kevin O'Neill followed in the All Star footsteps of his father, Liam, who won an award as a Galway wing-back in 1973. Derry celebrated their first All-Ireland success with seven awards, including all positions from No.4 to No.9.

Derry (7), Dublin (3), Cork (2), Armagh (1), Donegal (1), Mayo (1)

1994

John O'Leary
(Dublin)

Michael Magill   Seámus Quinn   Paul Higgins
(Down)   (Leitrim)   (Down)

Graham Geraghty   Steven O'Brien   D.J. Kane
(Meath)   (Cork)   (Down)

Jack Sheedy   Gregory McCartan
(Dublin)   (Down)

Peter Canavan   Greg Blaney   James McCartan
(Tyrone)   (Down)   (Down)

Mickey Linden   Tommy Dowd   Charlie Redmond
(Down)   (Meath)   (Dublin)

A first All Star award for Peter Canavan; Séamus Quinn won Leitrim's second award; Down took seven awards, their highest ever total.

Down (7), Dublin (3), Meath (2), Cork (1), Leitrim (1), Tyrone (1)

1995

John O'Leary
(Dublin)

Tony Scullion	Mark O'Connor	Fay Devlin
(Derry)	(Cork)	(Tyrone)

Paul Curran	Keith Barr	Steven O'Brien
(Dublin)	(Dublin)	(Cork)

Brian Stynes   Anthony Tohill
(Dublin)   (Derry)

Jarlath Fallon	Dessie Farrell	Paul Clarke
(Galway)	(Dublin)	(Dublin)

Tommy Dowd	Peter Canavan	Charlie Redmond
(Meath)	(Tyrone)	(Dublin)

Third successive award for both John O'Leary and Charlie Redmond; Jarlath Fallon won Galway's first award for five years.

Dublin (7), Cork (2), Derry (2), Tyrone (2), Galway (1), Meath (1)

1996

Finbarr McConnell
(Tyrone)

Kenneth Mortimer	Darren Fay	Martin O'Connell
(Mayo)	(Meath)	(Meath)

Pat Holmes	James Nallen	Paul Curran
(Mayo)	(Mayo)	(Dublin)

Liam McHale   John McDermott
(Mayo)   (Meath)

Trevor Giles	Tommy Dowd	James Horan
(Meath)	(Meath)	(Mayo)

Joe Brolly	Peter Canavan	Maurice Fitzgerald
(Derry)	(Tyrone)	(Kerry)

A fourth award for Martin O'Connell; Maurice Fitzgerald won his second award, eight years after taking his first; Peter Canavan made it three-in-a-row.

Meath (5), Mayo (5), Tyrone (2), Derry (1), Dublin (1), Kerry (1)

1997

Declan O'Keeffe
(Kerry)

Kenneth Mortimer	Davy Dalton	Cathal Daly
(Mayo)	(Kildare)	(Offaly)

Séamus Moynihan	Glenn Ryan	Eamonn Breen
(Kerry)	(Kildare)	(Kerry)

Pat Fallon   Niall Buckley
(Mayo)   (Kildare)

Pa Laide	Trevor Giles	Dermot McCabe
(Kerry)	(Meath)	(Cavan)

Joe Brolly	Brendan Reilly	Maurice Fitzgerald
(Derry)	(Meath)	(Kerry)

Dermot McCabe won Cavan's first award since 1978; Cathal Daly became Offaly's first recipient since 1983; Kildare won three awards for the first time.
Kerry (5), Kildare (3), Mayo (2), Meath (2), Cavan (1), Derry (1), Offaly (1)

1998

Martin McNamara
(Galway)

Brian Lacey	Seán Marty Lockhart	Tomás Mannion
(Kildare)	(Derry)	(Galway)

John Finn	Glenn Ryan	Seán Óg de Paor
(Kildare)	(Kildare)	(Galway)

Kevin Walsh   John McDermott
(Galway)   (Meath)

Michael Donnellan	Jarlath Fallon	Dermot Earley
(Galway)	(Galway)	(Kildare)

Karl O'Dwyer	Pádraic Joyce	Declan Browne
(Kildare)	(Galway)	(Tipperary)

Dermot Earley followed in the footsteps of his father, Dermot Snr (1974–79) and his uncle, Paul (1985), by winning an All Star; Declan Browne became Tipperary's first football recipient.
Galway (7), Kildare (5), Derry (1), Meath (1), Tipperary (1)

1999

Kevin O'Dwyer
(Cork)

| Mark O'Reilly | Darren Fay | Anthony Lynch |
| (Meath) | (Meath) | (Cork) |

Ciarán O'Sullivan
(Cork)

Kieran McGeeney
(Armagh)

Paddy Reynolds
(Meath)

John McDermott   Ciarán Whelan
(Meath)   (Dublin)

| Diarmaid Marsden | Trevor Giles | James Horan |
| (Armagh) | (Meath) | (Mayo) |

| Philip Clifford | Graham Geraghty | Ollie Murphy |
| (Cork) | (Meath) | (Meath) |

Meath's All-Ireland win earned them seven awards, their highest to date; Paddy Reynolds was chosen at left half-back, 28 years after his father Pat had been honoured in the same position.

Meath (7), Cork (4), Armagh (2), Dublin (1), Mayo (1)

2000

Declan O'Keeffe
(Kerry)

| Kieran McKeever | Séamus Moynihan | Michael McCarthy |
| (Derry) | (Kerry) | (Kerry) |

| Declan Meehan | Kieran McGeeney | Anthony Rainbow |
| (Galway) | (Armagh) | (Kildare) |

Anthony Tohill   Darragh O Sé
(Derry)   (Kerry)

| Michael Donnellan | Liam Hassett | Oisín McConville |
| (Galway) | (Kerry) | (Armagh) |

| Mike Frank Russell | Pádraic Joyce | Derek Savage |
| (Kerry) | (Galway) | (Galway) |

A fourth and final award for Anthony Tohill, eight years after winning his first.

Kerry (6), Galway (4), Armagh (2), Derry (2), Kildare (1)

2001

Cormac Sullivan
(Meath)

Kieran Fitzgerald	Darren Fay	Coman Goggins
(Galway)	(Meath)	(Dublin)

Declan Meehan	Francie Grehan	Seán Óg de Paor
(Galway)	(Roscommon)	(Galway)

Rory O'Connell   Kevin Walsh
(Westmeath)   (Galway)

Evan Kelly	Stephen O'Neill	Michael Donnellan
(Meath)	(Tyrone)	(Galway)

Ollie Murphy	Pádraic Joyce	John Crowley
(Meath)	(Galway)	(Kerry)

Rory O'Connell became Westmeath's first football All Star; Francie Grehan ended Roscommon's ten-year wait.

Galway (6), Meath (4), Dublin (1), Kerry (1), Roscommon (1), Tyrone (1), Westmeath (1)

2002

Stephen Cluxton
(Dublin)

Enda McNulty	Paddy Christie	Anthony Lynch
(Armagh)	(Dublin)	(Cork)

Aidan O'Rourke	Kieran McGeeney	Kevin Cassidy
(Armagh)	(Armagh)	(Donegal)

Darragh O Sé   Paul McGrane
(Kerry)   (Armagh)

Steven McDonnell	Eamonn O'Hara	Oisín McConville
(Armagh)	(Sligo)	(Armagh)

Peter Canavan	Ray Cosgrove	Colm Cooper
(Tyrone)	(Dublin)	(Kerry)

Armagh's first All-Ireland triumph earned them six awards; Eamonn O'Hara won Sligo's first award for 28 years.

Armagh (6), Dublin (3), Kerry (2), Cork (1), Donegal (1), Sligo (1), Tyrone (1)

2003

Fergal Byron
(Laois)

Francie Bellew	Cormac McAnallen	Joe Higgins
(Armagh)	(Tyrone)	(Laois)
Conor Gormley	Tom Kelly	Philip Jordan
(Tyrone)	(Laois)	(Tyrone)

Seán Cavanagh   Kevin Walsh
(Tyrone)   (Galway)

Brian Dooher	Brian McGuigan	Declan Browne
(Tyrone)	(Tyrone)	(Tipperary)
Steven McDonnell	Peter Canavan	Adrian Sweeney
(Armagh)	(Tyrone)	(Donegal)

Tyrone's first All-Ireland senior title helped them to the upper range of All Star representation with seven awards; Laois won three awards for the first time.

Tyrone (7), Laois (3), Armagh (2), Galway (1), Donegal (1), Tipperary (1)

ALL STAR HURLING TEAMS (1971–2003)

1971

Damien Martin
(Offaly)

Tony Maher	Pat Hartigan	Jim Treacy
(Cork)	(Limerick)	(Kilkenny)
Tadhg O'Connor	Mick Roche	Martin Coogan
(Tipperary)	(Tipperary)	(Kilkenny)

Frank Cummins   John Connolly
(Kilkenny)   (Galway)

Francis Loughnane	Michael 'Babs' Keating	Eddie Keher
(Tipperary)	(Tipperary)	(Kilkenny)
Mick Bermingham	Ray Cummins	Eamon Cregan
(Dublin)	(Cork)	(Limerick)

Seven counties from three provinces were represented on the inaugural All Star hurling team, led by All-Ireland finalists Tipperary and Kilkenny, who had four each.

Kilkenny (4), Tipperary (4), Cork (2), Limerick (2), Dublin (1), Galway (1), Offaly (1)

1972

Noel Skehan
(Kilkenny)

Tony Maher	Pat Hartigan	Jim Treacy
(Cork)	(Limerick)	(Kilkenny)

Pat Lawlor	Mick Jacob	Con Roche
(Kilkenny)	(Wexford)	(Cork)

Frank Cummins   Denis Coughlan
(Kilkenny)   (Cork)

Francis Loughnane	Pat Delaney	Eddie Keher
(Tipperary)	(Kilkenny)	(Kilkenny)

Charlie McCarthy	Ray Cummins	Eamon Cregan
(Cork)	(Cork)	(Limerick)

Kilkenny and Cork dominated the selection after their epic All-Ireland final clash; Mick Jacob became the first Wexford All Star; Noel Skehan won the first of seven awards.

Kilkenny (6), Cork (5), Limerick (2), Tipperary (1), Wexford (1)

1973

Noel Skehan
(Kilkenny)

Phil 'Fan' Larkin	Pat Hartigan	Jim O'Brien
(Kilkenny)	(Limerick)	(Limerick)

Colm Doran	Pat Henderson	Seán Foley
(Wexford)	(Kilkenny)	(Limerick)

Richie Bennis   Liam O'Brien
(Limerick)   (Kilkenny)

Francis Loughnane	Pat Delaney	Eamon Grimes
(Tipperary)	(Kilkenny)	(Limerick)

Martin Quigley	Kieran Purcell	Eddie Keher
(Wexford)	(Kilkenny)	(Kilkenny)

Limerick won the All-Ireland title for the first time since 1940, helping them to five awards, but they were still two behind beaten finalists, Kilkenny. Only four counties were represented.

Kilkenny (7), Limerick (5), Wexford (2), Tipperary (1)

1974

Noel Skehan
(Kilkenny)

Phil 'Fan' Larkin	Pat Hartigan	John Horgan
(Kilkenny)	(Limerick)	(Cork)
Ger Loughnane	Pat Henderson	Con Roche
(Clare)	(Kilkenny)	(Cork)

Liam O'Brien   John Galvin
(Kilkenny)   (Waterford)

Joe McKenna	Martin Quigley	Mick Crotty
(Limerick)	(Wexford)	(Kilkenny)
John Quigley	Kieran Purcell	Eddie Keher
(Wexford)	(Kilkenny)	(Kilkenny)

Ger Loughnane became Clare's first All Star; John Galvin earned a similar honour for Waterford; Kilkenny picked up seven more awards.

Kilkenny (7), Cork (2), Limerick (2), Wexford (2), Clare (1), Waterford (1)

1975

Noel Skehan
(Kilkenny)

Niall McInerney	Pat Hartigan	Brian Cody
(Galway)	(Limerick)	(Kilkenny)
Tadhg O'Connor	Seán Silke	Iggy Clarke
(Tipperary)	(Galway)	(Galway)

Liam O'Brien   Gerald McCarthy
(Kilkenny)   (Cork)

Martin Quigley	Joe McKenna	Eamon Grimes
(Wexford)	(Limerick)	(Limerick)
Mick Brennan	Kieran Purcell	Eddie Keher
(Kilkenny)	(Kilkenny)	(Kilkenny)

Pat Hartigan clinched his fifth successive award at full back; Galway's return as a major force earned them three awards.

Kilkenny (6), Galway (3), Limerick (3), Cork (1), Tipperary (1), Wexford (1)

1976

Noel Skehan
(Kilkenny)

Phil 'Fan' Larkin
(Kilkenny)

Willie Murphy
(Wexford)

Johnny McMahon
(Clare)

Joe McDonagh
(Galway)

Mick Jacob
(Wexford)

Denis Coughlan
(Cork)

Frank Burke
(Galway)

Pat Moylan
(Cork)

Mick Malone
(Cork)

Martin Quigley
(Wexford)

Jimmy Barry-Murphy
(Cork)

Mick Brennan
(Kilkenny)

Tony Doran
(Wexford)

Seán O'Leary
(Cork)

Jimmy Barry-Murphy became a dual All Star, having won two previous football awards in 1973 and 1974.

Cork (5), Wexford (4), Kilkenny (3), Galway (2), Clare (1)

1977

Séamus Durack
(Clare)

Johnny McMahon
(Clare)

Martin O'Doherty
(Cork)

John Horgan
(Cork)

Ger Loughnane
(Clare)

Mick Jacob
(Wexford)

Denis Coughlan
(Cork)

Tom Cashman
(Cork)

Mick Moroney
(Clare)

Christy Keogh
(Wexford)

Jimmy Barry-Murphy
(Cork)

P.J. Molloy
(Galway)

Charlie McCarthy
(Cork)

Ray Cummins
(Cork)

Seán O'Leary
(Cork)

Cork became the first county to win eight awards, six more than Wexford, whom they beat in the All-Ireland final. Clare won four awards for the first time.

Cork (8), Clare (4), Wexford (2), Galway (1)

1978

Séamus Durack
(Clare)

Phil 'Fan' Larkin	Martin O'Doherty	John Horgan
(Kilkenny)	(Cork)	(Cork)
Joe Hennessy	Ger Henderson	Denis Coughlan
(Kilkenny)	(Kilkenny)	(Cork)

Tom Cashman   Iggy Clarke
(Cork)   (Galway)

Jimmy Barry-Murphy	Noel Casey	Colm Honan
(Cork)	(Clare)	(Clare)
Charlie McCarthy	Joe McKenna	Tommy Butler
(Cork)	(Limerick)	(Tipperary)

A fourth award for 'Fan' Larkin; Cork's All-Ireland three-in-a-row helped them to six awards.

Cork (6), Clare (3), Kilkenny (3), Galway (1), Limerick (1), Tipperary (1)

1979

Pat McLoughney
(Tipperary)

Brian Murphy	Martin O'Doherty	Tadhg O'Connor
(Cork)	(Cork)	(Tipperary)
Dermot McCurtain	Ger Henderson	Iggy Clarke
(Cork)	(Kilkenny)	(Galway)

John Connolly   Joe Hennessy
(Galway)   (Kilkenny)

Johnny Callinan	Frank Burke	Liam O'Brien
(Clare)	(Galway)	(Kilkenny)
Mick Brennan	Joe McKenna	Ned Buggy
(Kilkenny)	(Limerick)	(Wexford)

John Connolly won his second award, eight years after taking his first; seven counties were represented, which was higher than usual.

Kilkenny (4), Cork (3), Galway (3), Tipperary (2), Clare (1), Limerick (1), Wexford (1)

1980

Pat McLoughney
(Tipperary)

Niall McInerney	Leonard Enright	Jimmy Cooney
(Galway)	(Limerick)	(Galway)
Dermot McCurtain	Seán Silke	Iggy Clarke
(Cork)	(Galway)	(Galway)

Joachim Kelly   Mossy Walsh
(Offaly)   (Waterford)

Joe Connolly	Pat Horgan	Pat Carroll
(Galway)	(Cork)	(Offaly)
Bernie Forde	Joe McKenna	Eamon Cregan
(Galway)	(Limerick)	(Limerick)

Galway's first All-Ireland title since 1923 earned them six awards; Pat McLoughney became the third goalkeeper to win more than one award; Mossy Walsh earned Waterford's second award.

Galway (6), Limerick (3), Cork (2), Offaly (2), Tipperary (1), Waterford (1)

1981

Séamus Durack
(Clare)

Brian Murphy	Leonard Enright	Jimmy Cooney
(Cork)	(Limerick)	(Galway)
Liam O'Donoghue	Seán Stack	Ger Coughlan
(Limerick)	(Clare)	(Offaly)

Steve Mahon   Liam Currams
(Galway)   (Offaly)

Johnny Callinan	George O'Connor	Mark Corrigan
(Clare)	(Wexford)	(Offaly)
Pat Carroll	Joe McKenna	Johnny Flaherty
(Offaly)	(Limerick)	(Offaly)

Offaly celebrated their first All-Ireland win with five awards, including three forwards; Joe McKenna won his sixth award, four at full forward, one at centre forward, one at right half-forward.

Offaly (5), Clare (3), Limerick (3), Galway (2), Cork (1), Wexford (1)

1982

Noel Skehan
(Kilkenny)

John Galvin	Brian Cody	Pat Fleury
(Waterford)	(Kilkenny)	(Offaly)

Aidan Fogarty	Ger Henderson	Paddy Prendergast
(Offaly)	(Kilkenny)	(Kilkenny)

Tim Crowley	Frank Cummins
(Cork)	(Kilkenny)

Tony O'Sullivan	Pat Horgan	Richie Power
(Cork)	(Cork)	(Kilkenny)

Billy Fitzpatrick	Christy Heffernan	Jim Greene
(Kilkenny)	(Kilkenny)	(Waterford)

Kilkenny were represented in every line, taking eight awards after winning the League-Championship double. Waterford won two awards for the first time.

Kilkenny (8), Cork (3), Offaly (2), Waterford (2)

1983

Noel Skehan
(Kilkenny)

John Henderson	Leonard Enright	Dick O'Hara
(Kilkenny)	(Limerick)	(Kilkenny)

Joe Hennessy	Ger Henderson	Tom Cashman
(Kilkenny)	(Kilkenny)	(Cork)

Frank Cummins	John Fenton
(Kilkenny)	(Cork)

Nicky English	Ger Fennelly	Noel Lane
(Tipperary)	(Kilkenny)	(Galway)

Billy Fitzpatrick	Jimmy Barry-Murphy	Liam Fennelly
(Kilkenny)	(Cork)	(Kilkenny)

Kilkenny become the first county to win nine awards, including a seventh for Noel Skehan, 11 years after winning his first. John Henderson joined brothers, Pat and Ger, as All Stars; Nicky English won the first of his six awards.

Kilkenny (9), Cork (3), Galway (1), Limerick (1), Tipperary (1)

1984

Ger Cunningham
(Cork)

Paudie Fitzmaurice	Eugene Coughlan	Pat Fleury
(Limerick)	(Offaly)	(Offaly)

Joe Hennessy	John Crowley	Dermot McCurtain
(Kilkenny)	(Cork)	(Cork)

John Fenton   Joachim Kelly
(Cork)   (Offaly)

Nicky English	Kieran Brennan	Paddy Kelly
(Tipperary)	(Kilkenny)	(Limerick)

Tomas Mulcahy	Noel Lane	Seán O'Leary
(Cork)	(Galway)	(Cork)

Cork celebrated the GAA's Centenary year with six awards; Ger Cunningham won the first of his four awards.

Cork (6), Offaly (3), Kilkenny (2), Limerick (2), Galway (1), Tipperary (1)

1985

Ger Cunningham
(Cork)

Séamus Coen	Eugene Coughlan	Sylvie Linnane
(Galway)	(Offaly)	(Galway)

Pete Finnerty	Pat Delaney	Ger Coughlan
(Galway)	(Offaly)	(Offaly)

Pat Critchley   John Fenton
(Laois)   (Cork)

Nicky English	Brendan Lynskey	Joe Cooney
(Tipperary)	(Galway)	(Galway)

Pat Cleary	Pádraig Horan	Liam Fennelly
(Offaly)	(Offaly)	(Kilkenny)

Pat Critchley became the first Laois All Star; Pete Finnerty and Joe Cooney each won the first of their five awards.

Galway (5), Offaly (5), Cork (2), Kilkenny (1), Laois (1), Tipperary (1)

1986

Ger Cunningham
(Cork)

Denis Mulcahy	Conor Hayes	Sylvie Linnane
(Cork)	(Galway)	(Galway)

Pete Finnerty	Tony Keady	Bobby Ryan
(Galway)	(Galway)	(Tipperary)

Richie Power   John Fenton
(Kilkenny)   (Cork)

Tony O'Sullivan	Tomás Mulcahy	Joe Cooney
(Cork)	(Cork)	(Galway)

David Kilcoyne	Jimmy Barry-Murphy	Kevin Hennessy
(Westmeath)	(Cork)	(Cork)

David Kilcoyne became Westmeath's first All Star; Galway filled four of the six defensive positions; All-Ireland champions Cork took four of the forward positions.

Cork (7), Galway (5), Kilkenny (1), Tipperary (1), Westmeath (1)

1987

Ken Hogan
(Tipperary)

Joe Hennessy	Conor Hayes	Ollie Kilkenny
(Kilkenny)	(Galway)	(Galway)

Pete Finnerty	Ger Henderson	John Conran
(Galway)	(Kilkenny)	(Wexford)

Steve Mahon   John Fenton
(Galway)   (Cork)

Michael McGrath	Joe Cooney	Aidan Ryan
(Galway)	(Galway)	(Tipperary)

Pat Fox	Nicky English	Liam Fennelly
(Tipperary)	(Tipperary)	(Kilkenny)

Joe Hennessy won his fifth award, this time at corner-back, having won three others at right half-back and one at midfield; Galway take six awards, their highest up to then.

Galway (6), Tipperary (4), Kilkenny (3), Cork (1), Wexford (1)

1988

John Commins
(Galway)

Sylvie Linnane	Conor Hayes	Martin Hanamy
(Galway)	(Galway)	(Offaly)
Pete Finnerty	Tony Keady	Bobby Ryan
(Galway)	(Galway)	(Tipperary)

Colm Bonnar   George O'Connor
(Tipperary)   (Wexford)

Declan Ryan	Ciarán Barr	Martin Naughton
(Tipperary)	(Antrim)	(Galway)
Michael McGrath	Nicky English	Tony O'Sullivan
(Galway)	(Tipperary)	(Cork)

Ciarán Barr became the first Ulster player to win a hurling All Star; Conor Hayes won a third successive award at full back; George O'Connor won a second award, seven years after winning his first.

Galway (7), Tipperary (4), Antrim (1), Cork (1), Offaly (1), Wexford (1)

1989

John Commins
(Galway)

Aidan Fogarty	Eamonn Cleary	Des Donnelly
(Offaly)	(Wexford)	(Antrim)
Conal Bonnar	Bobby Ryan	Seán Treacy
(Tipperary)	(Tipperary)	(Galway)

Michael Coleman   Declan Carr
(Galway)   (Tipperary)

Eanna Ryan	Joe Cooney	Olcan McFetridge
(Galway)	(Galway)	(Antrim)
Pat Fox	Cormac Bonnar	Nicky English
(Tipperary)	(Tipperary)	(Tipperary)

Conal and Cormac Bonnar were selected a year after their brother Colm was honoured; Des Donnelly and Olcan McFetridge made it Antrim's best ever All Star year; Nicky English won his sixth award.

Tipperary (6), Galway (5), Antrim (2), Offaly (1), Wexford (1)

1990

Ger Cunningham
(Cork)

John Considine   Noel Sheehy   Seán O'Gorman
(Cork)   (Tipperary)   (Cork)

Pete Finnerty   Jim Cashman   Liam Dunne
(Galway)   (Cork)   (Wexford)

Michael Coleman   Johnny Pilkington
(Galway)   (Offaly)

Michael Cleary   Joe Cooney   Tony O'Sullivan
(Tipperary)   (Galway)   (Cork)

Eamon Morrissey   Brian McMahon   John Fitzgibbon
(Kilkenny)   (Dublin)   (Cork)

Brian McMahon won Dublin's first award since the All Star's inaugural year in 1971; Pete Finnerty and Joe Cooney won their fifth awards in six seasons.
Cork (6), Galway (3), Tipperary (2), Dublin (1), Kilkenny (1), Offaly (1), Wexford (1)

1991

Michael Walsh
(Kilkenny)

Paul Delaney   Noel Sheehy   Seán Treacy
(Tipperary)   (Tipperary)   (Galway)

Conal Bonnar   Jim Cashman   Cathal Casey
(Tipperary)   (Cork)   (Cork)

Terence McNaughton   John Leahy
(Antrim)   (Tipperary)

Michael Cleary   Gary Kirby   D.J. Carey
(Tipperary)   (Limerick)   (Kilkenny)

Pat Fox   Cormac Bonnar   John Fitzgibbon
(Tipperary)   (Tipperary)   (Cork)

D.J. Carey won his first award; Tipperary picked up seven awards; Gary Kirby won Limerick's first award since 1984.
Tipperary (7), Cork (3), Kilkenny (2), Antrim (1), Galway (1), Limerick (1)

1992

Tommy Quaid
(Limerick)

Brian Corcoran	Pat Dwyer	Liam Simpson
(Cork)	(Kilkenny)	(Kilkenny)
Brian Whelahan	Ciarán Carey	Willie O'Connor
(Offaly)	(Limerick)	(Kilkenny)

Michael Phelan   Seánie McCarthy
(Kilkenny)   (Cork)

Gerard McGrattan	John Power	Tony O'Sullivan
(Down)	(Kilkenny)	(Cork)
Michael Cleary	Liam Fennelly	D.J. Carey
(Tipperary)	(Kilkenny)	(Kilkenny)

Gerard McGrattan won Down's first hurling All Star; Liam Fennelly won his fourth award, nine years after taking his first.

Kilkenny (7), Cork (3), Limerick (2), Down (1), Offaly (1), Tipperary (1)

1993

Michael Walsh
(Kilkenny)

Eddie O'Connor	Seán O'Gorman	Liam Simpson
(Kilkenny)	(Cork)	(Kilkenny)
Liam Dunne	Pat O'Neill	Pádraig Kelly
(Wexford)	(Kilkenny)	(Galway)

Pat Malone   Paul McKillen
(Galway)   (Antrim)

Martin Storey	John Power	D.J. Carey
(Wexford)	(Kilkenny)	(Kilkenny)
Michael Cleary	Joe Rabbitte	Barry Egan
(Tipperary)	(Galway)	(Cork)

Eddie O'Connor followed his brother, Willie (1992) onto the All Star honours list; Michael Cleary won his fourth successive award.

Kilkenny (6), Galway (3), Cork (2), Wexford (2), Antrim (1), Tipperary (1)

1994

Joe Quaid
(Limerick)

Anthony Daly	Kevin Kinahan	Martin Hanamy
(Clare)	(Offaly)	(Offaly)
David Clarke	Hubert Rigney	Kevin Martin
(Limerick)	(Offaly)	(Offaly)

Ciarán Carey   Mike Houlihan
(Limerick)   (Limerick)

Johnny Dooley	Gary Kirby	John Leahy
(Offaly)	(Limerick)	(Tipperary)
Billy Dooley	D.J. Carey	Damien Quigley
(Offaly)	(Kilkenny)	(Limerick)

'Hurler of the Year', Brian Whelahan, was omitted in one of the most controversial decisions in All Star history.

Offaly (6), Limerick (6), Clare (1), Kilkenny (1), Tipperary (1)

1995

Davy Fitzgerald
(Clare)

Kevin Kinahan	Brian Lohan	Liam Doyle
(Offaly)	(Clare)	(Clare)
Brian Whelahan	Seán McMahon	Anthony Daly
(Offaly)	(Clare)	(Clare)

Ollie Baker   Michael Coleman
(Clare)   (Galway)

Johnny Dooley	Gary Kirby	James O'Connor
(Offaly)	(Limerick)	(Clare)
Billy Dooley	D.J. Carey	Ger O'Loughlin
(Offaly)	(Kilkenny)	(Clare)

Clare's All-Ireland breakthrough earned them eight awards, including six of the first eight positions.

Clare (8), Offaly (4), Galway (1), Kilkenny (1), Limerick (1)

1996

Joe Quaid
(Limerick)

Tom Helebert	Brian Lohan	Larry O'Gorman
(Galway)	(Clare)	(Wexford)

Liam Dunne	Ciarán Carey	Mark Foley
(Wexford)	(Limerick)	(Limerick)

Adrian Fenlon   Mike Houlihan
(Wexford)   (Limerick)

Rory McCarthy	Martin Storey	Larry Murphy
(Wexford)	(Wexford)	(Wexford)

Liam Cahill	Gary Kirby	Tom Dempsey
(Tipperary)	(Limerick)	(Wexford)

Wexford won seven awards, their highest ever representation; Gary Kirby won his fourth award.

Wexford (7), Limerick (5), Clare (1), Galway (1), Tipperary (1)

1997

Damien Fitzhenry
(Wexford)

Paul Shelly	Brian Lohan	Willie O'Connor
(Tipperary)	(Clare)	(Kilkenny)

Liam Doyle	Seán McMahon	Liam Keoghan
(Clare)	(Clare)	(Kilkenny)

Colin Lynch   Thomas Dunne
(Clare)   (Tipperary)

James O'Connor	Declan Ryan	John Leahy
(Clare)	(Tipperary)	(Tipperary)

Kevin Broderick	Ger O'Loughlin	D.J. Carey
(Galway)	(Clare)	(Kilkenny)

A third successive award for Brian Lohan; Damien Fitzhenry became Wexford's first goalkeeper to win an award.

Clare (6), Tipperary (4), Kilkenny (3), Galway (1), Wexford (1)

1998

Stephen Byrne
(Offaly)

Willie O'Connor	Kevin Kinahan	Martin Hanamy
(Kilkenny)	(Offaly)	(Offaly)

Anthony Daly	Seán McMahon	Kevin Martin
(Clare)	(Clare)	(Offaly)

Tony Browne   Ollie Baker
(Waterford)   (Clare)

Michael Duignan	Martin Storey	James O'Connor
(Offaly)	(Wexford)	(Clare)

Joe Dooley	Brian Whelahan	Charlie Carter
(Offaly)	(Offaly)	(Kilkenny)

Joe Dooley followed his brothers, Billy and Johnny, onto the All Star roll of honour; Brian Whelahan was chosen at full forward, having won his previous two awards at right half-back.

Offaly (7), Clare (4), Kilkenny (2), Waterford (1), Wexford (1)

1999

Donal Óg Cusack
(Cork)

Fergal Ryan	Diarmuid O'Sullivan	Frank Lohan
(Cork)	(Cork)	(Clare)

Brian Whelahan	Brian Corcoran	Peter Barry
(Offaly)	(Cork)	(Kilkenny)

Andy Comerford   Thomas Dunne
(Kilkenny)   (Tipperary)

D.J. Carey	John Troy	Brian McEvoy
(Kilkenny)	(Offaly)	(Kilkenny)

Seánie McGrath	Joe Deane	Niall Gilligan
(Cork)	(Cork)	(Clare)

Cork won six awards, their highest since 1990; Frank Lohan followed his brother, Brian, into the All Star club.

Cork (6), Kilkenny (4), Clare (2), Offaly (2), Tipperary (1)

2000

Brendan Cummins
(Tipperary)

Noel Hickey	Diarmuid O'Sullivan	Willie O'Connor
(Kilkenny)	(Cork)	(Kilkenny)
John Carroll	Eamonn Kennedy	Peter Barry
(Tipperary)	(Kilkenny)	(Kilkenny)

Johnny Dooley   Andy Comerford
(Offaly)   (Kilkenny)

Denis Byrne	Joe Rabbitte	Henry Shefflin
(Kilkenny)	(Galway)	(Kilkenny)
Charlie Carter	D.J. Carey	Joe Deane
(Kilkenny)	(Kilkenny)	(Cork)

Nine awards for Kilkenny, their highest since 1983; Brendan Cummins became Tipperary's third All Star goalkeeper.

Kilkenny (9), Cork (2), Tipperary (2), Galway (1), Offaly (1)

2001

Brendan Cummins
(Tipperary)

Darragh Ryan	Philip Maher	Ollie Canning
(Wexford)	(Tipperary)	(Galway)
Eamonn Corcoran	Liam Hodgins	Mark Foley
(Tipperary)	(Galway)	(Limerick)

Thomas Dunne   Eddie Enright
(Tipperary)   (Tipperary)

Mark O'Leary	James O'Connor	Kevin Broderick
(Tipperary)	(Clare)	(Galway)
Charlie Carter	Eugene Cloonan	Eoin Kelly
(Kilkenny)	(Galway)	(Tipperary)

A fourth award for James O'Connor; a third for Thomas Dunne; just one award for Leinster champions, Kilkenny.

Tipperary (7), Galway (4), Clare (1), Limerick (1), Kilkenny (1), Wexford (1)

2002

Davy Fitzgerald
(Clare)

Michael Kavanagh	Brian Lohan	Philip Larkin
(Kilkenny)	(Clare)	(Kilkenny)
Fergal Hartley	Peter Barry	Paul Kelly
(Waterford)	(Kilkenny)	(Tipperary)

Colin Lynch   Derek Lyng
(Clare)   (Kilkenny)

Eoin Kelly	Henry Shefflin	Ken McGrath
(Waterford)	(Kilkenny)	(Waterford)
Eoin Kelly	Martin Comerford	D.J. Carey
(Tipperary)	(Kilkenny)	(Kilkenny)

The Kelly brothers from Tipperary were honoured in defence and attack; Waterford won three awards for the first time.

Kilkenny (7), Clare (3), Waterford (3), Tipperary (2)

2003

Brendan Cummins
(Tipperary)

Michael Kavanagh	Noel Hickey	Ollie Canning
(Kilkenny)	(Kilkenny)	(Galway)
Seán Óg Ó hAilpín	Ronan Curran	J.J. Delaney
(Cork)	(Cork)	(Kilkenny)

Tommy Walsh   Derek Lyng
(Kilkenny)   (Kilkenny)

John Mullane	Henry Shefflin	Eddie Brennan
(Waterford)	(Kilkenny)	(Kilkenny)
Setanta Ó hAilpín	Martin Comerford	Joe Deane
(Cork)	(Kilkenny)	(Cork)

Seán and Setanta Ó hAilpín joined the All Star brothers' club; eight awards for Kilkenny.

Kilkenny (8), Cork (4), Galway (1), Tipperary (1), Waterford (1)

Paul Galvin Honoured as 1000th All Star

(Kerry)

ALL STAR WINNER: 2004

The honour of becoming the 1000th All Star went to Paul Galvin, who was chosen at right half-forward on the football team after an outstanding season as Kerry swept to triple glory, winning the National League, Munster and All-Ireland titles.

Galvin, from the Finuge club, took his running game all over the field in search of responsibility, which he discharged with consistent efficiency. A player of great versatility, his high enterprise levels were central to Kerry's strategy as they set about making up for the disappointments of the previous three years.

Five of Galvin's colleagues also won awards on a team where seven counties were represented. Kerry's right half-back, Tomás Ó Sé was named as 'Footballer of the Year'.

In hurling, Brian Corcoran celebrated his return to the Cork team by being chosen at full forward, 12 years after winning his first award at corner-back. Colleague, Seán Óg Ó hAilpín, who was chosen at left half-back, picked up the 'Hurler of the Year' award on a team where five counties were represented, led by Cork who won seven awards.

2004 FOOTBALL ALL STARS

Diarmuid Murphy
(Kerry)

Tom O'Sullivan	Barry Owens	Michael McCarthy
(Kerry)	(Fermanagh)	(Kerry)
Tomás Ó Sé	James Nallen	John Keane
(Kerry)	(Mayo)	(Westmeath)

Martin McGrath   Seán Cavanagh
(Fermanagh)   (Tyrone)

Paul Galvin	Ciarán McDonald	Dessie Dolan
(Kerry)	(Mayo)	(Westmeath)
Colm Cooper	Enda Muldoon	Matty Forde
(Kerry)	(Derry)	(Wexford)

A first football All Star for Wexford; Westmeath and Fermanagh won two awards each for the first time.

Kerry (6), Fermanagh (2), Mayo (2), Westmeath (2), Derry (1), Tyrone (1), Wexford (1)

2004 HURLING ALL STARS

Damien Fitzhenry
(Wexford)

Wayne Sherlock	Diarmuid O'Sullivan	Tommy Walsh
(Cork)	(Cork)	(Kilkenny)
J.J. Delaney	Ronan Curran	Seán Óg Ó hAilpín
(Kilkenny)	(Cork)	(Cork)

Ken McGrath   Jerry O'Connor
(Waterford)   (Cork)

Dan Shanahan	Niall McCarthy	Henry Shefflin
(Waterford)	(Cork)	(Kilkenny)
Eoin Kelly	Brian Corcoran	Paul Flynn
(Tipperary)	(Cork)	(Waterford)

Seven awards for Cork to take their overall hurling total to 141, which extended their lead over closest pursuers, Kilkenny, to 22.

Cork (7), Kilkenny (3), Waterford (3), Tipperary (1), Wexford (1)